MAXIMIZE YOUR READING

4

Maximize Your Reading 4

Pearson Education, Inc., 221 River Street, Hoboken, NJ 07030 USA

Staff credits: The people who made up the **Maximize Your Reading** team are Pietro Alongi, Rhea Banker, Tracey Munz Cataldo, Mindy DePalma, Gina DiLillo, Niki Lee, Amy McCormick, Lindsay Richman, and Paula Van Ells.

Text composition: MPS North America LLC

Design: EMC Design Ltd

Photo credits: Cover: Moodboard/Getty Images. Page 32: S. Gatterwe/Fotolia; 43: Viz4biz/Fotolia; 65: Makar/Fotolia; 72: Juulijs/Fotolia; 144: nobeastsofierce/Shutterstock.

ISBN-13: 978-0-13-466135-3   ISBN-10: 0-13-466135-4

Printed in the United States of America

2   16

pearsonelt.com/maximizeyourreading

CONTENTS

Reading Level 4 – Advanced

Pre-Test..1
Comprehension Skills.................................12
  Previewing, Scanning, and Skimming.............12
    Previewing..................................12
    Scanning....................................18
    Skimming....................................22
    Combined Skills: Previewing, Scanning, and Skimming.................31
  Understanding Paragraphs.....................36
    Identifying the Topic of a Paragraph.........36
    Identifying the Main Idea....................38
    Identifying Key Details......................42
  Making Inferences............................47
    Facts vs. Inferences.........................47
    Making Inferences from Fiction...............49
    Facts and Opinions...........................53
    Tone and Point of View.......................56
  Patterns of Organization.....................59
    Text Organization: Thesis Statements, Main Points, and Supporting Details.......................59
    Comparison and Contrast Pattern..............61
    Cause and Effect Pattern.....................62
    Problem and Solution Pattern.................64
    Identifying Patterns.........................67
    Summarizing..................................72
  Comprehension Skills Practice Test...........76
Vocabulary Building..................................88
  Word Parts...................................88
    Roots..88
    Prefixes.....................................92
    Suffixes.....................................96
    Word Forms and Families......................99
  Inferring Meaning from Context..............101
    Using Context...............................101
    Inferring the Meaning of Words..............103
  Collocations and Idioms.....................107
    Common Collocations and Phrasal Verbs.................................107

    Idioms......................................112
    Collocations and Idioms in Context..........116
  Following Ideas in Text.....................119
    Signal Words and Phrases....................119
    Pronouns and Referents......................122
  Vocabulary Building Practice Test...........127
Reading Faster......................................134
  Introduction: Strategies for Reading Faster.....134
  Timed Reading Practice......................138
    Practice 1: Crime-Solving Techniques Throughout History..........................138
    Practice 2: Rock Legends: People Who Made a Difference in Music............147
    Practice 3: Unexplained Phenomena..........154
Study Skills..162
  Storing and Studying New Words..............162
  Study Strategies............................174
Language in Context.................................183
Appendices..200
  Appendix 1 Tips for Reading Tests...........200
  Appendix 2 Transition Words and Phrases..................................201
  Appendix 3 Reading Rate Table...............202
  Appendix 4 Reading Rate Log.................203
Post-Test...204
Answer Key..216

PRE-TEST

Part 1 Comprehension Skills

Preview and skim the passage quickly. Then circle the letter of the best answer for each question.

> **Boosting the Immune System Helps the Body Fight Cancer**
>
> The human immune system is a powerful and complex organism. Normally, the immune system is able to accurately target and attack harmful invaders in the body, but leaves the body's own tissues alone. Certain diseases, however, such as type 1 diabetes or multiple sclerosis, cause the immune system to attack the body, in effect weakening it even further. It is this malfunction that scientists are hoping may unlock the key to more effective cancer treatment in the future. A type of cell known as a Treg cell works to calm the immune system and keep it from overreacting and attacking the body. A recent study conducted on laboratory mice at the Children's Hospital of Philadelphia blocked Treg cell function, allowing the immune system to proceed unchecked. In cancer-infected mice, when Treg cells were hindered, the immune system began to attack the cancer first. The challenge for researchers is finding a way to let the immune system attack cancer, but not the body. Researcher Dr. Wayne Hancock remarked, "We needed to find a way to reduce Treg function in a way that permits anti-tumor activity without allowing autoimmune reactions." Hancock and other cancer researchers are hopeful that this breakthrough will lead to a new, effective option for cancer patients. However, much more research and testing is needed before the approach can be tried on humans.

1 The passage relates to the field of _____ .
   a law
   b economics
   c medicine
   d history

2 The passage is from _____ .
   a an advertisement
   b a college textbook
   c a scholarly journal
   d a personal email

3 The author of the passage intends to _____ .
   a inform people about the topic
   b give an opinion about the topic
   c teach people how to do something
   d persuade people to take some action

4 The purpose of the passage is to _____ .
   a compare two different types of cancer treatment
   b explain a new development in the field of cancer research
   c introduce one doctor's opinion about the future of cancer treatment
   d list the most popular types of cancer treatments today

Part 2 Comprehension Skills

Read the scanning questions. Then scan the text for the answers. Circle the letter of the correct answer.

Scanning Questions

1. Who was Helga Estby?
2. What two events caused the Estby family's financial problems?
3. What happened when Helga and Clara finally arrived at their destination?
4. What did Helga do after her journey was over?

Bold Spirit: Helga Estby's Journey across America

Bold Spirit is the heroic but tragic true tale of Helga Estby, a Norwegian immigrant to the United States, in the late 1800s. Helga emigrated from Oslo to Michigan with her mother in 1871. Five years later, she married another Norwegian immigrant, Ole Estby. Lured by the prospect of owning their own land on the western frontier, the couple bought a farm in Spokane, Washington, where they started their family and eventually had eight children. In 1893, the failure of a number of US banks set off widespread financial panic. Many people, including the Estbys, lost nearly all of their money and found themselves desperate and hungry. In addition, Ole Estby had suffered a serious back injury, making it impossible for him to work and support the family. In 1896, a businessman, whose identity to this day remains unknown, announced a challenge open to all women in the West: any woman who walked from the west coast to New York would be given $10,000. Desperate to save the family farm, 36-year-old Helga Estby and her 17-year-old daughter, Clara, took the stranger's wager. Their seven-month journey took them through 14 states, over mountains, across Native American reservations, through bitter storms and intense heat. Never begging, they worked hard to support themselves along the way. Their arrival in New York City on December 23, 1896 was not the joyous hero's welcome they had envisioned. The contest's sponsor refused to pay Helga and Clara their cash prize, saying that the women had not completed the trip before the established deadline. And most tragic of all, on arriving back in Washington, Helga Estby learned that two of her children had died of diphtheria during her absence. Sadly, the Estby family lost their farm, and many held Helga responsible for the tragedy. Embodying the book's title, *Bold Spirit,* Helga held her head high and went on to become an advocate for women's rights. She died in 1942 at the age of 82.

1 Why did Helga Estby make her journey?

  a to prove that women were strong

  b to save her family's future

  c to teach her daughter about the world

  d to find a new place for her family to live

2 What two events caused the Estby family's financial problems?

  a Ole's death; the loss of the family farm

  b Ole's injury; a national economic crisis

  c Helga's leaving; Clara's death

  d Helga's lack of farm experience; a fire at the farm

3 What happened when Helga and Clara finally arrived at their destination?
   a They were given a hero's welcome.
   b No one paid any attention.
   c They were told they had failed.
   d There was a big storm.

4 What did Helga do after her journey was over?
   a She deserted her family forever.
   b She became an activist for women.
   c She returned to a peaceful life on the farm.
   d She decided to get an education.

Part 3   Comprehension Skills

How would you like to lose weight, build muscle, and feel more energetic? The paleolithic diet could help you do all those things in a matter of a few short months or weeks. The paleolithic diet, or paleo diet for short, is a modern approach to nutrition that gets its inspiration from the caveman days. In essence, the approach involves following a diet similar to that of humans' ancient predecessors who lived 2.5 million years ago, during the Paleolithic era. In this pre-agrarian society, our cave-dwelling ancestors subsisted on the wild animals they hunted and the plants, fruit, seeds, and berries they gathered in nature. The modern version of the paleolithic diet consists primarily of protein in the form of meat, fish, and eggs, along with vegetables, fruits, roots, and nuts. Agricultural products such as harvested grains and dairy products are excluded, as are potatoes, refined salt and sugar, and processed oils, because those were not part of the original human diet. The philosophy behind the diet is that human genetics have remained largely the same since before agricultural techniques were developed. This means that our digestive system is better suited to a diet of proteins and plants than to one of grains, dairy, and other post-agricultural food products. This makes the paleo diet the ideal nutritional plan for general human health. Although there are differing opinions about the diet's health benefits, the vast majority of studies have shown overall improvements in health outcomes in those who have adopted the paleo diet over a period of several months. Find out how the paleo diet can change your life and improve your health. Our line of food products includes 20 frozen meals a week delivered right to your door for free. Order now and you'll also get access to our fabulous online library, including delicious recipes, video cooking tutorials, nutritional information, and the answers to all of your questions.

Read the passage and circle the letter of the correct answer.

1 What is the topic of the passage?
   a the development of agriculture during the Paleolithic Era
   b the paleolithic diet compared to other popular diets
   c the hunting techniques of paleolithic humans
   d the benefits of the modern paleolithic diet

2 What is the main purpose of the passage?

    a to generate sales of a product

    b to inform people about the topic

    c to warn people about something dangerous

    d to announce a scientific breakthrough in nutrition

3 What is the main idea of the passage?

    a The majority of experts are wrong about the paleolithic diet.

    b People should try the paleolithic diet to improve their health.

    c Buying meals online is more convenient than cooking them yourself.

    d Humans' health began to decline with the development of agriculture.

4 Which of the following is true about the paleo diet?

    a It includes a balance of items from all food groups.

    b It features mainly agricultural products.

    c It involves eating primarily animals and plants.

    d It mimics the diet of prehistoric animals.

Part 4 Comprehension Skills

Read the excerpt from a news blog. Circle the number of the sentence that expresses an inference (not a fact).

[1] The center of Rio de Janeiro was packed with more than 10,000 people over the weekend. [2] The group was made up of protesters demonstrating in support of teachers receiving higher wages. [3] For the most part, the demonstrations were peaceful, but as night fell, things took a violent turn when protesters threw firebombs at public buildings. [4] This is likely the type of attention Brazilian officials would prefer to avoid, with only eight months to go before Rio hosts the 2014 World Cup. [5] Federal and local authorities say they have already responded to many of the protesters' demands, for example, by promising to increase spending on healthcare and professional development for teachers.

Which sentence is NOT a fact?

Sentence 1

Sentence 2

Sentence 3

Sentence 4

Sentence 5

Part 5 Comprehension Skills

Read the passage from *The Curious Case of Benjamin Button*, by F. Scott Fitzgerald. Then circle the letter of the correct answer.

"Is the child born?" begged Mr. Button. Doctor Keene frowned. "Why, yes, I suppose so—after a fashion." Again he threw a curious glance at Mr. Button. "Is my wife all right?" "Yes." "Is it a boy or a girl?" "Here now!" cried Doctor Keene in a perfect passion of irritation, "I'll ask you to go and see for yourself. Outrageous!" He snapped the last word out in almost one syllable, then he turned away muttering: "Do you imagine a case like this will help my professional reputation? One more would ruin me—ruin anybody." "What's the matter?" demanded Mr. Button, appalled. "Triplets?" "No, not triplets!" answered the doctor cuttingly. "What's more, you can go and see for yourself. And get another doctor. I brought you into the world, young man, and I've been physician to your family for forty years, but I'm through with you! I don't want to see you or any of your relatives ever again! Good bye!" Then he turned sharply, and without another word, climbed into his phaeton, which was waiting at the curbstone, and drove severely away. Mr. Button stood there upon the sidewalk, stupefied and trembling from head to foot. What horrible mishap had occurred?

1 From the passage, we can infer that the two people are talking about _____ .
   a a car accident
   b a change of job
   c a baby's birth
   d a birthday party

2 From the passage, we can infer that Mr. Button is feeling _____ .
   a worried
   b happy
   c calm
   d sad

3 From the passage, we can infer that Doctor Keene feels _____ .
   a joyful
   b excited
   c satisfied
   d upset

4 From the passage, we can infer that _____ .
   a Mr. Button's wife is hurt
   b something is wrong with the baby
   c Dr. Keene was fired from his job
   d the babies are triplets

Part 6 Comprehension Skills

Read the passage. Then circle the letter of the correct answer.

Some call it vandalism, but others argue that graffiti has as much worth as any true work of art. In Long Island City, New York, graffiti, or aerosol art, as it's called, is definitely treated as a serious art form, and the respect is well-deserved. At least for the moment, the city is home to the 5Pointz Aerosol Art Center, a 200,000-square-foot factory turned outdoor exhibit space dedicated to displaying the artwork of graffiti artists from around the globe. Spray-can-wielding artists from Brazil, Canada, Japan, the Netherlands, and all over the US have ventured to 5Pointz to spray their panoramic murals on the sides of brick buildings around the industrial complex. The result is a gorgeous city block of giant paintings showcasing an astonishing variety of graffiti art, from cartoon characters to portraits of real people to terrifying science-fiction creatures. Sadly, however, as impressive and authentic as these works of art may be, a recent vote by the City Planning Commission has approved a plan to tear the 5Pointz complex down and build luxury apartments in its place. Building owner David Wolcoff proposed the new plan, calling the apartments "an exciting project for the neighborhood." Others in the community are already mourning the loss of a unique attraction. Tour company owner, Mark Levy, said, "We are unhappy to lose such a landmark—especially a place that's so welcoming to artists." "The fight isn't over," said 5Pointz founder Jonathan Cohen. But with the building's owner and the City Planning Commission standing firm, it's likely that graffiti fans and artists will have to find someplace else where they will be appreciated.

1 The writer of the article feels that graffiti _____.
  a is basically vandalism
  b can be considered a true art form
  c should only be displayed indoors
  d deserves more respect than other art

2 Which sentence expresses the writer's opinion about the city's plans?
  a At least for the moment, the city is home to the 5Pointz Aerosol Art Center, a 200,000-square-foot factory turned outdoor exhibit space.
  b The result is a gorgeous city block of giant paintings showcasing an astonishing variety of graffiti art.
  c Sadly, however, as impressive and authentic as these works of art may be, a recent vote by the City Planning Commission has approved a plan to tear the 5Pointz complex down.
  d "The fight isn't over," said 5Pointz founder Jonathan Cohen.

3 How does the writer feel about the future of 5Pointz?
  a optimistic
  b uncertain
  c frightened
  d happy

Part 7   Comprehension Skills

Read the passage and on page 8, circle the letter of the answer.

Fuel Cell Vehicles

Fuel cell vehicles (FCVs) run on hydrogen gas rather than gasoline and emit no harmful tailpipe emissions. Several challenges must be overcome before these vehicles will be competitive with conventional vehicles, but the potential benefits of this technology are substantial. FCVs look like conventional vehicles from the outside, but inside they contain technologically advanced components not found on today's vehicles. The most obvious difference is the fuel cell stack that converts hydrogen gas stored on board with oxygen from the air into electricity to drive the electric motor that propels the vehicle. The major components of a typical FCV are described below.

Benefits

Fewer Greenhouse Gas Emissions

Gasoline- and diesel-powered vehicles emit greenhouse gases (GHGs), mostly carbon dioxide (CO_2), that contribute to global climate change. Fuel cell vehicles (FCVs), powered by pure hydrogen, emit no GHGs from their tailpipes, only heat and water.

Fewer Air Pollutants

Highway vehicles emit a significant share of the air pollutants that contribute to smog and harmful particulates in the US. FCVs powered by pure hydrogen emit no harmful pollutants. If the hydrogen is produced from fossil fuels, some pollutants are produced, but much less than the amount generated by conventional vehicle tailpipe emissions.

Reduced Oil Dependence

FCVs could reduce our dependence on foreign oil, since hydrogen can be derived from domestic sources, such as natural gas and coal, as well as renewable resources, such as water. That would make our economy less dependent on other countries and less vulnerable to oil price shocks from an increasingly volatile oil market.

Challenges

Onboard Hydrogen Storage

Some FCVs store enough hydrogen to travel as far as gasoline vehicles between fill-ups—about 300 miles—but this must be achievable across different vehicle makes and models, and without compromising customer expectations of space, performance, safety, or cost.

Vehicle Cost

FCVs are currently more expensive than conventional vehicles and hybrids. Manufacturers must bring down production costs, especially the costs of the fuel cell stack and hydrogen storage, to compete with conventional technologies.

Fuel Cell Durability and Reliability

Fuel cell systems are not yet as durable as internal combustion engines, especially in some temperature and humidity ranges.

Getting Hydrogen to Consumers

The extensive system used to deliver gasoline from refineries to local filling stations cannot be used for hydrogen.

Public Acceptance

Finally, fuel cell technology must be embraced by consumers before its benefits can be realized. Consumers may have concerns about the dependability and safety of these vehicles, just as they did with hybrids.

1 This paragraph describes _____ .
   a the steps in a process
   b a sequence of events over time
   c a comparison between two people or things
   d different causes and effects

2 Choose the best thesis statement for the passage.
   a Fuel cell vehicles (FCVs) have the potential to significantly reduce our dependence on foreign oil and lower harmful emissions that contribute to climate change.
   b Producing the hydrogen to power FCVs can generate greenhouse gases, but much less than that emitted by conventional gasoline and diesel vehicles.
   c Public doubt must be overcome before fuel cell vehicles (FCVs) will be a successful, competitive alternative for consumers.
   d New facilities and systems must be constructed for producing, transporting, and dispensing hydrogen to consumers.

Part 8 Comprehension Skills

Read the passage. Then circle the letter of the correct answer.

El Niño

El Niño is the nickname of a naturally occurring weather event in the equatorial region which causes temporary changes in the world climate. Originally, El Niño was the name used for warmer than normal sea surface temperatures in the Pacific Ocean off the coast of South America. Now, El Niño has come to refer to a whole complex of Pacific Ocean sea surface temperature changes and global weather events. The ocean warming off South America is just one of these events. In normal, non-El Niño conditions, trade winds blow in a westerly direction along the equator. These winds pile up warm surface water in the western Pacific, so the sea surface is much higher in the western Pacific than in the eastern Pacific. These trade winds are one of the main sources of fuel for the Humboldt Current. The Humboldt Current is a cold ocean current which flows north along the coasts of Chile and Peru, then turns west and warms as it moves out into the Central Pacific. So, the normal situation is warmer water in the western Pacific, cooler in the eastern. In an El Niño, the equatorial westerly winds diminish. As a result, the Humboldt Current weakens and this allows the waters along the coast of Chile and Peru to warm and creates warmer than usual conditions along the coast of South America. El Niños occur irregularly approximately every two to seven years. A strong El Niño is often associated with flooding rains and warm weather in Peru, drought in Indonesia, Africa, and Australia, torrential downpours and mudslides in southern California, a mild winter in the northeast, and fewer hurricanes in the southeast. In non-El Niño years, upwelling of deep, cold ocean water brings up nutrients that lie near the bottom. Fish living in the upper waters feed on plankton that are dependent on these nutrients. Kelp forests also depend on cool, nutrient-rich water for survival and growth. An El Niño reduces the upwelling of cold water off the coast of the Americas. When this happens, fish either die or migrate into areas where they'll find more to eat. With the fish gone, sea birds that depend on them may die or go elsewhere. Kelp forests are often destroyed by storms and ocean swells. Fish populations may also be reduced, and marine mammals, such as seals and sea lions, that feed on fish may be affected.

This passage primarily describes _____ .

a a comparison between two things

b different causes and effects

c a problem and a solution

d steps in a process

Part 9 Comprehension Skills

Read the passage and circle the letter of the correct answer.

TO: Jessica Gelter, Marketing Manager
FROM: Nate Terrill, Market Research Assistant
DATE: October 10, 2014
SUBJECT: Spring Fashion Promotion

New data from market research and analysis shows that the proposed advertising plan for the new spring fashion campaign needs to be reviewed and updated. Findings from consumer surveys and focus groups indicate a need to modernize our advertising approach to align it with the interests and sensibilities of today's young adults. The previous ad campaigns on which this one is based placed a heavy emphasis on network TV ads as the primary media. However, with more and more young people canceling cable TV accounts and watching on-demand shows by subscription on laptops and mobile devices, it is increasingly important that we use the Internet as the primary tool to introduce new products to the public and communicate our brand message. Rather than continuing to throw budget money at ineffective TV ads that don't reach our target audience, we need to focus on websites that appeal to young people. According to recent surveys, 78% of our target market watches Internet TV four hours or more per week on both free network sites and paid subscription sites. It is clear that the time has come to move our ad placements from our other media sources such as network TV, radio, and magazines to these Internet sites in order to more effectively promote our product sales. As the trend for cultural icons is to go digital, so must our marketing plans. By repositioning our marketing efforts in time for our new spring clothing line, we will maximize our exposure to potential customers and increase our sales.

This passage primarily describes _____ .

a a comparison between two things
b different causes and effects
c a problem and a solution
d steps in a process

Part 10 Vocabulary Building

Circle the letter of the correct meaning for the underlined word.

1 A type of cell known as a Treg cell works to calm the immune system and keep it from overreacting and attacking the body. A recent study conducted on laboratory mice at the Children's Hospital of Philadelphia blocked Treg cell function, allowing the immune system to proceed unchecked. In cancer-infected mice, when Treg cells were <u>hindered</u>, the immune system began to attack the cancer first.

    a created   **b** blocked   **c** strengthened   **d** removed

2 Fuel cell vehicles look like conventional vehicles from the outside, but inside they contain technologically advanced components not found on today's vehicles. The most obvious difference is the fuel cell stack that converts hydrogen gas stored on board with oxygen from the air into electricity to drive the electric motor that <u>propels</u> the vehicle.

    a moves   **b** starts   **c** repairs   **d** cleans

Part 11 Vocabulary Building

Circle the letter of the correct form of the word to complete the sentence.

1 In order to make a _____ decision, you have to consider all options carefully.

    a ration   **c** rationalize
    b rationale   **d** rational

2 It's important to try new things and stay physically active, _____ of your age.

    a regarding   **c** regard
    b regardless   **d** disregard

3 These kinds of situations must be handled with _____ to avoid hurting someone's feelings.

    a sensitive   **c** sensitivity
    b insensitive   **d** sensory

4 _____ to recent research, texting while driving impairs driving performance as much as or more than driving while under the influence of alcohol.

    a Due   **c** Contrary
    b According   **d** In addition

5 The study found a dramatic increase in fatal automobile accidents in states where there was no existing legislation against texting while driving. In _____ , the interruptions effectively doubled the number of fatalities.

    a response   **c** short
    b fact   **d** a way

Part 12   Vocabulary Building

For each group of sentences, circle the letter of the word or words that the underlined text refers to.

1 Supporters of the "Tea Party Movement" advocate lowering the national debt and federal budget deficit by curbing government spending and taxes. <u>These individuals</u> have organized a number of protests and have even sponsored political candidates.

   a national debt and federal budget deficit
   b government spending and taxes
   c supporters of the Tea Party Movement
   d political candidates

2 For families wishing to adopt a pet and help reduce the number of stray animals, there are a number of lower-cost and socially-conscious options. <u>These</u> include adopting from local animal shelters such as the Humane Society, privately-run animal rescue organizations, or Internet-based pet adoption services.

   a local animal shelters
   b lower-cost and socially-conscious options
   c families wishing to adopt a pet
   d Internet-based pet adoption services

Part 13   Vocabulary Building

Circle the letter of the correct pronoun that completes each sentence.

1 In 1896, a businessman, _____ identity to this day remains unknown, announced a challenge open to all women in the West.

   a which
   b whose
   c that
   d whom

2 El Niño is the nickname of a naturally occurring weather event in the equatorial region _____ causes temporary changes in the world climate.

   a who
   b which
   c whose
   d whom

COMPREHENSION SKILLS

Previewing, Scanning, and Skimming
PREVIEWING

Previewing Articles and Essays

Previewing a text before you read it can give you a sense of its purpose, main idea, and organizational structure. This can help you read more efficiently and save time.

When previewing an article or essay, you quickly read only certain parts of the text, for example:

- the title and any bold headings
- any visuals (maps, charts, graphs) that include key information
- the entire first paragraph
- the first sentence of each paragraph
- the concluding sentence

Ask yourself the following questions as you preview:

- How is the text organized? Are there separate sections? If so, what is the focus of each one?
- What is the purpose? (to define, explain, or describe, to inform, to give an opinion, to persuade the reader to do something)
- Are there any important bold or italicized terms?

Practice 1

Preview the article by reading only the underlined parts. Preview the article for one minute. Then answer the questions on p. 13. Note how much you remember after just previewing.

Citizenship and Naturalization

Citizenship (also called *nationality*) means having the legal right to live and work in a particular country and participate in politics. Naturalization is the process by which a person acquires legal citizenship of a country other than the original citizenship held at birth.

How Nationality Is Determined

Depending on the citizenship laws, a country may use one of two ways to determine who does or does not have citizenship at birth:

1) *Jus soli* is the Latin term meaning *right of territory*. This means that a person is a citizen of a country if he or she is born within that country or its territories, regardless of the nationality of his or her parents.

2) *Jus sanguinis* means *right of blood* in Latin, and indicates that a person holds the same nationality of his parents, regardless of where he or she is born.

Some countries, such as Canada, the UK, and the US allow citizens to hold dual or multiple nationalities. Other countries forbid multiple nationalities and require that naturalization applicants agree to give up their original citizenship.

Typical Naturalization Applicant

There are no typical characteristics of a citizenship applicant. Individuals may come from any country, and may be applying for naturalization for many different reasons. They may have left their home countries for political, economic, or humanitarian reasons, such as during a time of war or following a natural disaster. Or they may have their own personal or pragmatic reasons for immigrating to a new country. For example, they may want to join other family members already living in the country, or to attend university.

Naturalization Application Procedures

Each country has its own laws and policies regarding the requirements and procedures necessary to fulfill in order to apply to become a citizen. In general, however, most countries require that a person be a full time, legal resident for a minimum period of time (ranging between 2 to 12 years). In addition, the applicant must pledge to respect and obey the laws of his or her new country of citizenship.

1 What is this article about?

  a the author's experience applying for naturalization

  b how and why people apply for citizenship in another country

  c naturalization laws and procedures around the world

2 What is the purpose of this text?

  a to inform or explain

  b to give an opinion

  c to persuade people to take some action

3 How many ways are there to determine citizenship at birth?

  a many different ways

  b two main ways

  c 2–12 ways

4 Who is a typical naturalization applicant?

  a There is no such thing.

  b Someone attending university.

  c A member of a large family.

5 Which of the following is true about naturalization procedures in different countries?

  a They vary somewhat.

  b Every country is completely different.

  c They are the same around the world.

Previewing Research Materials

When you are preparing to do research, previewing can help you work efficiently to decide which texts will be most useful for your report.

When previewing a text, you quickly read only certain parts of it, for example:

- the title and any bold headings
- any visuals (maps, charts, graphs) or sidebars (boxes along the side of the text) that include key information
- the entire first paragraph
- the first sentence of each paragraph
- the concluding sentence

Then, ask yourself the following previewing questions:

- What do I know about the topic? What do I need to know for my research?
- How does the text relate to or inform my research? Are there useful facts or details to support my topic?
- What is the purpose of this text? (to define, explain, or describe, to inform, to give an opinion, to persuade the reader to do something)
- Are there any important bold or italicized terms?

Practice 2

A student is choosing research texts for a paper entitled "Should Spanish be an official language of the United States?" Preview the following three different research texts. Then answer the questions on p. 18.

Text 1

Spanish Should be Second Language in the US, Advocates Say

Spanish in the US

- 45 million people living in the United States speak Spanish as their first or second language; 37 million people aged five or older use Spanish as their primary language at home.

- Spanish is the second most common language in the United States, after English.

- In the US, more people speak Spanish than Chinese, French, German, Hawaiian, Italian, and all Native American languages combined.

Total U.S. Hispanic Population = 50.5 million

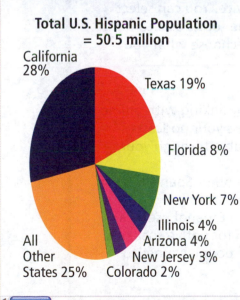

California 28%
Texas 19%
Florida 8%
New York 7%
Illinois 4%
Arizona 4%
New Jersey 3%
Colorado 2%
All Other States 25%

The immigration debate

Immigration has been a major topic of political debate in the last several US presidential elections, fueling the age-old debates about national security, employment, health care, and social security, among others. But another immigration-related question being raised by some is whether the US should create legislation to make both Spanish and English the official languages of the US.

What is the official language of the US?

Being the primary language of the US for over 200 years, many might guess that English is the country's official language. However, the truth is that the country does not have a legal official language.

Spanish to Overtake English in US

While a large number of proponents would like to make English the one-and-only official language of the United States, there are a growing number of cities and regions around the country—in particular in the Mexican-border states—that are being dominated by Spanish-speakers. Some experts predict that Spanish will overtake English as the most used language in these areas of the country soon. As a result, many jobs require some Spanish-speaking ability, and Spanish is the most commonly studied language among English speakers in the US.

All of this makes it clear why some groups are suggesting that Spanish should be the official second language of the country.

Enhance Your Professional Skills by Studying a Second Language

More and more Americans are studying the Spanish language as a way to enhance their résumés, broaden their marketable professional skills, and open more job possibilities. There are a wide variety of options for those wishing to study Spanish, from face-to-face classes, to self-study books, to DVDs or online options. The optimal method depends on the individual, and on what each person's needs and preferred learning styles are.

Learn Spanish on the Go

Now there's a new, easy way to study Spanish anywhere, anytime with **Radio Español**. Our patented program offers students a novel way to enjoy learning the Spanish language. Instead of sitting in a classroom listening to and repeating a teacher, or sitting in front of your computer at home, you can use your cell phone or mobile device anywhere you go to listen to real Spanish-speakers talking about real-life situations like being at a soccer match, shopping at an outdoor market, or going to the doctor. Radio Español allows you to work online at your own pace to improve your Spanish vocabulary, comprehension, and fluency. Our course units consist of high-quality, professionally produced podcasts that are convenient to access from any computer or mobile device. You can select from a wide variety of topics and proficiency levels. The topics and content are educational and entertaining, and, best of all, you choose what you want to listen to.

> **10 Jobs That Require Bilingual Spanish Skills**
> 1. Retail Sales Representative
> 2. Bank Teller
> 3. Customer Service Representative
> 4. Assistant Manager
> 5. Administrative Assistant
> 6. Medical Assistant
> 7. Production Supervisor
> 8. Human Resources Manager
> 9. Dental Assistant
> 10. Social Worker

Radio Español: Functions and Features

- Radio Español makes use of the latest technology by linking with online media stores. This means you can conveniently access your podcasts from anywhere, anytime. Our lessons are also available through your favorite social media account.
- Discussion forums - Connect and communicate with other Spanish learners through our online discussion forums pages.
- TV dramas - As a new addition to our content, Radio Español users can now access telenovelas - Spanish TV dramas created for native speakers.
- Music – Learners can choose from a great variety of popular tunes to listen to.

Text 3

Jared27 | **Spanish an Official Language of the U.S. - Porque No? (Why not?)**

I've been thinking about this question and wanted to get others' opinions on it:

The Latino population is growing rapidly in this country. Hispanic culture is everywhere—in music, on TV, radio, and other aspects of American life. Many states, such as California, Arizona, Texas, and Florida, as well as large cities like New York and Miami, have large Latino populations.

Spanish is quickly catching up to English as a prominent language. Although some would like to make English the official language of the US, saying we should "protect" America's English heritage, I argue that it may be time to recognize both English and Spanish as official languages.

What do you think?

Lanaron | **NO! NO! NO!**

The US is a mix of people from different backgrounds and cultures. Making Spanish an official language will only divide people more on the topic. Throughout history, immigrants like myself have come to the US and learned English, and they were better off for it. Making Spanish an official language sends a message to Spanish speakers that they don't need to learn English, a skill that only benefits them. There is no need to fix something that is not broken.

FreddieRug | **Spanish Is Already Here – Why Fight It?**

Whether you like it or not, Spanish is here to stay. English-speaking Americans should not only accept it as an official language; they should look at it as an educational opportunity. I think it's sad that most Americans can't speak a language other than English. Especially when most Europeans grow up speaking two—and some three or four—anguages from birth! Let's adopt Spanish as our official language and start requiring it as a school subject, the same way we do English!!

1 Which two texts would be most helpful for the student's research paper?
   a Texts 1 and 2
   b Texts 2 and 3
   c Texts 1 and 3

2 What is the purpose of Text 1?
   a to explain or inform
   b to express an opinion
   c to persuade the reader to do something

3 Which text would provide useful quotations from individuals to include in the report?
   a Text 1
   b Text 2
   c Text 3

4 What is the purpose of Text 2?
   a to explain or inform
   b to express an opinion
   c to persuade the reader to do something

5 Which information from Text 2 would be most useful for the student's report?
   a the information in the first paragraph
   b the information listed in the sidebar
   c the bulleted information at the end

SCANNING

Presentation

Scanning

You scan a text when you only need specific information, such as a name, date, or number. You move your eyes very quickly over the page until you find what you are looking for. You don't read all of the words. You just look for the necessary information in the text.

You probably already use scanning, for example, when you are looking for information on a website, course syllabus, or train schedule.

When scanning a text for information, you are usually looking for the answers to "Wh-" questions (*who*, *what*, *why*, *where*, *when*, and *how*). For example if the question begins with:

"Who....?" look for a person's name.

"When....?" look for a time, day, or date.

"How many...?" look for a number.

"Where...?" look for the name of a place.

Practice 1

Read these questions. Then scan the chemistry syllabus on p. 19 and answer the questions.

1 Which days does the course meet?

2 How many exams are there?

3 How many undergraduate courses are required before taking this course?

4 During which week are the research project presentations?

5 What is happening during Week 13?

6 Who is the guest lecturer during Week 5?

7 How much does the presentation count toward the final grade?

8 Where is the class held?

Organic Chemistry (CHEM 223)

Fall Semester 2016

Meets Mondays and Wednesdays 1:30-2:45, Smith Research Center, Room 321

Instructor: Taoling Xie, email: xie@pearson.edu

Office hours by appointment only

The curriculum for this course is based primarily upon recent research in the field of chemical biology. We will use recent articles and literature in the field as reference material. This course emphasizes the processes involved in making new discoveries.

Please note: For students taking this class, undergraduate Organic Biochemistry 105 and Physical Chemistry 117 are required courses.

Required Textbook: Bioorganic Chemistry, by Von Krusenstiern and Heller

Schedule:
Week 1 (Aug 29, 31) Introduction to Chemical Biology
Week 2 (Sept 5, 7) Bio-molecular structure
Week 3 (Sept 12, 14) DNA structures
Week 4 (Sept 19, 21*) Nucleic acids
Week 5 (Sept 26, 28) Guest Lecturer: Prof. Jackie Barstow
Week 6 (Oct 5, 7) Proteins and peptides
Week 7(Oct 12, 14) Natural enzymes
Exam I
Week 8 (Oct 19, 21) Guest Lecturer: Prof. John Lane
Week 9 (Oct 26, 28) Artificial enzymes, antibodies
Week 10 (Nov 2, 4) Chemical genetics and small molecules
Week 11(Nov 9, 11) Medicinal chemistry/Approaches to drug design
Exam II
Week12 (Nov 16, 18) Research project proposals reviewed
Week 13(Nov 23, 25) Fall Break
Week 14 (Nov 30, Dec 2) Research project presentations
Week 15 (Dec 7, 9) Review / ** Final Exam**

Grading:
20 % Research project proposal
20% Research project presentation
10% Class participation
50% Three exams

1 Which days does the course meet? _____

2 How many exams are there? _____

3 How many undergraduate courses are required for students taking this course?

_____

4 During which week are research project presentations? _____

5 What is happening during Week 13? _____

6 Who is the guest lecturer during Week 5? _____

7 How much does the presentation count toward the final grade? _____

8 In what room is the class held? _____

Practice 2

Read the previewing questions below. Then scan the job listing and write the answers in the blank.

1 Where is the job located?

2 When is the application deadline?

3 How many ways are there to apply for the job?

4 What is the job title?

5 How much work experience is required?

6 What level of education is required?

Bull's Eye Stores
Current Employment Openings
Date: May 17, 2016
Location: Toronto, Canada
Category: Apparel, Merchandising, Marketing
Position: Fashion Buyer

About this Opportunity
Be part of a dynamic team in a fast-paced, exciting work environment. Help us create happy, satisfied customers. You'll be responsible for developing business strategies and marketing plans, and selecting quality, cost-effective merchandise to help maintain profits, value, quality, and style.
Use your skills and experience to be a part of innovative, goal-oriented marketing strategy.

Job Description
As a Fashion Buyer for Bull's Eye Stores, you'll take the lead as you...
- Develop merchandise selections, and stay on top of the latest trends
- Take on general management duties and be responsible for a $100-$250,000 budget including apparel, jewelry, shoes, and accessories
- Work closely with our Design and Development team members, gaining vast experience with various areas of merchandising, such as product development, multi-channel marketing, label development, and imports
- Develop business strategies and marketing plans to drive profitable sales

Requirements
- Four-year college degree
- Five to seven years of previous work experience, retail apparel or accessories background strongly preferred
- Independent with strong decision-making and organizational skills
- Team player with creative problem-solving skills
- Ability to pay attention to detail
- Excellent leadership and communication skills

Benefits
Competitive pay, comprehensive insurance coverage, retirement plan, flexible scheduling, professional development, and many other perks. Bull's Eye is an Equal Opportunity Employer and is a drug-free workplace.
Application deadline: June 7, 2016
Apply online now or email resume and cover letter to Human Resources Director Darlene Smith at humanresources@bestores.biz

1 Where is the job located? _____

2 When is the application deadline? _____

3 How many ways are there to apply for the job? _____

4 What is the job title? _____

5 How much work experience is required? _____

6 What level of education is required? _____

Presentation

Scanning for Key Words

You can scan a longer piece of text to learn its main idea. To do this, you scan for key words – words that are repeated several times in the text because they are important to its meaning.

As you scan for information, move your eyes quickly as you look for key words and phrases. The key words or phrases can often be found in the title and are related to the important ideas in the passage.

You do not need to try to understand all of the ideas in the passage as you scan it. Do not worry about comprehension or trying to read unfamiliar words. Just scan for words that are repeated throughout the text.

Practice 3

Read the list of key words. Then scan the text and underline each key word in the text as you see it.

Key Words:

citizen / citizens / citizenship

legal / legally

nationality / nationalities

country / countries

1 Naturalization

Naturalization is the process by which a person acquires legal nationality or citizenship of a country other than the original citizenship held at birth. Each country has its own laws and policies regarding the requirements and procedures necessary to fulfill in order to apply to become a citizen. In general, however, most countries require that a person be a full-time legal resident for a minimum period of time (ranging between 2 to 12 years, depending on the country). In addition, the applicant must pledge to respect and obey the laws of the new country of citizenship.

2 How Nationality Is Determined

Depending on the citizenship laws, a country may use one of two ways of determining who does or does not have citizenship at birth:

1) *Jus soli* is the Latin term meaning "right of territory." This means that a person is a citizen of a country if he or she is born within that country or its territories, regardless of the nationality of his or her parents.

2) *Jus sanguinis* means "right of blood" and indicates that a person holds the same nationality of his or her parents, regardless of where he or she is born.

Some countries, such as Canada, the U.K., or the U.S. allow citizens to hold dual or multiple citizenships. Others forbid multiple citizenships and require that naturalization applicants agree to give up their original citizenship.

3 Typical Naturalization Applicant

There are no typical characteristics of a citizenship applicant. Individuals may come from any country, and may be applying for naturalization for many different reasons. They may have left their home countries for political, economic, or humanitarian reasons, such as during a time of war or following a natural disaster. Or they may have their own personal or pragmatic reasons for immigrating to a new country, for example, to join other family members already living in the country, or to attend university.

SKIMMING

Presentation

Skimming a News Article

When you skim, you read a passage quickly just to get the general idea. You read quickly by reading only some parts of the text and skipping others.

To skim, follow these steps:

- Look at the title.
- Think about the type of passage (news article, opinion essay, review, etc.).
- Think about what information might be important.
- Look at the first paragraph.
- Read the first sentence of each paragraph.
- Read the last paragraph.
- Note key words or words that are repeated frequently in the passage.
- For a news article, ask yourself *Wh-* questions as you look through the text.

Practice 1

Look at the title of the news article. Skim the text for 45 seconds to find out what it is about. Then answer the questions.

Breakthrough in Search for First Web Page

The European Organization for Nuclear Research, the birthplace of the World Wide Web, (also known as CERN), recently launched an online search for the very first web site ever created. This first webpage was created in 1990 by a British computer scientist named Sir Tim Berners-Lee, who is considered the founding father of the Internet.

In late April, CERN sent out a request to the public via its website for computer files, hardware, and software from the earliest days of the Web. The organization plans to use the materials to create an online exhibit that would let the public experience what the Internet was like when it was first in use. The timing of the exhibit marks the 20th anniversary of the Web's release to the public for free and open use. "The first live webpage was created in 1990, but unfortunately," said Mr. Noyes, "there is no copy of that page at CERN. The oldest copies the organization has date from 1992. The real original page is missing because the web's creators wrote over their earlier work, rather than saving, when they upgraded." Dan Noyes, web manager at CERN's communications group said, "They had no idea their work would be so influential. They saw no need to keep copies or records."

"The public appeal to recover an older version has been successful," he said, "as it has resulted in a demonstration copy of the webpage created by Sir Tim Berners-Lee in 1991, when he was gathering support for his idea of the World Wide Web." According to Noyes, re-creating the first website will enable future generations to understand, explore, and think about how the web has changed modern life.

1 In which section of the newspaper would this article appear?

   a Business

   b Technology

   c Health

   d Environment

2 What is the main purpose of the article?

   a To invite people to an upcoming event at CERN

   b To announce a new manager at CERN

   c To inform people about current work at CERN

   d To explain the work of Sir Tim Berners-Lee at CERN

3 Which sentence best describes the main idea?

   a CERN is the organization responsible for creating the first website.

   b CERN is creating an online exhibit for people to learn the history of the Web.

   c CERN is asking the public to share their first experiences using the Web.

   d CERN has kept detailed records about all of its past work.

Practice 2

Part 1   Product Reviews

Quickly skim the review of a new computer game for not more than 30 seconds. Then answer the questions on p. 24.

gamereviews.com

Palace Storm *by Gengro Electronics*

Palace Storm is the new computer game from Gengro Electronics. In recent years, these types of tower defense games have begun to lose their appeal among experienced gamers who say the action is too predictable, and there's too little variety and not enough competition. However, the new version of Palace Storm delivers enough excitement, challenge, and wild combat action for even the highest-level gamer. Unlike some other tower games, which focus mainly on defense, Gengro Electronics has managed to put out a game with a balance of offense and defense. The visuals and effects are also high-quality and attractive.

The primary goal in Palace Storm is to protect the palace from enemy invaders. In this case, the enemy is in the form of powerful Vikings from a neighboring country, who arrive both by ship and land to try to overthrow the king and take over the palace. What makes this game stand apart from the others is that it not only requires defensive strategy, but players also get to build their offensive capabilities as their forces make their way closer to the enemy's castle and try to take it over.

With all this back and forth action, it definitely gets tricky to keep track of all the details of the game. For that reason, I wouldn't recommend it to beginning-level gamers. The first few times I played, I got confused switching between the different locations. But I got used to it after a while. Overall, this one is well-done and worth the $40.00 price tag.

1 What is the reviewer's overall opinion of the product?

   a positive

   b negative

   c mixed

2 According to the reviewer, what is a negative aspect of the product?

   a It is too predictable.

   b It is too easy.

   c It is confusing.

3 What recommendation does the reviewer make?

   a Buyers should not pay more than $40.

   b Players should be experienced gamers.

   c Games should focus mainly on defense.

Part 2 Entertainment Reviews

Quickly skim the review of a new album for not more than 30 seconds. Then answer the questions.

tunesreview.net

Daren Rider's first jazz single, "Swing in Line," helped a retired rock star turn his life around and reinvent his career. Rider, the former lead singer of the well-known Australian rock band Lionhead, has been out of the spotlight for the past 10 years. "I had to take a break and focus on my personal life for awhile," said Rider in a recent interview, citing difficulties in his marriage caused by the challenges of being away from home while on tour with Lionhead. The time away from the band allowed Rider to focus on another area of musical passion – Jazz.

On his latest album, *Rosie's Groove*, the artist proves that he has some potential in the jazz genre, with a few well- written, original tunes hidden among the primarily uninspiring cover songs, which Rider seems to have copied exactly. However, he has a long way to go before he can be considered a true jazz musician. One positive point to the album is the thing that made Rider famous in the rock world: his incredible voice. Amazingly, it's still as strong as ever, and listening to the album brought back great memories of seeing Rider on stage with Lionhead in the old days. The problem is that his vocals are really better-suited to rock than jazz. After listening to about half of the songs on the new album, I'd heard enough, and I went and got out my old copy of Lionhead's first CD, *Rock Safari*.

I think it's great that Rider's back from retirement. It's too early for a talented songwriter and vocalist to just disappear from the music scene. He still has a lot of good years left in him... just not as a jazz musician. If you want to hear the best of Daren Rider, don't buy *Rosie's Groove*, instead, wait for the Lionhead box set of greatest hits, which hits music stores later this summer.

1 What is the reviewer's overall opinion of the album?

   a Positive

   b Negative

   c Mixed

2 Which sentence best describes the reviewer's main point?

   a Daren Rider is better at playing rock than jazz.

   b Musicians should not try to switch genres of music.

   c Lionhead is one of the best rock bands of all time.

3 What recommendation does the reviewer make?

   a People should go see Daren Rider in concert.

   b People should buy Daren Rider's old albums.

   c People should only buy Daren Rider's best jazz songs.

Part 3   Travel Reviews

Quickly skim the review of a tour company for not more than 30 seconds. Then answer the questions on p. 27.

Traveltourreviews.net

Thank you for this opportunity to post comments on your website about our recent trip to China. I am happy to offer you feedback on the tours conducted by your company.

When we began to plan our trip to Beijing and Xian, I searched a number of websites, looking for reputable tour companies. Your website seemed to offer the most tour options, but none of your scheduled group tours coincided with our desired travel dates. On writing an email to your customer service department, your agent's response was quick, clear, and thorough. She kindly offered us a private tour at a reasonable price.

As our trip approached, I requested several changes and additions. Your representatives always responded quickly and politely, and were willing to bend over backward to give us the trip we really wanted. They also made helpful recommendations for airline reservations and handled all the domestic transport, hotel accommodations, and meal reservations for us. This saved us time and money and we greatly appreciated your expertise. All transportation during our trip was on time, the hotels were comfortable, and the food and the service were generally excellent.

We made a huge mistake in planning our trip during a Chinese public holiday week. All the sites we visited were impossibly crowded with visitors, both foreign and Chinese. In many cases, the crowds were so large that we could not even get close to the actual site, and had to view it from a great distance. We spent hours on the bus due to traffic jams in Beijing, and parking lots were full at several sites, so we had to come back during the evening hours. Although we had reservations, we still had to wait a long time to sit down and be served in the restaurants. Our guide, Ms. Li, was very kind and tried to find alternatives for us when there were issues. Of course, we don't blame any of that on your company, but I hope you will advise other customers in the future to avoid traveling to China during that week.

Overall, we were satisfied with the trip. It was reasonably priced, and the guides were pleasant and knowledgeable and spoke excellent English. I would highly recommend your company to anyone wishing to travel to China. When we return, we will certainly come to you first for our travel needs. Thank you and your staff for a memorable journey.

Mrs. Joan Bonnett

1 How was the reviewer's overall experience with the tour company?

   a Positive

   b Negative

   c Mixed

2 What was one negative aspect of the reviewer's trip?

   a The bus was too slow.

   b The sites were too crowded.

   c The guide did not speak English.

3 Which statement best describes the reviewer's recommendation?

   a She highly recommends the tour company to anyone.

   b She recommends it only to people who have traveled to China before.

   c She recommends choosing a different tour company.

Presentation

Skimming Blogs

There are blogs on every subject imaginable. Blogs are a great way to get information and ideas, and to learn about different people's opinions on a topic. Skimming is a useful way to decide quickly if a blog contains information that is interesting or useful to you. As with new articles, it's helpful to ask yourself *Wh-* questions to get the main idea of the blog. For example, ask yourself

- Who is the blog written by?
- Who is the target audience?
- What is the blogger's opinion or main point?
- Why did the person write the blog?

When you skim, read the main title or heading and any bold subheadings. Then quickly skim the first paragraph, the first and last line of the middle paragraphs, and the whole last paragraph.

Practice 3

Skim the blog and circle the letter of the best answer that completes each sentence on p. 29.

Students of the World Blog

Best Ways to Keep Your Memories of Your Study Abroad Experience
Posted on May 31th, 2014 by Johann Franken

Busy college students have enough to keep track of, especially when they're studying overseas. Of course your experiences will be memorable, and you'll want to share them with family and friends in your home country. Today's guest blogger, Johann Franken, shares his thoughts on the best ways to make your memories last a lifetime.

Traveling to a new country can be a life-changing experience. We see the world in new ways and we make fascinating discoveries about our own culture and about ourselves. In short, it changes our global outlook. Of course, it's important to document these experiences so you can share them with loved ones and look back and remember them throughout your life. Unless you hire a reality show film crew, it's impossible to capture every important moment, but by combining some simple, old-fashioned memory-keeping techniques with today's technology, you can create long-lasting memories of your trip that are easy to share with others.

Here are a few options for documenting your adventures:

Journaling

Keeping a journal is a great way not only to document memories, but also to express how you're feeling about living and studying far from home and adjusting to a new culture.

Carrying a notepad with you at all times is probably the best way to keep an accurate record of your experiences. That way you can write brief notes in real time, rather than waiting until later when you've forgotten the details of the situation and your true feelings.

Blog

Writing a blog may help you write more frequently, as you have an audience waiting to read your posts. But you need to be the type of person who doesn't mind sharing your private thoughts and feelings openly. Of course, you can allow only certain people to view your blog, but that may include your friends as well as your parents and grandparents. We all share different things with the different people in our lives; for example, there are things you would tell your friends that you wouldn't tell your grandparents. With a blog, you'll have to choose topics carefully and use a tone for your writing that works for all readers. It can be hard to keep your writing truly open and candid when you have such a broad audience.

Photos

They say a picture is worth a thousand words. Cell phone cameras, tablets, and photo-sharing sites make it easy to remember the places you visit and what people look like. These images are important, and great to give the people back home a virtual tour of where you've been. Over time, however, the images alone don't necessarily help you keep a detailed record of the events and your feelings about them.

Video

With images and sound combined, video provides the most accurate representation of your experiences. Watching your video later may also help you remember the moment more clearly. Video editing takes some skill and time though, so make sure you're ready to take on that challenge.

The Ideal Combination

If you really want to do things right, I feel a combination of all of the above is the best approach. Carry a notebook and a video camera with you and write down things that strike you and things you want to remember. Most cameras, and even cell phones these days have the option of taking both video and audio. From your journal entries, choose certain things you want to share with family and friends and post them on a blog along with photos and video of the people, places, and experiences. Your blog will be there forever so you can look back and remember your experiences and share them with whomever you choose.

1 The most likely audience for this blog is
   a all university students everywhere.
   b students studying in a foreign country.
   c first-year university students in the US.

2 The purpose of this blog is mainly to
   a share memories.
   b entertain the reader.
   c suggest ideas.

3 The blogger's advice is to
   a take photos of only important experiences.
   b use a combination of different approaches.
   c avoid sharing private information online.

Presentation

Skimming for Research

When you need to write a research report, you should first preview the materials to determine whether they are useful or not. Then you can skim to find out more about the content and which parts will be most relevant for your research.

Rather than reading whole articles, skimming helps you save time when you do research by allowing you to focus on the sections that are relevant to your topic. Here is how to skim research materials:

- Skim the heading or title and any bold subheadings.
- Then skim over any graphics or charts.
- Then read the first paragraphs, first and last line of each middle paragraph, and the whole last paragraph.

Practice 4

Skim the text from a website. Then circle the letter of the best answer to each question on p. 31.

NATIONAL OCEANIC AND ATMOSPHERIC ADMINISTRATION

Data Helps New York City Prepare for Climate Change

New York City is America's largest coastal community at risk from the effects of a changing climate. Temperature increases and sea level rise are already occurring and, along with other climate changes, are likely to accelerate. As a city of more than 8 million people situated along 520 miles of coastline, with an extensive underground infrastructure prone to flooding, and lack of easy evacuation routes, it is particularly vulnerable to coastal storms and sea level rise. Recognizing the seriousness of climate change, city planners and decision-makers have started to take action.

As part of PlaNYC New York City's long-term sustainability plan, Mayor Michael Bloomberg convened the New York City Panel on Climate Change (NPCC) to advise the city on issues related to climate change and adaptation. The panel of experts used climate data to analyze the current climate and project future climate scenarios. This climate information was a key part of the coordinated adaptation plan for the city's critical infrastructure developed by the New York City Climate Change Adaptation Task Force, comprised of public agencies and private companies. The NPCC used observed weather data from the National Oceanic and Atmospheric Administration (NOAA's) National Climatic Data Center (NCDC) to complete a historical climate analysis for temperature and precipitation. NPCC used these analyses to identify observed trends in both mean climate and climate extremes, such as hot or cold temperatures and intense precipitation events. Their analysis for Central Park has determined that the observed trend for temperature is increasing by 0.25 degrees Fahrenheit per decade and increasing for precipitation by 0.72 inches per decade.

A similar historical analysis for sea-level rise, conducted with data collected from the NOAA tide gauge at The Battery, indicates that the net sea level has been rising relative to the land since 1900, at a rate of 1.2 inches per decade. Future climate projection scenarios for temperature, precipitation, sea level rise, and extreme events were developed by the NPCC using a suite of global climate models and greenhouse gas emissions scenarios. By comparing climate projections with the observed data analysis, the NPCC was able to determine whether current climate risks can be expected to continue into the future, how risk frequency and severity may change, and how to identify new climate hazards.

NPCC projections indicate that sea level may rise approximately 1 to 2 feet by the middle of this century, and as a result, more frequent coastal flooding can be anticipated. For a city that has a significant amount of infrastructure in coastal areas, climate projections are necessary to adequately prepare and plan for a more resilient future. New York City has taken several steps to begin preparing for rising sea level and more frequent coastal flooding. For example, the New York City Department of Environmental Protection (NYCDEP) is raising pumps at the Rockaway Wastewater Treatment plant from 25 feet below the existing sea level to 14 feet above the existing sea level. Design plans for higher water levels have also been used in the development of a park on Governors Island in New York Harbor, much of which lies below the elevation where the NPCC projects the flood level could be by the end of the century. In the design plans for the new park, a significant portion of the new parkland will be raised above the projected flood level by reusing construction debris. Other steps under consideration to address these climate risks include utilizing saltwater-tolerant plants that can thrive on brackish groundwater and replacing impervious paved surface with plants and permeable materials.

1 What kind of information or ideas would you expect to find on this website?

    a travel and tourism

    b weather and environment

    c jobs and careers

2 What is the main topic of the article?

    a climate change and flooding in US city parks

    b effects of climate change on city planning in New York

    c organizations that do research on climate change

3 What is the purpose of the article?

    a to inform the reader about the subject

    b to entertain the reader

    c to persuade the reader to take some action

COMBINED SKILLS: PREVIEWING, SCANNING, AND SKIMMING

Presentation

Combined Skills: Previewing, Scanning, and Skimming

When you read longer texts, you can combine different reading strategies to help you read faster and understand better.

- Remember to preview the text before you begin reading: Look at any pictures or bold headings, and think about the type of writing it is.
- Skim the text quickly to get the main idea.
- Think about the important information you want to know and scan the text quickly to find that information.

Practice 1

Read each question on p. 33 and follow the instructions for reading the textbook excerpt. Then circle the letter of the correct answer.

Black Ships and Japanese Isolation

The Black Ships (*kurofune* in Japanese) were the ships that arrived in Japan from the West during the 16th and 19th centuries. The term "black ships" was first used to identify Portuguese ships, which were the first Western vessels to arrive in Japan in 1543 when they began a trade route between Goa, India and Nagasaki, Japan. These vessels were painted black with tar pitch to enhance waterproofing. This period of peaceful trading with the West lasted approximately a century.

Then, in 1639, a rebellion erupted in Japan, which the ruling Tokugawa shogunate blamed on the influence of Christianity. As a result, the shogun closed off trade and contact with all Westerners, and enforced a strict isolationist policy called "Sakoku."

For 200 years, despite the requests of various Western leaders, Japan remained a primarily locked state, and trade with other nations was practically non-existent, aside from China and an allowance of one ship per year from the Dutch East India Company (based in Indonesia).

The End of Self-imposed Isolation

In the present day, the term "Black Ships" refers in particular to the four U.S. Navy warships—*Mississippi, Plymouth, Saratoga,* and *Susquehanna*—commandeered by United States Commodore Matthew Perry, which arrived in the Bay at Edo (present-day Tokyo) in July of 1853. In this case, black refers not only to the color of the sailing vessels, but also to the black smoke coming from the coal-powered American ships.

Perry's Mission

US President Millard Fillmore sent Commodore Matthew Perry to Japan to try to secure trading rights with Japan for eager American merchants. In addition, the American military wanted the Japanese to help shipwrecked sailors who washed up on their shores, who under Japan's isolationist period, had been either killed or left to die. Perry presented the Japanese with a letter from President Fillmore requesting that Japan open its ports for both diplomatic and commercial purposes.

External Pressure and Internal Revolt

Perry told Japanese leaders he would return the following year, with an even larger fleet, for the shogun's reply. A year later, in July of 1854, Perry arrived with seven ships. This massive display of power, combined with the ships' loud, booming cannons shocked the shoguns and the Japanese people. After some debate among the shogun's advisors, the Japanese leadership determined that Japan could not defend itself against the US Navy. The government conceded, marking the end of Japan's two centuries of isolation.

In the Treaty of Kanagawa, the shogun agreed to open two ports to American ships, though at first, not for trade. After a few years, the United States gained trading rights, leading the way for several European nations to do the same. The Japanese people were angered by the terms of the treaty, which they found unequal and humiliating. Many citizens criticized the shogun for not fighting against the aggressive foreign invaders.

1 Preview the text. What type of textbook is it from?

   a Economics

   b History

   c Engineering

2 From the picture, title, and bold headings, which best describes the topic of the excerpt?

   a the fishing industry in 19th-century Japan

   b Japanese-Chinese trade relations throughout history

   c the arrival of Perry's Black Ships in Japan

3 Skim the excerpt quickly. Which statement best describes the main idea of the text?

   a The arrival of Perry's Black Ships in the 19th century helped resume Japanese trade relations with the West.

   b 19th century American coal-powered warships were modeled after Portuguese ships from the 15th century.

   c International trade relations have improved considerably as a result of American military operations.

4 Scan the excerpt. What happened in 1639?

   a President Millard Fillmore sent Commodore Matthew Perry to Japan.

   b The Japanese began trading with the Dutch East India Company.

   c The Japanese government stopped allowing contact with outside nations.

5 Scan the excerpt. For how long did Japan forbid trade with the West?

   a for two centuries

   b from 1543 to 1639

   c until it stopped trading with China

6 Scan the excerpt. What kind of fuel did the American warships use?

   a steam

   b coal

   c both steam and coal

7 Scan the excerpt. How many ships did Perry bring in 1854?

   a 4

   b 7

   c 47

Practice 2

Read each question on p. 35 and follow the instructions for reading the textbook excerpt. Then circle the letter of the correct answer.

Wolf Kahn, The Early Years

Wolf Kahn, was born in Stuttgart, Germany in 1927. He moved to England at the start of World War II in 1939 and then to New York City in 1940 at age 12. After graduating from the High School of Music and Art, Kahn entered the private art school of German abstract expressionist Hans Hofmann. Sharing their German heritage, Kahn and Hofmann struck up a friendship and Kahn soon became Hofmann's studio assistant. He worked and trained at Hofmann's studio for two years, often helping his fellow artists-in-training by translating Hofmann's frequent use of mixed German and English during his lectures.

"A lot of time I translated for him," Kahn said of Hofmann in an interview, "Hofmann would go up to someone, and he'd say about his or her color, "Your color, this is too bunt." People would look at each other in total incomprehension. What does he mean by that?" Then I'd come in—and say, "Well, it's a German word, *bunt*, which means disorganized color—color that doesn't make any sense, like circus color, or color that's just put together for noise. That's the word *bunt*."

Influence of Nature

Under Hofmann's guidance, Kahn developed his practice of using nature as the primary inspiration for his paintings. Working mainly in oils and pastels, Kahn's works combine color and light in unique ways to create texture and patterns that mimic our natural surroundings. Kahn manages to juxtapose unexpected color combinations, not often in nature—bright magenta, oranges, and pinks with cool and neutral tones—to enhance particular features of nature and portray simultaneous energy and tranquility.

Chicago and Beyond

After two years of training under Hofmann, Kahn was having doubts about his life's direction and felt the need to move on. In 1950, he left New York, relocating to Chicago, where he enrolled in the Bachelor's Degree program at the University of Chicago. He completed his studies in only one year, receiving his degree in 1951.

Now a university graduate, Kahn was determined to become a professional artist. He and a group of other former Hofmann students established the Hansa Gallery in New York, where Kahn had his first solo exhibition.

Personal Life

In 1956, he met Emily Mason, daughter of the founder of the American Abstract Artists organization. Mason was on her way to study in Italy on a Fulbright Scholarship. Kahn later joined Mason in Venice and the two were married there in March 1957. In late 1958, the couple returned to New York. Emily gave birth to their first daughter, Cecily, in 1959. In 1963, the family returned to Italy. Their daughter, Melany, was born in Rome in 1964.

Over the course of his life, Kahn and his family traveled extensively, and he has painted landscapes in Egypt, Greece, Hawaii, Italy, Kenya, Maine, Mexico, and New Mexico.

Kahn has received numerous honors such as the Fulbright Scholarship, a John Simon Guggenheim Fellowship, and an Award in Art from the American Academy of Arts and Letters. His works can be found in the permanent collections of major museums, including the National Museum of American Art, the Metropolitan Museum of Art, and the Boston Museum of Fine Arts. In 2010, he returned to Germany for the first time since his childhood for an exhibition of his pastels at the Museum für Kunst und Gewerbe in Hamburg.

He and Mason still currently live in New York for part of the year, and they spend their summers and autumns on a farm in West Brattleboro, Vermont.

1 Preview the text. What type of text is it?

a a business letter

b a biography

c a newspaper article

2 Skim the text for the general idea. What is Wolf Kahn known for?

a his German translation work

b his abstract landscape paintings

c his marriage to Emily Mason

3 Scan the text. Who was Hans Hofmann?

a Kahn's first English teacher

b Kahn's childhood friend from Germany

c Kahn's art teacher

4 Scan the text. According to the author, what is unique about Kahn's artwork?

a his use of color combinations

b his use of light and shadow

c his use of nature as his inspiration

5 Scan the text. Where did Kahn attend university?

a New York

b Chicago

c Venice

6 Scan the text. How many children did Kahn have?

a two

b one

c three

Understanding Paragraphs

IDENTIFYING THE TOPIC OF A PARAGRAPH

Identifying the Topic of a Paragraph

A paragraph is a group of sentences that all relate to the same topic. Knowing the topic you are reading about is important. When you know the topic, you can make connections to what you already know about it. This helps you make sense of the passage.

The topic sentence, which is usually the first sentence, gives the first clue about the topic. Then the topic is often repeated several times in the passage.

A topic should not be too general, nor too specific. It should be broad enough cover all of the information in the passage.

Practice 1

Read each paragraph and circle the letter of the correct topic.

There are a large number of proponents who would like to make English the official language of the United States. However, there are a growing number of cities and regions around the country, especially those that border Mexico, that are being dominated by Spanish speakers. Some experts predict that Spanish will soon overtake English as the most used language in these areas of the country. As a result, many jobs require some Spanish language ability, and Spanish has become the most commonly studied language among English speakers in the U.S.

1 a the prevalence of the Spanish language in the U.S.
  b jobs that require Spanish language ability
  c Mexicans who come to study English in the U.S.

On Wednesday, a group of eight Senators released the full text of their newly proposed immigration reform legislation, entitled, the "Border Security, Economic Opportunity, and Immigration Modernization Act." The 844-page document addresses border security, undocumented immigrants, and the legal immigration system. The new legislation would allow undocumented immigrants to become citizens after a lengthy application process. It would also require employers to check job applicants using an online system to ensure that they are authorized to work in the U.S.

2 a a newly proposed immigration law
  b documents required for immigration
  c jobs for undocumented immigrants

Practice 2

Read each paragraph and circle the letter of the correct topic.

A constitutional monarchy is a modern system of government used in many countries around the world, such as Thailand and the UK. This model of government employs a monarch (king or queen) as head of government, as well as a parliamentary system with democratically elected members. While the monarch serves as the head of government, he or she typically has limited powers or strictly ceremonial duties. Under most modern constitutional monarchies, a prime minister serves as the official head of state and exercises political decision-making power.

1 **a** an explanation of the government system in the UK
   b the definition of a constitutional monarchy
   c a description of the Thai monarch's duties

The world-famous Songkran Festival happens during the month of April, Thailand's hottest month. Known as the festival of water, Songkran celebrates the Thai New Year. It is a wet and wild celebration that lasts three to five days (up to a full week or more in some parts of the country). City streets are closed off during the festivities when friends and strangers alike gather in the streets to toss water-filled balloons, pour buckets of water on one another, and spray each other with hoses. In addition to throwing water, people may also visit a wat (Buddhist temple) to pray and give food offerings to monks. They may also wash statues and images of Buddha at temples or in their homes, gently pouring water mixed with a Thai fragrance over them in order to bring prosperity for the New Year.

2 **a** the New Year festival in Thailand
   b weather patterns in Thailand
   c Thai religious ceremonies

In many cultures, it is important that food be both delicious and pleasing to look at when it is served. The art of plate garnishing (or decorating) began thousands of years ago in Japan, when food was typically served on plain clay dishes. The Thai art of fruit and vegetable carving is one example of a method used to beautify dishes. Expert carvers use specially made tiny knives to cut intricate patterns into colorful fruits and vegetables such as melons, squash, radishes, carrots, ginger, etc., to make beautiful arrangements that look like amazing floral displays. Some carvers create other shapes, carving letters into the fruit or creating animal shapes. Carvers take great pride in their works of art, and each tries to develop his or her own personal style.

3 **a** the history of decorating dishes
   b traditional Japanese and Thai cooking
   c Thai fruit and vegetable carving

Thai, the official language of Thailand, is a member of the Tai–Kadai language family, and is spoken by over 20 million people. Similar to some other East Asian languages, like Mandarin Chinese or Vietnamese, Thai is a tonal language, having five different tone patterns. These tones are like musical notes and can change the meaning of the words, even if the pronunciation of the word is the same. English and almost all other European languages are not tonal languages. Thai has a complex alphabet consisting of 44 basic symbols, each representing a consonant/vowel sound combination. There are also about 25 additional vowels and vowel combinations. Like English, Thai is written from left to right in horizontal lines.

4 **a** a comparison of East Asian tonal languages
   b a description of the Thai writing system
   c an explanation of the language of Thailand

IDENTIFYING THE MAIN IDEA

Presentation

Main Idea Sentences

A paragraph has one topic and one main idea. The main idea is usually expressed in a sentence that tells you more about the topic. It describes what the writer wants to say about the topic. For example,

Topic: The effects of stress

Main Ideas

- Stress helps people perform better at work.
- People experience stress differently.
- Stress is dangerous and shortens people's lives.

The main idea sentence often appears at the beginning of the paragraph as the first or second sentence, but it may appear in the middle or at the end, depending on the style of writing. It often expresses the writer's opinion about the topic, or gives a summary of the paragraph.

As with topics, the main idea should be neither too general, nor too specific. The main idea sentence should be broad enough to cover all of the information in the paragraph.

Practice 1

Read each paragraph. Write the number of the sentence that expresses the main idea.

[1] It is a commonly held belief that lightning never strikes twice in the same place, but this is not exactly accurate. [2] Forest rangers in some mountainous areas have reported several lightning strikes to the same lookout tower, all within minutes of one another, during particularly strong electrical storms. [3] Recent meteorological research shows that that cloud-to-ground lightning frequently strikes in two or more places and that the chances of being struck are about 45 percent higher than what people commonly assume.

1 _____

[1] The gypsy moth, the Asian long-horned beetle, and the giant African snail are all examples of invasive species. [2] Patterns of human movement around the globe, such as planes flying from country to country, ships sailing to and from different ports, or cars driving up and down highways, create opportunities for these species to relocate and create problems in new areas. [3] Some traits of invasive species, such as rapid reproductive cycles, high levels of adaptability, and tolerance to different weather and temperatures, make it almost impossible to stop their spread once they have arrived in a new area. [4] These species, when transported to a new habitat, can grow out of control and completely take over, killing off native plants and animals. [5] One thing is for sure, in today's globally independent society, the spread of invasive species is highly likely to continue.

2 _____

[1] White-tailed deer and wild turkey are abundant in the region. [2] This entire area is excellent for those who enjoy outdoor sports such as fishing and hunting. [3] There are ample woodlands and open fields with long grasses where animals come to graze. [4] In addition, one can easily find many clean streams, rivers, and ponds filled with rainbow trout and large-mouth bass.

3 _____

[1] The word "coyote" is borrowed from Mexican Spanish and originated from the Aztec word cóyotl, meaning "trickster". [2] The coyote, also sometimes called the American jackal, is a species of wild canine found throughout North and Central America. [3] The color of the coyote's fur may vary from grayish-brown to tawny gray on the upper areas, while the throat and underbelly are generally beige or white in color. [4] Coyotes live in groups, called packs, and communicate with high-pitched calls, consisting of sustained howls, short yips and yelps, as well as barks. [5] Their calls are usually heard at dusk or night, but can also sometimes be heard during daylight hours.

4 _____

[1] In 1979, an Indian teenager named Jadav "Mulai" Payeng began a part-time job with the local government. [1] He worked on a team, planting trees in a sandy, barren 200-acre plot near his hometown in the Assam region of northern India. [2] When the job was completed, the other members of Payeng's team moved on and found work elsewhere. [3] But Payeng decided to stay, even moving to an apartment next to the land. [4] For three decades, Payeng cared for the newly planted trees and plants and continued planting more and more, eventually turning the area into a large forest. [5] Amazingly, today, the location is a lush 1,360-acre jungle which houses four Bengal tigers, three rhinoceros, over 100 deer and rabbits, several apes, and countless species of birds. [6] The area is named the Mulai Forest, after the man who created it nearly single-handedly. [7] Jadev Mulai Payeng's story is proof that one person has the power to make a big difference in the world.

5 _____

Presentation

Main Ideas in Longer Passages

A paragraph has one topic and one main idea. Each paragraph in a longer passage has one topic and one main idea. The main idea is usually expressed in a sentence that tells you more about the topic. It describes what the writer wants to say about the topic. For example:

   Topic: The effects of stress

Main Ideas

- Stress helps people perform better at work.
- People experience stress differently.
- Stress is dangerous and shortens people's lives.

As with topics, the main idea should be neither too general, nor too specific. The main idea should be broad enough to cover all of the information in the paragraph.

Practice 2

Read the essay. Then read the main idea sentences on p. 41. Write the number of the paragraph that each main idea belongs to.

1   Something strange was happening in northern Canada, in the early- and mid-1940s. There began to be a sudden, rapid decline of the caribou population. The government, unable to find another reason, blamed this decline on Arctic wolves, which inhabited the region. To combat these "ruthless" predators, the government hired teams of professional "wolfers," and sent them to kill wolves in massive numbers. During this time, regular citizens who saw wolves were allowed, and even encouraged, to kill them. People began to view wolves as aggressive, dangerous, ruthless predators.

2   Farley Mowat is a Canadian environmentalist and author of the book, *Never Cry Wolf*, which journals Mowat's experiences living in the Canadian Arctic and studying Arctic wolves. The book, which was made into a film in 1983, changed people's understandings and perceptions of the wolf forever. Mowat spent many months living among the wolves and studying their habits. He observed all aspects of the animal's lives—how they raised their young, how they communicated, and how they hunted. One thing he very rarely saw, however, was wolves killing caribou. In *Never Cry Wolf*, he documented that Arctic wolves usually prey on smaller mammals, such as rabbits and rodents, even choosing them over caribou. In the cases where Mowat did observe wolves preying on caribou, the caribou was an older, sick, or weak animal, making it easier for the wolves to catch it. Because of the small numbers of caribou he saw wolves hunting, Mowat concluded that it was impossible for wolves to be the true cause of the declining caribou population.

3   Over the course of his time in the Arctic, Mowat did see large numbers of caribou killed, but not by wolves, by human hunters. This, he concluded, was the real cause of the declining caribou population. In *Never Cry Wolf*, he writes, "We have doomed the wolf not for what it is, but for what we deliberately and mistakenly perceive it to be—the mythological epitome of a savage, ruthless killer—which is, in reality, no more than the reflected image of ourself."

4   After the publication of *Never Cry Wolf* in 1963, The Canadian Wildlife Service received a flood of letters from angry citizens urging them to stop its policy of killing Arctic wolves. When the book was translated into other languages, its influence spread to other countries, such as Russia, where people began to protest against similar anti-wolf policies. Mowat's time in the Arctic and his subsequent book gave the world a view of wolves we may have never seen otherwise, and helped protect these beautiful, intelligent animals from the fiercest enemy they have ever faced—humans.

1 _____ The book, *Never Cry Wolf* documents Farley Mowat's observation of the Arctic wolf's habits, which did not include hunting large amounts of caribou.

2 _____ Mowat made the startling conclusion that human hunters were actually responsible for the dropping caribou population.

3 _____ The Canadian government began the systematic killing of wolves because of a decline in the number of caribou in the 1940s.

4 _____ People and governments around the world adopted a more positive attitude toward the wolf after the publication of Farley Mowat's book.

Practice 3

Read the passage. Circle the numbers of the statements on p. 42 that reflect main ideas expressed in the passage.

Kakenya Ntaiya grew up in Kenya, the oldest of eight children born to Maasai parents. In Maasai culture, girls must grow up quickly. They begin at an early age learning to cook, clean, gather firewood, carry water from the river, and tend the farm. They will continue to perform this hard work after marriage and throughout their adulthood. Maasai marriages are typically arranged by the parents. Families of boys and girls as young as five or six agree that their children will marry in the future. Each family promises gifts, such as money and livestock, to the other family and to the new couple. Maasai girls often must stop their education at 12 or 13 in order to marry.

Like most Maasai girls, Kakenya was engaged to be married by the age of five to a boy her parents had chosen for her. She attended elementary school until, at the age of 13, her father told her it was time to stop her education and get married. Although Kakenya knew this day would come, the idea of leaving school was too difficult to bear. Since the day she entered, school had been the only thing that brought Kakenya true happiness. She studied hard and got excellent grades. She admired her teachers in their crisp, clean clothes and she dreamed of someday becoming one herself. "I lived in a hut made of grass and mud that we shared with goats and sheep. But I had dreams. I kept pictures of beautiful green places with nice homes and somehow knew there was a different life out there."

Kakenya thought about her future as a married woman in her village. She thought about how hard her own mother had worked all her life. "I looked at this boy," she recalls, "whose family was even poorer than my own. I looked at all my mother's anger and pain. I looked at this hopeless future in front of me and I said, 'No way.'" What Kakenya did next created a chain of events that changed the future for all girls in her village. She went to her father and told him she would get married, but only if he would allow her to finish high school. This was an act of courage and optimism other girls in her village could not imagine. To her surprise, her kind father agreed.

After her graduation, Kakenya was accepted to a teachers college in Kenya, and then to a university in the United States. At that time, however, her father was gravely ill and lay paralyzed in the hospital. She said, "My mother had sold almost everything to pay for his care, so there was no money for college, especially in the US." In Maasai culture, it is said that in bad times, the person who arrives before the sunrise will bring good news. Kakenya decided to be that person. One morning, by the faint light of dawn, she visited the leader of her village. She told him of her acceptance to university in the US. The village leader knew Kakenya's father was sick, and that the rest of her family would need someone to help care for them. He consulted with the other leaders and gathered the financial and community support for Kakenya to continue her education.

Kakenya was the first woman from her village to graduate from college. She completed her Ph.D. in education in the US and then returned to her village to build Ntaiya's Academy for Girls, the first primary school only for girls. The school now has 60 girls and five teachers and plans to accept 30 new girls each year. Along with fostering strong academics, Kakenya's school nurtures leadership skills. "After just a few months here, they become completely different people," Kakenya observes. "In a girls-only environment, they lead, make decisions, speak up, and gain confidence. They're smart and thriving. They just needed a chance." Thanks to one young girl's courage, patience, and persistence, they'll get one.

Which statements reflect main ideas expressed in the passage?

1 In Maasai culture, most women do not have much choice in their lives.

2 For Kakenya Ntaiya, education was the greatest priority in life.

3 In a typical African marriage, women take care of the children while men tend to the farm.

4 The education system in Africa has changed rapidly over the past few decades.

5 Kakenya Ntaiya's actions have improved the lives of many girls in her village.

IDENTIFYING KEY DETAILS

Presentation

Key Details

Certain details in a text may have more or less importance, depending on the type of text you are reading and your purpose for reading it. Think about what you want and need to know from a text and which details are important to you before you begin reading.

Scanning is a useful skill to help you locate key details because you read quickly for specific information.

Practice 1

Read the passage. Which key details are included? Circle the letter for *True, False,* or *It doesn't say*.

The History of Fingerprints

We take it for granted now, but at the turn of the twentieth century, the use of fingerprints to identify criminals was still in its infancy.

More popular at the time was the Bertillon system, which measured dozens of features of a criminal's face and body and recorded the series of precise numbers on a large card along with a photograph. After all, law enforcement officials thought, what were the chances that two different people would look the same and have all of the identical measurements logged by the Bertillon method?

Very small, of course. But inevitably, a case came along to beat the odds.

It happened this way: In 1903, a convicted criminal named Will West was taken to Leavenworth federal prison in Kansas. The clerk at the admissions desk, thinking he recognized West, asked if he'd ever been to Leavenworth. The new prisoner denied it. The clerk took his Bertillon measurements and went to the files, only to return with a card for a "William" West. It turns out, Will and William bore an uncanny resemblance (they may have been identical twins). And their Bertillon measurements were a near match.

The clerk asked Will again if he'd ever been to the prison. "Never," he protested. When the clerk flipped the card over, he discovered Will was telling the truth. "William" was already in Leavenworth, serving a life sentence for murder! Soon after, the fingerprints of both men were taken, and they were clearly different.

It was this incident that caused the Bertillon system to eventually be replaced. The next year, Leavenworth abandoned the method and started fingerprinting its inmates. Thus began the first federal fingerprint collection.

1 Before fingerprinting, the Bertillion method was used to identify criminals.
   a True
   b False
   c It doesn't say.

2 Law enforcement officials thought the Bertillion method was too complicated to use.
   a True
   b False
   c It doesn't say.

3 Will West was a clerk at Leavenworth prison.

   a True

   b False

   c It doesn't say.

4 Will and William West may have been brothers.

   a True

   b False

   c It doesn't say.

5 The Bertillion method is still in use in some places.

   a True

   b False

   c It doesn't say.

Presentation

Supporting Information

As you know, paragraphs have one main idea. All of the information in the paragraph gives more detail to support the main idea. After you identify the main idea of a paragraph, look for details, facts, and examples that support it. Understanding the relationship between the main idea and supporting information will help your reading comprehension.

Practice 2

Part 1

Read the paragraph and circle the letter of the best answer.

A Brief History of Indian Film

The Indian film industry began in the 1920s and 1930s. The first color film, entitled *Kisan Kanya*, was released in 1937 by director Ardeshir Irani; however, color was not widely used in Indian filmmaking until the 1950s. The late 1940s to the 1960s marked an important period in Hindi cinema. Several of the best-known Indian films were produced during this time. In 1957, the film *Mother India*, directed by Mehboob Khan, was nominated for an Academy Award for Best Foreign Language Film. During the 1960s and 1970s, Bollywood's traditional romantic films became adventure/action movies, but the 1980s and 1990s saw a shift back to the musical love stories that are still typical today. The early 2000s saw a rapid growth in the popularity of Bollywood cinema and Hindi music.

1 Which statement about the Indian film industry in the 1940s–1960s is true?

   a Musical love stories were popular.

   b It was an important time.

   c It was when the industry first started.

2 Which detail from the paragraph supports the answer to question 1?

  a The Indian film industry began in the 1920s and 1930s.

  b Several of the best-known Indian films were produced during this time.

  c The early 2000s saw a rapid growth in the popularity of Bollywood cinema and Hindi music.

Part 2

Read the paragraph and circle the letter of the best answer.

Climate Change and New York City

New York City is America's largest coastal community at risk from the effects of a changing climate. Temperature increases and sea level rise are already occurring and, along with other climate changes, are likely to accelerate. As a city of more than 8 million people, situated along 520 miles of coastline with an extensive underground infrastructure prone to flooding and lack of easy evacuation routes, it is particularly vulnerable to coastal storms and a rise in sea level. Recognizing the seriousness of climate change, city planners and decision-makers have started to take action.

1 Which statement about New York City is true?

  a Officials there are not concerned about climate change.

  b Climate change is likely to have widespread negative effects.

  c Climate change has had very little effect so far.

2 Which detail supports the answer to question 1?

  a Recognizing the seriousness of climate change, city planners and decision-makers have started to take action.

  b Temperature increases and sea level rise are already occurring and, along with other climate changes, are likely to accelerate.

  c As a city of more than 8 million people, situated along 520 miles of coastline with an extensive underground infrastructure prone to flooding and lack of easy evacuation routes, it is particularly vulnerable to coastal storms and a rise in sea level.

Presentation

Organizing Details

Some texts contain numerous details, which can be difficult to keep track of and understand. It is helpful to take notes and sort or organize the details to help you determine which ones are important. This is particularly helpful when doing research.

Practice 3

Read the descriptions of the two candidates for mayor of Newton. Write the number of the detail about each person in the correct box on p. 46.

While Tom Fredrickson and Carol Newman agree on some issues, the two candidates running for mayor of Newton differ in a number of key areas. First, Fredrickson has been called the "green candidate" and has said he plans to assemble a committee of citizen volunteers to research ways the city can be more efficient in terms of its energy usage. He also proposed spending $1,000,000 on a new transportation center designed to encourage more use of the city's public transportation system. On the other hand, Carol Newman has focused more on education reform. She says she wants to renovate and modernize the city's high school, which was built over 40 years ago. Her proposed project would cost about $500,000. Fredrickson and Newman agree that property taxes should be lowered. However, Newman would like to impose a new higher toll for cars traveling on Highway 97. Fredrickson has not proposed raising any taxes so far. The main issue the two candidates disagree on is the idea of installing cameras on the city's street corners. Although Fredrickson says that the cameras will save money because the city will need fewer police officers, Newman opposes the idea because she says the cameras and their maintenance will cost just as much or more than hiring a few more officers.

1. has not proposed raising taxes
2. wants a higher highway toll
3. called the green candidate
4. thinks cameras downtown will save money
5. focused on education reform
6. feels property taxes should be lowered
7. thinks cameras downtown will cost too much
8. wants to renovate the high school
9. wants to build a transportation center

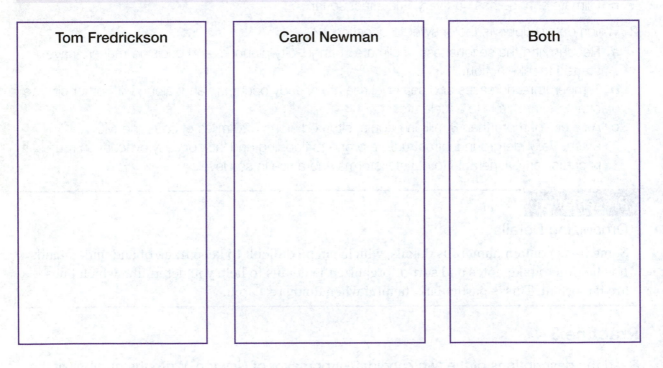

Tom Fredrickson	Carol Newman	Both

Making Inferences

FACTS VS. INFERENCES

Presentation

Facts vs. Inferences

In many types of writing, authors present factual (true) information about a topic, as well as make inferences from those facts. This means that in addition to presenting important facts, they also include information and ideas that come from their own imaginations or experiences with the world.

Facts are statements that can be proven true. For example:

On February 25, 2013, Park Geun-hye became the eleventh president of South Korea. She is the country's first woman to assume this post.

Inferences use one or more facts to make an assumption. For example:

South Korea has become less politically conservative in recent years. (The facts above were used to make this assumption. This is the writer's opinion.)

It is useful to recognize the distinction between facts and inferences so that you can use both facts and inferences to more thoroughly evaluate and analyze information in texts.

Practice 1

Read the newspaper article. Then read each statement on p. 48. Write *F* next to a fact, and write *I* next to an inference.

Police Release Photograph of Mysterious "Forest Boy"

BERLIN—June 11, 2012 Police in Berlin, Germany have released a photograph of the English-speaking boy known as "Ray," nearly a year after he arrived in the city. The boy, who police say is between the ages of 16-20, arrived in Berlin under mysterious circumstances in September 2011 claiming he been living with his father in the nearby woods, and except for his first name, "Ray," had no idea who he was. The boy had previously not given permission for his photo to be released. The Berlin police have been growing frustrated by the lack of leads in the case. "He has finally given us permission to release a photograph of him and we are appealing for information about who he is," said Thomas Neuendorf of the Berlin police.

Language specialists analyzed Ray's speech and accent in an attempt to identify where he came from. Neuendorf said, "At first he spoke just English, but from his accent the specialists could not determine where he was from." Neuendorf added that the boy was sticking to his original story—one that has captivated the world's attention—that his mother, Doreen, died in a car accident when he was 12, and his father Ryan had taken him to live in the woods for about five years. They slept in a tent or found shelter in hunting sheds. Ray says that one day after a sudden illness, his father died. He then says he followed his father's emergency instructions—to walk north until he found the city and ask for help.

1 _____ "Ray" speaks English.

2 _____ Ray came to Berlin in September 2011.

3 _____ The Berlin police have been growing frustrated by the lack of leads in the case.

4 _____ Language specialists analyzed Ray's speech.

5 _____ The boy's story has captivated the world's attention.

Practice 2

Read the newspaper article. Then read each statement. Write *F* next to a fact, and write *I* next to an inference.

"Forest Boy" Mystery Revealed

BERLIN—June 15, 2012   Police in Germany reported that the individual who claimed to be a 17-year-old named "Ray" who had been living wild in the woods for five years, is actually a 20-year-old Dutch runaway. After his photograph was released earlier this week, the man's step-mother contacted Berlin police and identified him as Robin Van Helsum, who was reported missing by his family five days before he turned up in Berlin in September 2011.

Van Helsum's initial story was that he had been living in the woods with his father since his mother was killed in a car crash five years earlier, and that his father had subsequently died following a fall. After his father's death, he claimed to have walked for days until he reached the city.

Investigators were unable to confirm details of the story. There were no records of the car crash and the body of the father was never found, which raised doubts about his account. The man had initially refused to allow his picture to be issued, which prevented officials from making progress in identifying him until recently.

"He has admitted that he is a fraud," Thomas Neuendorf of the Berlin police told the press. Van Helsum's friends told the media that he had personal problems and suggested that his disappearance was an effort to start a new life. The man is now facing charges of fraud for the money he cost the city while being in the care of the youth welfare office. The sum is reported at over $40,000.

1 _____ The man is twenty years old.

2 _____ The man left home five days before he arrived in Berlin.

3 _____ The police and the general public felt something was strange about Van Helsum's story.

4 _____ After seeing his photo, Van Helsum's step-mother contacted German police.

5 _____ Van Helsum's disappearance was an attempt to start a new life.

MAKING INFERENCES FROM FICTION

Presentation

Making Inferences from Fiction

Fiction writers often use details to give hints about a situation or about character's feelings. They can use dialogue between characters, descriptions of body language or setting, or use descriptive phrases to give more information about a situation.

When you make inferences about fiction, you use information you know along with clues from the passage (descriptive words, dialogue, punctuation, etc.) to make assumptions about a situation or character's feelings.

Practice 1

Read the passage from *The Secret Garden* by Frances Hodgson Burnett. Then circle the letter of the answer that completes each inference on p. 50.

Mary put down her candle on the table near the bed and sat down on the cushioned stool. She did not want to go away at all. She wanted to stay in the mysterious hidden-away room and talk to the mysterious boy.

"What do you want me to tell you?" she said.

He wanted to know how long she had been at Misselthwaite; he wanted to know which corridor her room was on; he wanted to know what she had been doing; if she disliked the moor as he disliked it; where she had lived before she came to Yorkshire. She answered all these questions and many more and he lay back on his pillow and listened. He made her tell him a great deal about India and about her voyage across the ocean. She found out that because he had been an invalid he had not learned things as other children had. One of his nurses had taught him to read when he was quite little and he was always reading and looking at pictures in splendid books.

Though his father rarely saw him when he was awake, he was given all sorts of wonderful things to amuse himself with. He never seemed to have been amused, however. He could have anything he asked for and was never made to do anything he did not like to do.

"Everyone is obliged to do what pleases me," he said indifferently.

"It makes me ill to be angry. No one believes I shall live to grow up."

He said it as if he was so accustomed to the idea that it had ceased to matter to him at all. He seemed to like the sound of Mary's voice. As she went on talking he listened in a drowsy, interested way. Once or twice she wondered if he were not gradually falling into a doze. But at last he asked a question which opened up a new subject.

"How old are you?" he asked.

"I am ten," answered Mary, forgetting herself for the moment, "and so are you."

"How do you know that?" he demanded in a surprised voice.

"Because when you were born the garden door was locked and the key was buried. And it has been locked for ten years."

Colin half sat up, turning toward her, leaning on his elbows.

"What garden door was locked? Who did it? Where was the key buried?" he exclaimed as if he were suddenly very much interested.

"It—it was the garden Mr. Craven hates," said Mary nervously.
"He locked the door. No one—no one knew where he buried the key."
"What sort of a garden is it?" Colin persisted eagerly.
"No one has been allowed to go into it for ten years," was Mary's careful answer.
But it was too late to be careful. He was too much like herself. He too had had nothing to think about and the idea of a hidden garden attracted him as it had attracted her. He asked question after question. Where was it? Had she never looked for the door? Had she never asked the gardeners?
"They won't talk about it," said Mary. "I think they have been told not to answer questions."
"I would make them," said Colin.
"Could you?" Mary faltered, beginning to feel frightened. If he could make people answer questions, who knew what might happen!
"Everyone is obliged to please me. I told you that," he said.
"If I were to live, this place would sometime belong to me. They all know that. I would make them tell me."

1 The characters are in
  a a hospital room.
  b the boy's bedroom.
  c the girl's bedroom.

2 The two children
  a know each other from school.
  b are meeting for the first time.
  c are the same age.

3 The girl has recently
  a moved to a new home.
  b taken a vacation.
  c finished school.

4 The boy is
  a lost.
  b sick.
  c shy.

5 After this conversation, the children will probably
  a look for the garden together.
  b begin to dislike each other.
  c plan to escape to India.

Practice 2

Excerpt 1

Read the excerpt from the book *Pollyanna* by Eleanor H. Porter. Then circle the letter of the answer to complete each inference on p. 51.

Miss Polly Harrington entered her kitchen a little hurriedly this June morning. Miss Polly did not usually make hurried movements; she specially prided herself on her repose of manner. But today she was hurrying—actually hurrying. Nancy, washing dishes at the sink, looked up in surprise. Nancy had been working in Miss Polly's kitchen only two months, but already she knew that her mistress did not usually hurry.

"Nancy!"

"Yes, ma'am." Nancy answered cheerfully, but she still continued wiping the pitcher in her hand.

"Nancy,"—Miss Polly's voice was very stern now—"when I'm talking to you, I wish you to stop your work and listen to what I have to say."

Nancy flushed miserably. She set the pitcher down at once, with the cloth still about it, thereby nearly tipping it over—which did not add to her composure.

"Yes, ma'am; I will, ma'am," she stammered, righting the pitcher, and turning hastily. "I was only keeping on with my work because you specially told me this morning to hurry with my dishes, you know."

Her mistress frowned.

"That will do, Nancy. I did not ask for explanations. I asked for your attention."

1 Polly Harrington is
  a the head servant.
  b a wealthy woman.
  c one of the maids.

2 Nancy is feeling
  a angry and irritable.
  b calm and carefree.
  c nervous and uneasy.

3 The two women are
  a enjoying spending time together.
  b preparing for an important event.
  c cleaning up after dinner as usual.

Excerpt 2

Read another excerpt from the book *Pollyanna* by Eleanor H. Porter. Then circle the letter of the answer that completes each inference on p. 52.

"Yes, ma'am." Nancy stifled a sigh. She was wondering if ever in any way she could please this woman. Nancy had never worked before; but a sick mother suddenly widowed and left with three younger children besides Nancy herself, had forced the girl into doing something toward their support, and she had been so pleased when she found a place in the kitchen of the great house on the hill—Nancy had come from "The Corners," six miles away, and she knew Miss Polly Harrington only as the mistress of the old Harrington homestead, and one of the wealthiest residents of the town. That was two months before. She knew Miss Polly now as a stern, severe-faced woman who frowned if a knife clattered to the floor, or if a door banged—but who never thought to smile even when knives and doors were still.

> "When you've finished your morning work, Nancy," Miss Polly was saying now, "you may clear the little room at the head of the stairs in the attic, and make up the cot bed. Sweep the room and clean it, of course, after you clear out the trunks and boxes."
>
> "Yes, ma'am. And where shall I put the things, please, that I take out?"
>
> "In the front attic."

1 Polly Harrington's character can be described as
  a grumpy.
  b cheerful.
  c gentle.

2 Nancy is
  a a relative of Miss Harrington's.
  b a girl from a poor family.
  c from a wealthy part of town.

3 What is happening soon?
  a Miss Harrington is planning to move.
  b Nancy is going to go back to The Corners.
  c Someone is coming to stay at the house.

Excerpt 3

Read another excerpt from *Pollyanna*. Then circle the letter of the answer to complete each inference.

> Miss Polly hesitated, then went on: "I suppose I may as well tell you now, Nancy. My niece, Miss Pollyanna Whittier, is coming to live with me. She is eleven years old, and will sleep in that room."
>
> "A little girl—coming here, Miss Harrington? Oh, won't that be nice!" cried Nancy, thinking of the sunshine her own little sisters made in the home at "The Corners."
>
> "Nice? Well, that isn't exactly the word I should use," rejoined Miss Polly, stiffly. "However, I intend to make the best of it, of course. I am a good woman, I hope; and I know my duty."
>
> Nancy colored hotly. "Of course, ma'am; it was only that I thought a little girl here might—might brighten things up for you," she faltered.
>
> "Thank you," rejoined the lady, dryly. "I can't say, however, that I see any immediate need for that."
>
> "But, of course, you—you'd want her, your sister's child," ventured Nancy, vaguely feeling that somehow she must prepare a welcome for this lonely little stranger.

1 Polly Harrington
  a does not have any children of her own.
  b is looking forward to her niece's arrival.
  c does not have a lot of space in her house.

2 Miss Harrington's niece, Pollyanna, will probably
  a feel welcome at the house.
  b become friends with Nancy.
  c be happy to leave her home.

FACTS AND OPINIONS

Presentation

Distinguishing Fact from Opinion

Writers often present information blending facts with their own opinions. It is important to be able to distinguish between these two types of statements when you read.

Facts are statements that are known to be true, and can be confirmed. For example:

> *In March 2010, the US government passed a law requiring fast food restaurants to display the number of calories next to every item on their menus.*

> *The law applies to restaurants that have more than 20 locations.*

Opinions express a personal belief or preference that cannot be proven true or false. For example:

> *Although the new law may help some people make healthy choices, it is unlikely it will have a great effect anytime soon.*

> *The US has a long battle ahead in the fight against obesity.*

Certain key words and phrases can let a reader know that a statement is an opinion. In the first example above, the word *unlikely* tells the reader that this is an opinion. The second example is a statement that cannot be proven true or false.

Practice 1

Read the passage. Then read each statement from the passage and decide if it is a fact or an opinion. Write the number of the statement in the correct box on p. 54.

"Nanny state" is an expression which originated in Britain. The term is used to describe laws and policies that aim to control people's behavior in an effort to protect them from danger. Policies such as mandatory seatbelt laws, motorcycle and bicycle helmet laws, and high taxes on junk food are examples of the government overstepping its power. According to officials who adhere to these policies, it is the government's duty to protect citizens from their own dangerous behavior. These authorities assume that the government, not the citizens themselves, should be the judge of what constitutes "dangerous behavior."

   Recent attempts at regulating retail food and beverages are particularly disturbing. Last year, New York City Mayor Michael Bloomberg proposed a ban on selling soft drinks over 16 ounces. Bloomberg defended the ban, saying it would help curb childhood obesity and promote better health in general. Recent research has shown that large-sized sweetened drinks are a major contributing factor in childhood obesity. However, a government-imposed ban on soda size is likely to be an ineffective response. Instead, the government should institute more programs to educate parents and children about the dangers of junk food and high-sugar beverages.

1. "Nanny state" is an expression which originated in Britain.

2. The government should institute more programs to educate parents and children about the dangers of junk food and high-sugar beverages.

3. Recent attempts at regulating retail food and beverages are particularly disturbing.

4. These authorities assume that the government, not the citizens themselves, should be the judge of what constitutes "dangerous behavior."

5. Last year, New York City Mayor Michael Bloomberg proposed a ban on selling soft drinks over 16 ounces.

6. Recent research has shown that large-sized sweetened drinks are a major contributing factor in childhood obesity.

7. A government-imposed ban on soda is likely to be an ineffective response.

8. Policies such as mandatory seatbelt laws, motorcycle and bicycle helmet laws, and high taxes on junk food are examples of the government overstepping its power.

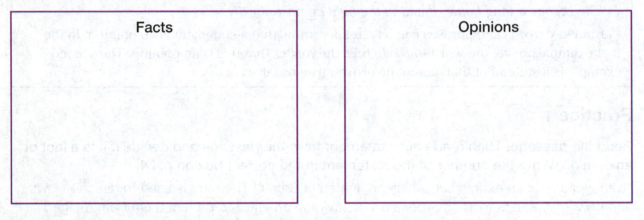

Facts	Opinions

Practice 2

Read the passage. Then read each statement from the passage and decide if it is a fact or an opinion. Write the number of the statement in the correct box on p. 55.

Pull up your pants, or get a ticket... Has the government gone too far?

Officials in the seaside town of Wildwood, New Jersey on the famous Jersey Shore have just passed a new law that bans the wearing of overly saggy pants on its boardwalk. The hip-hop fashion known as "sagging," involves wearing pants very low around the hips, and is a popular style among some of Wildwood's young male residents. In recent years, the Wildwood boardwalk has become crowded with groups of wild, partying young people. The new legislation was prompted by the large number of complaints from visitors, especially families with young children, who said they are offended by the groups and their fashion.

Some influential people are encouraging Wildwood "saggers" to fight the system, saying the government doesn't have the right to tell them how to wear their clothes. The hip-hop artist known as "The Game" has offered to personally pay the tickets for the first five violators of the new law, which goes into effect July 2.

The saggy pants law isn't the only surprising news in New Jersey politics. Last spring, the city of Fort Lee passed a "distracted walking" law, banning pedestrians from texting while crossing the street. Violators must pay an $85 fine. It's no shock that nearly all US states now have "distracted driving" laws that restrict cell phone use and texting while operating motor vehicles. However, making "distracted walking" a crime may be stretching the government's power over us a bit too much.

1. Violators must pay an $85 fine.

2. The saggy pants law isn't the only surprising news in New Jersey politics.

3. It's no shock that nearly all US states now have "distracted driving" laws that restrict cell phone use and texting while operating motor vehicles.

4. Officials in the seaside town of Wildwood, New Jersey on the famous Jersey Shore have just passed a new law that bans the wearing of overly saggy pants on its boardwalk.

5. In recent years, the Wildwood boardwalk has become crowded with groups of wild, partying young people.

6. The hip-hop artist known as "The Game" has offered to personally pay the tickets for the first five violators of the new law, which goes into effect July 2.

Facts	Opinions

TONE AND POINT OF VIEW

Practice 1

Read the paragraph and write the best answer from the box to complete each sentence.

> While Tom Fredrickson and Carol Newman agree on some issues, the two candidates running for mayor of Newton differ in a number of key areas. Fredrickson already has proven track record on environmental issues. He has been called the "green candidate" and has said he plans to assemble a committee of citizen volunteers to research ways the city can be more efficient in terms of its energy usage. He also voted "yes" to the proposed Transportation Center project, which would encourage greater use of the city's public transportation system. On the other hand, when it comes to the environment, Carol Newman still has a long way to go. Newman voted 'no' to the transportation center project, and 'yes' to the new Highway 97 construction project, which would only bring more traffic (and pollution) into the city.

1

Tom Fredrickson   Carol Newman
neither Fredrickson nor Newman

The writer thinks _____
should be the mayor.

2

highway repairs   environmental issues
transportation costs

The writer thinks _____ are
important for the city.

3

present	against	for

The writer would have voted _____ the Highway 97 construction project.

4

neither Newman nor Fredrickson	
Tom Fredrickson	Carol Newman

The writer already knows what _____ has done for the environment.

Practice 2

Read the blog post and circle the letter of the best answer to complete each sentence.

With hundreds of accidents and fatalities every year resulting from the use of cell phones while driving, it's no surprise that nearly all US states have now passed laws restricting cell phone use and texting while operating motor vehicles. However, officials in cities across the country have decided to take an even more drastic step in passing "distracted walking" laws, which ban people from texting while crossing the street. Yes, that means walking—not driving—across the street.

With new legislation comes after a recent increase in the number of pedestrians being hit by cars while texting and crossing the street. Fort Lee, New Jersey, the first city to pass the ban, has already had three such deaths this year. In one three-month period, 23 people were injured there, all as a result of being distracted by technology while walking.

Officials say that by passing the law, they're just doing their job to keep citizens safe, and it's clear that something should be done. But do citizens really need a law to tell them to watch where they're going? What's next? If the government can tell us how to walk across the street, before you know it, they'll be telling women they can't wear high heels because they might fall down.

1 The writer thinks laws banning cell phone use while driving are _____ .
 a surprising
 b necessary
 c strict

2 The writer _____ that being distracted by technology is dangerous.
 a agrees
 b does not agree
 c does not know

3 The writer thinks the "distracted walking" law _____ .
 a will be useful
 b is too restrictive
 c will not work

Presentation

Tone and Point of View

In some types of writing, such as news articles or academic papers, the writer includes just facts, without including his or her personal point of view or opinion. However, other pieces of writing, such as letters to the editor of a newspaper, personal blog posts, or comments on online news articles, the writer may express a clear opinion or point of view.

It is important to recognize the writer's point of view to help you analyze and evaluate the information he or she presents. This will help you form your own opinions about what you read. Certain words and phrases may give clues to the writer's opinion. For example, the opinion words *think* and *believe*, as well as evaluative adjectives such as *good, bad, true, false, wrong, right*, and *excellent*, are used to express an opinion.

Note: In general, writing that includes strongly expressed points of view or opinions is considered to be less reliable to use for academic research papers. You may wish to use it simply for quotations to illustrate one side of an issue in your paper, not for supporting points.

Practice 3

Read the text and underline the phrases that indicate the writer's opinion or point of view about the topic.

Over the past couple of decades, the Internet has literally opened up the world, paving the way for citizens of the world to freely express their ideas and opinions and exchange information with others around globe; but all this virtual freedom hasn't been without its price. Terrorists, cyber-spies, bootleggers, and other cyber-criminals are constantly finding new ways to use information on the web to their advantage, creating a desperate need for heightened Internet security.

Some governments around the world have been monitoring people's Internet usage and imposing restrictions and controls on certain types of content since the Web's early days, but recent stories in the news have revealed that Internet security is getting tighter everywhere, and with good reason. As hackers continue to get more advanced and efficient at breaking through even the most complex up-to-date security systems, governments need to respond quickly to prevent intellectual property rights, prevent cyber-espionage, and avoid national security threats.

Patterns of Organization
TEXT ORGANIZATION: THESIS STATEMENTS, MAIN POINTS, AND SUPPORTING DETAILS

Presentation

Thesis Statements

In longer passages with multiple paragraphs, the writer usually expresses the main point of the passage in a sentence called a *thesis statement*. The thesis statement tells the overall idea of the entire passage.

The thesis statement usually

- is a complete sentence
- tells the topic of the passage
- is found in the first paragraph
- often includes the writer's opinion about the topic
- gives a preview of how the passage will be organized
- is supported by all of the facts and details in the passage

Practice 1

Read each paragraph. Write the number of the sentence that is the thesis statement in the blank.

[1] Over the past couple of decades, the Internet has literally opened up the world, paving the way for citizens of the world to freely express their ideas and opinions and exchange information with others around globe. But all this virtual freedom hasn't come without a price. [2] Terrorists, cyber-spies, bootleggers, and other cyber-criminals are constantly finding new ways to use information on the Web to their advantage, creating a desperate need for heightened Internet security.

1 _____

[1] It's a fact. [2] The world is getting older. In 2012, 810 million people were ages 60 or over. By 2050, that number will reach 2 billion. [3] Around the world, advancements in health care and medicine are allowing people to stay healthy and live longer than ever before. [4] In some ways, the fact that these developments have helped to extend our lives is good news, but in the future, the growing elderly population may create serious social and economic challenges.

2 _____

[1] Ecotourism, also known as "ecological" or "green" tourism, has become a popular way to travel in recent years. [2] It is one of the fastest-growing sectors of the tourism industry, growing annually by 10–15% worldwide (Miller, 2007). [3] Ecotourism refers to an eco-conscious travel experience with the aim of learning about and having a positive impact on the local people and environment. [4] Supporters of ecotourism say it's both fun and educational; however, this relatively recent travel trend has not been without its detrimental side effects.

3 _____

Main Points and Supporting Details

The *thesis statement* gives the overall idea of a passage and tells the main points that will be discussed. As you have learned, each paragraph then includes one main idea that supports the thesis statement. The rest of the paragraph then contains facts and information that support the main idea. These are the *supporting details*.

Supporting details may include facts, statistics, quotations, or other examples and information which help to clarify and support the main idea of that paragraph, as well as the thesis statement of the entire passage.

Practice 2

Read the passage and write the number of the supporting details in the correct places in each paragraph.

1. For many nations, such as Costa Rica, Madagascar, and Nepal, income from ecotourism makes up a large portion of the economy

2. Costa Rica, for example, has placed strict limits on the numbers of visitors allowed in particular areas

3. Very often, there are no limits on the number of visitors to a location

4. It is one of the fastest-growing sectors of the tourism industry, growing annually by 10–15% worldwide (Miller, 2007)

5. An important feature is the idea that visitors should not disturb the local environment and culture, but rather, their presence and activities should have a positive impact

6. In addition, animals have become accustomed to human presence and have changed their behaviour and eating habits

Ecotourism, also known as "ecological" or "green" tourism, has become a popular way to travel in recent years. _____ . Ecotourism refers to an eco-conscious travel experience with the aim of learning about and having a positive impact on the local people and environment. Supporters of ecotourism say it's both fun and educational; however, this relatively recent travel trend has not been without its detrimental side effects.

A typical eco-tour may include opportunities to study local plants and animals, do volunteer work, such as planting trees or teaching in schools, and learn about local culture and heritage. _____ .

Ecotourism can be especially good for developing countries. _____ . It also helps to educate both visitors and local people about the need to conserve and protect land and natural resources.

Not all the effects of ecotourism have been positive. _____ . Over time, the constant presence of large numbers of people has an effect on the natural surroundings and wildlife. More hotels, restaurants, and shops are often built near protected natural areas in order to accommodate more visitors. _____ .

Some countries are trying to address the issues and challenges presented by ecotourism. _____ . Indian officials issued a ban on tiger ecotourism after a local environmentalist reported that ecotourism was harming the tigers' environment and breeding grounds when hotels and shops were built in reserves without permission. However, if the travel trend continues to gain popularity, much more will have to be done to ensure that it leads to the positive effects rather than negative ones.

COMPARISON AND CONTRAST PATTERN

Presentation

Comparison/Contrast Pattern

Writers use the comparison/contrast pattern to discuss the similarities and differences between two or more things. Readers can look for signal words and phrases to recognize this pattern of organization.

To show similarities, writers use the words: *similar to, like, alike, both, also, too, the same, in common, as well as*

To show differences, writers use the words: *different from, unlike, however, while, although, on the other hand, instead, rather than*

Practice 1

Read the paragraph. Then write the number of each phrase in the appropriate box.

There are two primary factors that differentiate asteroids from comets: chemical composition and orbit. Firstly, in terms of chemical composition, comets contain a volatile (unstable) material on the surface. This material produces a temporary atmosphere when the comet passes near the Sun. Solar radiation and winds cause the comet's surface to lose some of this compound. In contrast, asteroids do not produce any type of atmosphere at all. With regard to orbit, asteroids have a fairly regular, elliptical-shaped orbit path, and therefore, they remain within approximately the same distance from the Sun wherever they are in that path. Comets, on the other hand, have an irregular orbit, so their distance from the Sun tends to vary greatly.

There are other secondary ways in which asteroids and comets are different. These have to do with the way the two are named when they are discovered. While asteroids are named by their discoverers, comets are named after their discoverer. For example, the famous comet discovered by English astronomer Edmund Halley, is called Halley's Comet. However, when the first asteroid was discovered by Italian astronomer Giuseppe Piazzi, he named it Ceres.

1. have an irregular orbit
2. are named by their discoverers
3. stay the same distance from the Sun
4. produce a temporary atmosphere
5. have a regular orbit
6. are named after their discoverers
7. vary in distance from the Sun
8. produce no atmosphere

Asteroids	Comets

Practice 2

Read the passage. Underline the signal words and phrases that indicate the comparison/contrast pattern.

Anthropologist Edward T. Hall first introduced the idea of "high-context" and "low-context" cultures to explain differences in communication styles between different cultures. According to Hall, high context cultures are more common in the Eastern countries such as Japan and China, while most Western countries are low-context cultures. Of course, communication between members of a society is important in high-context as well as in low-context cultures. Hall's pretext is that intercultural communication falls under two main umbrellas: high and low context.

Hall states that both types of culture use a mix of spoken words and non-verbal cues to communicate. People in low-context cultures, the U.S. and Germany for example, rely heavily on spoken words to convey meaning. On the other hand, conversation in high-context cultures involves a larger amount of non-verbal features, including voice tone and gestures. In addition, although those from low-context cultures tend to state their thoughts, ideas, and opinions directly, people from high-context cultures like Japan or China often communicate more indirectly.

The way in which conversation is used to begin personal relationships is similar in the two cultures. People from high-context cultures share a lot of detailed personal information with friends and co-workers. In contrast, low-context cultures generally share necessary information with smaller select groups of people.

CAUSE AND EFFECT PATTERN

Presentation

Cause and Effect Pattern

The cause and effect pattern is used to show the relationship between two events. The *cause* is the first event that makes another event happen (the *effect*). Readers can look for signal words and phrases to identify the cause and effect pattern.

Signals for causes: *so, cause, help, start, create, produce, affect, make, lead to, result in, responsible for, increase, decrease, reduce*

Signals for effects: *because, a result of, caused by, due to, consequence of, as a result, as a consequence*

Practice 1

Read the passage. Then choose the best signal word or phrase to complete each sentence on p. 63.

Attention Deficit Disorder (ADD) and Attention Deficit Hyperactivity Disorder (ADHD) are neuro-phychological or behavioral disorders that affect a person's ability to function normally, particularly in situations which require extended periods of sustained concentration. Diagnoses of these disorders are becoming more and more common, affecting up to 16% of school-aged children. As a result, school officials are looking for ways to better serve the needs of these children.

ADD/ADHD and related disorders can create serious challenges for children in traditional school environments. The symptoms may cause an inability to sit or stay at rest, difficulty concentrating for extended time periods, and disruptive behavior. At school, children suffering from ADD may miss important details, have trouble staying organized, daydream, or become easily confused. These issues very often result in serious difficulties in the classroom. Without proper diagnosis and support, they can lead to academic failure.

Due to the fact that symptoms and needs vary from individual to individual, many schools have hired additional support staff to work with students with ADD/ADHD. One-on-one support and tailored accommodations can help students stay focused and on task and lead to greater academic success.

1 ADD and ADHD are disorders which _____ a person's ability to concentrate.
   a result in
   b affect
   c cause

2 The disorders are becoming more common. _____ , schools are looking for ways to better serve these students.
   a Due to
   b Because
   c As a consequence

3 Proper accommodations and academic support can _____ academic success for those suffering from ADD/ADHD.
   a reduce
   b lead to
   c decrease

4 The symptoms of ADD and ADHD can _____ challenges at school.
   a cause
   b help
   c reduce

5 Academic failure is sometimes a _____ of ADD/ADHD.
   a consequence
   b cause
   c start

Practice 2

Read the passage. Underline the words and phrases that indicate the cause and effect pattern.

It is well known that martial arts such as karate, tae kwon do, and judo have numerous health benefits. Regular martial arts training results in increased stamina, strength, and flexibility. In addition, it can reduce stress and lower blood pressure. Many long-time martial artists claim that frequent practice creates a heightened sense of overall calm, and experts conclude that it improves mental function and positively affects psychological well-being.

The whole-body movements characteristic of martial arts require significant focus and practice to learn properly. As a consequence, those who practice martial arts have enhanced concentration and learn to decrease distraction. Learning the *kata*, or choreographed series of movements, helps build motor control and coordination. In addition, the time and effort necessary to perfect these skills very often leads to a deeper sense of personal values such as patience, responsibility, and diligence.

Finally, the martial arts practice gym, or *dojo*, often has a family-like atmosphere, with children and adults practicing and studying together. This environment frequently serves to build confidence, self-esteem, respect for others, and positive interpersonal relationships.

PROBLEM AND SOLUTION PATTERN

Presentation

Problem/Solution Pattern

In passages with a problem/solution pattern, the writer presents one or more difficult situations. The passage explains the problem(s), and then offers examples or details about one or more solutions to the problem.

Common Signal Words and Phrases for the Problem/Solution Pattern:

- Words that indicate a problem: *problem, situation, trouble, crisis, issue, question, dilemma*
- Words that indicate a solution: *solution, suggestion, solve, resolution, resolve, decide, take action, plan*

Practice 1

Read the passage. Then read the list of sentences on p. 66 from the passage. Write *P* in the blank before the sentences that relate to the problem. Then write *S* in the blank before the sentences that relate to the solution.

It's a fact: The world is getting older. In 2012, 810 million people were ages 60 or over. By 2050, that number will reach 2 billion. Around the world, advancements in health care and medicine are allowing people to stay healthy and live longer than ever before. The fact that these developments have helped to extend our lives may seem like good news, but in the future, the growing elderly population may create serious social and economic challenges around the globe.

The statistics are alarming: Almost 58 million people worldwide will turn 60 this year. If current birth and death rates continue, by 2050, there will be more old people than children under the age of 15 for the first time in history. The most rapidly growing elderly populations are in developing countries in Africa, Asia, and other regions where resources and access to medical care may already be limited.

The simple truth is this: With so many people living longer, some with disabilities or chronic medical conditions, the caregiving responsibilities of family members will be extended, as will the required medical care costs for each individual. Unless world leaders begin planning how to address the potentially devastating caregiving challenges and financial strain of this demographic shift, there will be grave consequences.

Programs that allow the elderly to continue to be active members of their communities have been shown to keep older members of society healthier and happier for longer. When older people have opportunities to work or volunteer and remain productive in society, they feel valued and respected. Sustained activity and involvement helps them stay physically fit and experience fewer emotional problems such as depression. These programs are also beneficial because they allow others to benefit from their elderly co-workers' wisdom and experience.

Another successful tactic being used in some countries (the Russian Federation, the Slovak Republic, Turkey, the United Kingdom, and Canada) is offering paid allowances for family members who take on caregiving responsibilities for their elderly parents or grandparents. This helps people more easily make the choice to work less at their jobs in order to care for their elderly relatives. As a result, these relatives are able to live independently for longer and fewer elderly end up in government-funded nursing homes.

In an ideal future, we'll be able to have our cake and eat it too. People will live longer, remain healthy, and be respected members of society in their workplaces, communities, and families well into their old age.

But whatever the actions, strategic planning must begin now.

1 _____ In the future, the growing elderly population may create serious social and economic challenges around the globe.

2 _____ Programs that allow the elderly to continue to be active members of their communities have been shown to keep older members of society healthier and happier for longer.

3 _____ By 2050, there will be more old people than children under the age of 15 for the first time in history.

4 _____ When older people have opportunities to work or volunteer and remain productive in society, they feel valued and respected.

5 _____ Another successful tactic being used in some countries (the Russian Federation, the Slovak Republic, Turkey, the United Kingdom, and Canada) is offering paid allowances for family members who take on caregiving responsibilities for their elderly parents or grandparents.

6 _____ With so many people living longer, some with disabilities or chronic medical conditions, the caregiving responsibilities of family members will be extended, as will the required medical care costs for each individual.

Practice 2

Read the letter. Then circle the letter of the best answer.

LETTERS TO THE EDITOR

Dear Editor:

While walking down King Street today, I encountered several people panhandling—standing on the street corners asking others for money. A few were old and a few were young. Some sat on the sidewalk with signs saying "Homeless. Please help," or "Please support an unemployed veteran," while others boldly approached passersby, asking, "Can you spare a few dollars?" Further down the street, one young guy, probably a college student, was standing in front of the subway entrance busking—playing his guitar and singing (quite well, I thought)— his guitar case open on the ground with a few bucks in it. I stopped to listen. Toward the end of one song, a police officer approached the young busker and asked to see his permit. "You need to get a permit from City Hall if you want to play on the street," he said sternly. The man politely explained that he was unaware of that policy. The officer proceeded to tell the busker that if he did not pack up and leave, he would have to issue him a ticket.

I cannot comprehend a law enforcement officer who would bother a polite young man who is trying to make an honest living by providing viable entertainment while a few steps away, five people are just asking strangers on the street for money.

I consider myself a generous and kind person. I donate food and clothing to the local homeless shelter and I give money to various charities, and I always give a few dollars to buskers, if their music is good enough to make me stop and listen. However, I refuse to give money to panhandlers who, although they may need it, are not contributing anything positive to society.

I propose that City Hall stop requiring permits for busking. Unlike some panhandlers, buskers do not bother anyone. Their performances liven the downtown atmosphere and are often high quality entertainment. In addition, while it may be difficult to stop panhandling completely, I would also like to see the police discourage panhandlers from approaching people directly, as it makes a walk down the street less pleasant.

Sincerely,
Isabella Takacs

1 What does the writer think is the problem?
   a people living on the street
   b people asking for money on the street
   c not enough police officers on the street

2 Which statement describes the writer's opinion about the police officer's actions?
   a The officer should have arrested the panhandlers.
   b The officer should have let the busker continue playing.
   c The officer should have asked the panhandlers for their permits.

3 Why does the writer think busking is OK?
   a She views it as entertainment.
   b It is mostly done by college students.
   c It requires a permit.

4 Which sentence best summarizes the writer's suggestion?
   a Require permits for busking as well as panhandling.
   b Add more police officers to areas where there are panhandlers.
   c Don't require permits for busking and control panhandlers better.

IDENTIFYING PATTERNS

> **Presentation**
>
> ## Choosing the Correct Pattern
>
> You have learned about the following common patterns used in English paragraphs:
> - Comparison/Contrast Pattern
> - Cause and Effect Pattern
> - Problem/Solution Pattern
>
> For each pattern, you learned signal words and phrases to help you identify the pattern. Identifying the pattern will help you better understand what you read and help you read more quickly.

Practice 1

Read the passage and circle the letter of the correct pattern.

What Kind of Small Business Is Right for You?

New owners of small businesses must consider which type of business model will work best for their company. Two of the most common business models are Limited Liability Companies (LLCs) and Subchapter S Corporations (S-Corps). Although they are similar in some ways, they do have several differences. An owner must consider operational ease, administrative requirements, profit-sharing and employment tax implications before choosing one of these options. The needs of every business are different so it's worth investigating all of the issues that will affect it.

One of the features that distinguishes the LLC from an S-Corp is its operational ease. There are far fewer forms required for registering, and there are fewer start-up costs. Filing taxes happens once a year, and LLC owners do not need to file a separate tax document for themselves and their business. Moreover, LLCs are not required to have formal meetings and keep minutes. There are also fewer restrictions on profit-sharing within an LLC, as members can distribute profits as they see fit.

An S-Corp is a corporation that is considered by law to be a unique entity, separate from those who own it. Therefore, the tax process is more complex than with LLCs. While LLCs can be started relatively quickly and with low registration and start-up fees, S-Corps are a bit more costly. Finally, unlike owners of LLCs, S-Corp owners must file their own personal income taxes in addition to a separate business tax return.

1 Which best describes the pattern of the passage?
   a comparison/contrast
   b cause-effect
   c problem-solution

Big Drinks and Childhood Obesity

Recent attempts at regulating retail food and beverages are particularly disturbing. Last year, New York City Mayor Michael Bloomberg proposed a ban on selling soft drinks over 16 ounces. Bloomberg defended the ban, saying it would help curb childhood obesity and promote better health in general. Recent research has shown that large-sized sweetened drinks are a major contributing factor in childhood obesity. However, a government-imposed ban on soda size is likely to be an ineffective response. Instead, a more effective way to address the issue would be for the government to institute more programs to educate parents and children about the dangers of junk food and high-sugar beverages.

2 Which best describes the pattern of the passage?
   a comparison/contrast
   b cause and effect
   c problem/solution

Monitoring the Web

Over the past couple of decades, the Internet has literally opened up the world, paving the way for citizens of the world to freely express their ideas and opinions and exchange information with others around globe, but all this virtual freedom hasn't been without its price. Terrorists, cyber-spies, bootleggers, and other cyber-criminals are constantly finding new ways to use information on the web to their advantage, creating law enforcement issues and a desperate need for heightened Internet security.

Internet security is getting tighter everywhere, and with good reason. As hackers continue to get more advanced and efficient at breaking through even the most complex up-to-date security systems, the only way for governments to solve the problem is to continue to monitor Internet usage in order to protect intellectual property rights, prevent cyber-espionage, and avoid national security threats.

3 Which best describes the pattern of the passage?

 a comparison/contrast

 b cause and effect

 c problem/solution

The Black Ships

The term "black ships" was first used when Portuguese ships first arrived in Japan in 1543 and began a trade route between Goa, India and Nagasaki, Japan. These vessels were painted black with tar pitch to enhance waterproofing. This period of peaceful trading with the West lasted approximately a century. Then, in 1639, a rebellion erupted in Japan, which the ruling Tokugawa shogunate blamed on the influence of Christianity. As a result, the shogun closed off trade and contact with Westerners, and enforced a strict isolationist policy, called "Sakoku."

For 200 years, despite the requests of various Western leaders, Japan remained a primarily locked state. Trade with other nations was practically non-existent, aside from China and an allowance of one ship per year from the Dutch East India Company (based in Indonesia).

4 Which best describes the pattern of the passage?

 a comparison/contrast

 b cause and effect

 c problem/solution

Endangered Orangutans

Humans pose a great threat to orangutans. Many orangutans are killed by humans, in particular because of the production of palm oil. In the process of clearing large areas of rainforest to plant the palm trees, the palm oil companies leave the orangutans with nowhere to live and nothing to eat. In addition, the companies often burn large areas of land for clearing, which results in the deaths of many of the animals from inhaling smoke or being burned to death.

Some sources have reported that 6–12 endangered orangutans are killed every day due to the palm oil industry's actions. An estimated 50,000 orangutans have already died as a result of deforestation because of palm oil in the past 20 years. In Sumatra alone, the orangutan population is now 6,000—down from 100,000 fifty years ago.

Animal rights activists say that if the pattern is allowed to continue, orangutans in the wild could be extinct within 10–12 years. And in 20 years, their rainforest habitat, home to thousands of other species of plants and animals, will also be completely gone.

5 Which best describes the pattern of the passage?

 a comparison/contrast

 b cause and effect

 c problem/solution

Climate Change in New York

New York City is America's largest coastal community at risk from the effects of a changing climate. Temperature increases and sea level rise are already occurring and, along with other climate changes, are likely to accelerate. As a city of more than 8 million people situated along 520 miles of coastline with an extensive underground infrastructure prone to flooding and lack of easy evacuation routes, it is particularly vulnerable to coastal storms and sea level rise.

Recognizing the seriousness of climate change, city planners and decision-makers have started to take action. As part of PlaNYC, New York City's long-term sustainability plan, Mayor Michael Bloomberg convened the New York City Panel on Climate Change (NPCC) to advise the city on issues related to climate change and adaptation. The panel of experts used NOAA's climate data to analyze the current climate and project future climate scenarios. This climate information was a key part of the coordinated adaptation plan for the city's critical infrastructure developed by the New York City Climate Change Adaptation Task Force, comprised of public agencies and private companies.

6 Which best describes the pattern of the passage?
  a comparison/contrast
  b cause and effect
  c problem/solution

Thoreau and Emerson

The two authors Henry David Thoreau and Ralph Waldo Emerson are alike in a number of key ways. First, both loved nature and appreciated their natural surroundings. In fact, though at different times, both spent time living on Walden Pond in Massachusetts in the northeastern US, writing and living what Thoreau called "the right life"—one which was close to nature.

While the two writers had different views about the government system, both were somewhat rebellious at heart. Thoreau believed strongly that citizens had the right to disagree with and speak out against government policies. In *Civil Disobedience*, he encourages people to gather and take action against the government in order to impart change. On the other hand, Emerson's views on public protesting were somewhat milder, but he also felt that change needed to happen.

7 Which best describes the pattern of the passage?
  a comparison/contrast
  b cause and effect
  c problem/solution

Tips for Investing Your Money

Not all types of investments are created equally or work for your personal financial goals. Some provide steady income and are low risk but yield small returns on investment; others may provide significant returns, but require a long-term investment commitment. There is a wide assortment of investment vehicles available. Some of the most popular include: mutual funds, individual retirement accounts (IRAs), savings bonds, stocks, and certificates of deposit.

Some investments pay out earnings on a regular (quarterly, monthly, or annual) basis, while others pay out earnings at the end of the investment period or may have age requirements for when you can withdraw your money without a penalty. Make sure your investment income stream matches your investment timeline.

8 Which best describes the pattern of the passage?

   a comparison/contrast

   b cause and effect

   c problem/solution

British and French Conflict in Acadia

In the late 1600s and early 1700s, conflicts arose between the French and the British governments over territory in eastern Canada. Because the land that the French had settled in Canada was a border area between French and British territories, the two powers had started to fight over the right to govern the region known as Acadia. These conflicts resulted in many battles and significant losses of British and French forces over a period of about 75 years.

In 1710, the British Navy, led by General Charles Lawrence, succeeded in beating the French, leading to a 45-year period of British rule over Acadia. During that time, the French, now known as "Acadians," lived under British rule with few problems. However, everything changed for the Acadians in 1755, which was the start of the French and Indian War. Between 1755 and 1763, thousands of Acadians were driven out of Canada by the British. The Acadians' homes and villages were set on fire and burned to the ground, families were separated and men put on ships and sent away to labor building other new British colonies. Their wives and children were loaded onto other ships and sent back to France or other areas of Europe. Approximately one-third of the Acadians either drowned or died from disease.

Many Acadians who survived made their way south to Louisiana, which was still ruled by France at the time. Some made the entire journey on foot, taking many months and relying on kind strangers for food and a bed for the night. In Louisiana, they were safe. Once again there was land where they could farm and hunt, and rivers and swamps where they could trap animals and fish. And once again, they made friends and shared the land with the local Native Americans; many from both cultures even married each other. Over time, as the Acadian culture and language blended with the Native American as well as that of the local Africans who had been brought to Louisiana as slaves, the Louisiana Cajun culture emerged.

9 Which best describes the pattern of the passage?

   a comparison/contrast

   b cause and effect

   c problem/solution

SUMMARIZING

Presentation

Summarizing

A *summary* is a shorter version of a passage that includes only the most important information. In a university setting, students often need to summarize articles and reading assignments from course textbooks.

Writing a summary of what you have read is also a useful way to check your understanding of the ideas in a text and to help you remember them.

A good summary...

- is shorter than the original text.
- includes only the most important facts and ideas from the text.
- does not include a lot of detail.
- does not include any extra information that is not in the text.
- does not use exact words or sentences from the text.
- does not include your own opinion of the ideas in the text.

Practice 1

Read the textbook excerpt. Then read the passage and write the number of the missing sentence in the correct place in the summary on p. 74. There are two extra sentences that do not belong in the summary.

GRANT—A PEACEFUL VICTORY

In 1869, General Grant, who had made such a great name for himself during the Civil War, became President. Grant was a brave and honest soldier. He knew little, however, about politics. But now that Lincoln was gone, the people loved him better than any other man. So he became President.

His was a simple trusting soul. He found it hard to believe evil of any one, and he was easily misled by men who sought not their country's good, but their own gain. So mistakes were made during his Presidency. But these may be forgotten while men must always remember his greatness as a soldier, and his nobleness as a victor. He helped to bring peace to his country, and like his great leader he tried after war was past to bind up the nation's wounds.

When Grant came into power, the echoes of the great war were still heard. The South had not yet returned into peaceful union with the North, and there was an unsettled quarrel with Britain. The quarrel arose in this way. During the Civil War, the British had allowed the Confederates to build ships in Britain; these ships had afterwards sailed out from British ports, and had done a great deal of damage to Union shipping.

The British had declared themselves neutral. That is, they had declared that they would take neither one side nor the other. But, said the Americans, in allowing Confederate ships to be built in Britain, the British had taken the Confederate side, and had committed a breach of neutrality. And for the damage done to their ships, the Americans now claimed recompense from the British Government. The ship which had done the most damage was called the *Alabama* and from this the claims made by America were called the Alabama Claims.

At first, however, the British refused to consider the claims at all. For years letters went to and fro between the two governments, and as the British still refused to settle the matter, feelings in America began to run high.

But at length the British consented to talk the matter over, and a commission of five British and five Americans met at Washington. After sitting for two months, this commission formed what is known as the Washington Treaty. By this Treaty it was arranged that the Alabama Claims should be decided by arbitration. A Court of Arbitration was to be formed of five men; and of this court the President of the United States, the Queen of England, the King of Italy, the President of Switzerland, and the Emperor of Brazil, were each to choose a member.

The men chosen by these rulers met at Geneva in Switzerland, and after discussing the matter for a long time they decided that Britain had been to blame, and must pay the United States $15,500,000. Thus the matter was settled in a peaceful way. Fifty years before, a like quarrel might have led to war between the two countries. Even at this time, with less wise leadership on either side, it might have come to war. But war was avoided and a great victory for peace was won.

Besides the Alabama Claims, the last dispute about boundaries between the United States and Canada was settled at this time. This also was settled by arbitration, the new-made German Emperor being chosen as arbiter. "This," said President Grant, "leaves us for the first time in the history of the United States as a nation, without a question of disputed boundary between our territory and the possessions of Great Britain."

Grant was twice chosen as President and it was during his second term that Colorado was admitted to the Union as the thirty-eighth state. The new state was formed partly out of the Mexican Concession, partly out of the Louisiana Purchase, and was named after the great river Colorado, two branches of which flow through it. It was admitted as a state in August, 1876.

1. Grant was faced with two major problems in his terms as President: healing and reuniting the nation after the war, and a dispute with England.
2. At first, Britain refused to address these claims and tensions mounted between the countries.
3. Britain paid the US $15,500,000 as a result of the Alabama Claims.
4. When Grant came into power, the echoes of the great war were still heard.
5. Though Grant didn't have much political experience, he helped bring the country back together and avoid further international conflict.

Ulysses S. Grant was a beloved Civil War hero who became president after the assassination of Abraham Lincoln. _____ The Alabama Claims were made against Britain because they allowed Confederate ships to be built in England during the Civil War, despite having declared themselves neutral. These claims asked for money for the damage caused by these British-built ships during the war. _____ This dispute could have escalated into another war, but Grant chose to have the claims settled by an international group in arbitration. Britain was found guilty and paid the damages. _____

Practice 2

Read the passage. Then circle the letters of the sentences on p. 75 that belong in the summary.

Black Ships and Japanese Shogun

The Black Ships (*kurofune* in Japanese) were the ships that arrived in Japan from the West during the 16th and 19th centuries. The term "black ships" was first used for Portuguese ships, the first Western vessels which arrived in Japan in 1543 and began a trade route between Goa, India and Nagasaki, Japan. These vessels were painted black with tar pitch to enhance waterproofing. This period of peaceful trading with the West lasted approximately a century. Then, in 1639, a rebellion erupted in Japan, which the ruling Tokugawa shogunate blamed on the influence of Christianity. As a result, the shogun closed off trade and contact with Westerners, and enforced a strict isolationist policy, called Sakoku.

For 200 years, despite the requests of various Western leaders, Japan remained a primarily locked state. Trade with other nations was practically non-existent, aside from China and an allowance of one ship per year from the Dutch East India Company (based in Indonesia).

The End of Self-imposed Isolation

In the present day, the term "Black Ships" refers in particular to the four US Navy warships—the *Mississippi, Plymouth, Saratoga,* and *Susquehanna*—commandeered by United States Commodore Matthew Perry, which arrived in the Bay at Edo (present-day Tokyo) in July of 1853. In this case, *black* refers not only to the color of the sailing vessels, but also to the black smoke from the coal-powered American ships.

Perry's Mission

US President Millard Fillmore sent Commodore Matthew Perry to Japan to try to secure trading rights with Japan for eager American merchants. As well, the American military wanted the Japanese to help shipwrecked sailors who washed up on their shores, who under Japan's isolationist period had been either killed or left to die. Perry presented the Japanese with a letter from President Fillmore, requesting that Japan open its ports for both diplomatic and commercial purposes.

External Pressure and Internal Revolt

Perry told Japanese leaders that he would return the following year, with an even larger fleet, for the shogun's reply. A year later, in July of 1854, Perry arrived with seven ships. This massive display of power combined with the ships' loud, booming cannons shocked the shoguns and the Japanese people. After some debate among the shogun's advisors, the Japanese leadership had determined that Japan could not defend itself against the US Navy. The government conceded, marking the end of Japan's two centuries of isolation.

In the Treaty of Kanagawa, the shogun agreed to open two ports to American ships, though at first not for trade. After a few years, the United States gained trading rights, leading the way for several European nations to do the same. The Japanese people were angered by the terms of the treaties, which they found unequal and humiliating. Many citizens criticized the shogun for not fighting against the aggressive foreign invaders.

a The mid 1500s to the mid 1600s marked a century of peaceful trade between Japan and the West, most notably the Portuguese.

b However, a 1639 Japanese rebellion resulted in the ruling Japanese shogun shutting down all trade with Westerners.

c This may have been an overreaction on the part of the shogun, and was probably the wrong choice for the Japanese people.

d For the 200-year period that followed, Japan remained nearly completely cut off from other nations.

e In the summer of 1853, American President Millard Fillmore sent a fleet of four warships led by Commodore Matthew Perry into Toyko Bay.

f Perry delivered a letter from Fillmore requesting that Japan open its doors to trade with the US.

g Fillmore was the 13th president of the United States and was from the Finger Lakes region of upstate New York.

h One year later, Perry returned to Tokyo for the shogun's answer.

i Feeling a lack of confidence about its ability to overcome the US Navy, the Japanese government agreed to Perry's demands.

j The subsequent Treaty of Kanagawa led the way for Japan to trade openly with the West again.

k Over the century and half that followed, Japan rose to become one of the world's greatest economic powers.

Comprehension Skills Practice Test

Part 1   Previewing and Skimming

Preview and skim the text below (do not read it carefully). Then circle the letter of the best way to complete each sentence on p. 77.

Internet Use and Electronic Communication

The following policies have been established for the use of the Internet, company-owned devices such as smartphones, cell phones, and email in an appropriate, ethical and professional manner:

- The Internet and company-owned devices (e.g., smartphones, tablets, laptops, computers) and services may not be used for transmitting, retrieving, or storing any communications or images that are of an offensive, threatening, or discriminatory nature.

- The following actions are prohibited: using abusive or offensive language; viewing or distributing materials that could negatively reflect upon the company; and engaging in any manner of illegal activity online

- Do not copy, download, edit, or forward copyrighted materials without written permission or as a single copy for reference only.

- Do not use the Internet or company-owned devices in a way that prevents or hinders its use by others, for example, sending or receiving large document or media files. Employees are forbidden to send or receive any computer files that do not relate directly to work.

- Never open emails from unknown sources. Contact the IT Department at extension 22 with any questions or concerns in order to reduce the risk of computer viruses.

- Internal and external emails are considered business records and are subject to monitoring or may be used as evidence in the event of a legal case. Be aware of this possibility when sending email within and outside the company.

Right to Monitor

All company-owned devices and work-related documents and records are the property of the company. The company has the right to monitor use of company supplied technology and all types of electronic communication by and between employees. Illegal or inappropriate use of electronic communications may result in disciplinary action or termination of employment.

Social Media Use

The following are guidelines for use of social media:

- Do not post information of a personal, confidential, or sensitive nature about the company or its clients, employees, or applicants.

- Do not post offensive language or personal attacks that could damage the public image of the company, clients, or employees.

- The company may monitor content on any social media site. Policy violations may result in disciplinary action or termination of employment.

1 The text is from _____ .
   a a university student handbook
   b a computer instruction manual
   c a handbook for new employees
   d a website's privacy policy

2 The main purpose of the text is to _____ .
   a suggest ways to solve problems
   b provide a set of rules to follow
   c explain reasons for changes
   d announce upcoming events

3 Which statement best summarizes the main idea of the text?
   a Employees should use electronic communication appropriately and responsibly.
   b The use of the Internet and social media sites is strictly prohibited by the company.
   c Employees are responsible for reporting inappropriate use of electronic communication.
   d The company is not responsible for information posted on the Internet by employees.

Part 2   Scanning

Read the scanning questions. Then scan the text for the answers to the questions on p. 78.

Scanning Questions

1. Which types of electronic communication does the company have the right to monitor?

2. When is it OK to download copyrighted materials?

3. Which types of computer files can employees send and receive?

4. What may be used as evidence in a legal case?

5. Which department can be reached at extension 22?

Internet Use and Electronic Communication

The following policies have been established for the use of the Internet, company-owned devices such as smartphones, cell phones, and email in an appropriate, ethical, and professional manner:

- The Internet and company-owned devices (e.g., smartphones, tablets, laptops, computers) and services may not be used for transmitting, retrieving, or storing any communications or images that are of an offensive, threatening, or discriminatory nature.

- The following actions are prohibited: using abusive or offensive language; viewing or distributing materials that could negatively reflect upon the company; and engaging in any manner of illegal activity online

- Do not copy, download, edit, or forward copyrighted materials, without written permission or as a single copy for reference only.

- Do not use the Internet or company-owned devices in a way that prevents or hinders its use by others, for example, sending or receiving large document or media files.

- Employees are forbidden to send or receive any computer files that do not relate directly to work.

- Never open emails from unknown sources. Contact the IT Department at extension 22 with any questions or concerns in order to reduce the risk of computer viruses.

- Internal and external emails are considered business records and are subject to monitoring, or may be used as evidence in the event of a legal case. Be aware of this possibility when sending email within and outside the company.

Right to Monitor

All company-owned devices and work-related documents and records are the property of the company. The company has the right to monitor use of company supplied technology and all types of electronic communication by and between employees. Illegal or inappropriate use of electronic communications may result in disciplinary action or termination of employment.

Social Media Use

The following are guidelines for use of social media:

- Do not post information of a personal, confidential, or sensitive nature about the company or its clients, employees, or applicants.

- Do not post offensive language or personal attacks that could damage the public image of the company, clients, or employees.

- The company may monitor content on any social media site. Policy violations may result in disciplinary action or termination of employment.

1 Which types of electronic communication does the company have the right to monitor?
- **a** email messages
- **b** social media accounts
- **c** smart phone text messages
- **d** all electronic communication

2 Which types of computer files can employees send and receive?
- **a** files that relate to work
- **b** files that are very large
- **c** files that do not have attachments
- **d** files that contain personal information

3 When is it OK for employees to download copyrighted materials?
- **a** when they have obtained permission
- **b** when they are for personal use
- **c** when they are owned by the company
- **d** It is never allowed.

4 According to the text, what may be used as evidence in a legal case?
- **a** employees' records
- **b** text messages
- **c** email messages
- **d** voicemail messages

Part 3   Identifying Main Ideas and Details

Read the text. Then circle the letter of the best answer.

If you like to escape with a good movie, you'll love our International Film Festival Tour Package. Visit some of the world's most thrilling destinations and make the rounds at the most popular and prestigious international film festivals. This extended eight-week tour is designed for those who love the art of great filmmaking and who want to explore our wonderful planet—perfect for retired couples and anyone who wants to take a break from the daily routine. This round-the-world package runs between mid-September and mid-November and includes air transportation, lodging, and film festival tickets.

Tour itinerary:

September 20: Tour begins at New York's Coney Island Film Festival. A relatively new festival, the Coney Island event started 13 years ago as a fundraiser for the non-profit arts organization Coney Island, USA. It features amateur independent films from all over the US and the world.

October 3: Fly to South Korea for the Busan International Film Festival. This event promotes first-time directors and never-before-seen movies and is held in the Busan Cinema Center, featuring a 4,000-seat outdoor theater and four indoor screens under an LED-covered roof.

October 15: London International Film Festival. One of Europe's largest public film events, this festival highlights about 300 films from 60 different countries.

October 30: Toronto International Film Festival. Over four decades, this festival has developed a reputation for being one of the top venues for international and foreign language film debuts in North America.

November 15: Return to New York

Total tour cost: $5,575

1 The passage is _____ .
   a a film festival's schedule of events
   b an advertisement for a travel agency
   c a review of several film festivals
   d an airline's list of travel destinations

2 How long do travelers spend at each destination?
   a exactly seven days
   b as long as they want
   c roughly two weeks
   d about a month

3 Which of the following is NOT included in the tour's price?
   a hotel accommodations
   b meals and snacks
   c airplane tickets
   d festival tickets

4 How many continents does the tour include?

  a 1

  b 3

  c 5

  d 6

5 Which event raises money for a local organization?

  a Coney Island Film Festival

  b Busan Film Festival

  c London Film Festival

  d Toronto Film Festival

Part 4 Combined Skills

Read the text. Then circle the letter of the best answer.

Gabon, a beautiful country on the West African coast, is a haven for many different species of plants and wildlife. About three-quarters of Gabon's land is covered by dense rainforest, which is home to gorillas, antelopes, and many tropical birds. In addition, Gabon is home to more than half of Africa's 40,000 forest elephants. Unfortunately, the lush, pristine environment that makes Gabon an ideal home for animals also attracts some very unwanted guests: poachers. A growing demand for ivory products, particularly in Asia, has fueled a rapid rise in poaching in recent years, leading to the illegal killing of many animals in Gabon's national parks. Contrary to the image many people may have of a few poachers hiding out in the forest and killing one or two elephants, poaching is a huge global business network, netting millions each year in the ivory trade. The statistics are sickening. According to a recent survey conducted by the Gabonese National Parks Agency, WWF, and the Wildlife Conservation Society (WCS), over 11,000 elephants—more than half of the entire population—have been slaughtered by poachers in Gabon over the past decade and a half. If the issue of poaching is left unaddressed, Central Africa's elephants will follow the fate of the black and the white rhinoceroses, both of which were hunted to extinction. What can be done to prevent the horrific slaughter of thousands of innocent animals in Gabon and around the African continent? Officials from Gabon and surrounding countries, such as Chad and Cameroon, have sent armed soldiers to fight the poachers, but that has had little effect. Government leaders from all corners of the globe must know about the poaching crisis, and come together to identify, track, and arrest those involved in these global criminal networks. The demand and the market for ivory products will most likely always exist. However, if governments in the countries that import ivory take a stand, the future of Central African elephants may stand a chance.

1 Choose the best title for the passage based on the topic.

  a Ivory Shortage Creates Problems for Asian Art Dealers

  b Elephant Poaching in Africa Becoming a Global Crisis

  c Governments Send Soldiers to Combat Poaching in Gabon

  d Elephant Poachers Reveal the Secrets of Their Trade

2 The passage _____.

   a compares two things

   b describes cause and an effect

   c introduces a problem and a solution

   d gives instructions for how to do something

3 From the passage, we can infer that the writer _____.

   a is a resident of Gabon, Africa

   b is strongly against the poaching of elephants

   c believes that ivory trade should continue

   d hopes to become a politician someday

4 Which statement best describes the main idea of the passage?

   a Poaching is a serious problem in Gabon and can only be stopped through international efforts.

   b Poachers in Gabon must be made aware that they are endangering the future of the African elephant.

   c Elephants in Gabon are being illegally killed at a rate faster than that of the white and black rhinoceros.

   d International government leaders have not done enough to prevent poaching in Gabon.

5 Which sentence from the passage describes an opinion (not a fact)?

   a About three-quarters of Gabon's land is covered by dense rainforest, which is home to gorillas, antelopes, and many tropical birds.

   b The demand and the market for ivory products will most likely always exist.

   c A growing demand for ivory products, particularly in Asia, has fueled a rapid rise in poaching in recent years.

   d In addition, Gabon is home to more than half of the world's 40,000 forest elephants.

Part 5   Making Inferences

Read the text. Then circle the letter of the best way to complete each sentence on p. 82.

On a drizzle-gray Saturday, Henry Jacobs had fallen asleep on the sofa while watching the cable shopping channel. The telephone's high-pitched ring sent an electric current through him and he bolted upright, eyes ablaze. His heart still thumping in his chest, he groped clumsily for the cordless handset on the side table, knocking over the photo of his wife, Lydia. "Hello?" he said, his voice cracking.

"Hey, Dad, it's me... How are you?"

"Oh, hi, honey. I wasn't expecting…." As reality sank in, Henry picked up the photo frame, rubbed the dust off with his shirt, and set it upright on the table. "What is it? Everything OK?"

"Yeah, I'm fine. I just wanted to hear your voice. It's just… I know I've been awful about calling. I've been so busy, you know, with looking for a place to live and figuring out the new job."

"I know, honey. That's OK. I understand. It's not as though I've been calling you every day either. It's sure nice that you called now, though. It's been pretty quiet around here… I miss your surprise visits. Are you all settled in San Diego? How's the job?"

"I'm getting used to it, I guess. I miss being at school, though. Everything seemed a lot easier somehow—Work is a lot of pressure. I mean; I don't want to get fired."

"Ah, you're going to do great, Sarah. You're learning something new; you don't have to be perfect right away, you know."

"Thanks, Dad. I know—Mom always used to say I was too hard on myself." Henry sighed, glancing at Lydia's picture on the table. Sarah continued, "Anyway, I feel like being here is giving me a chance to do a lot of thinking. I've been having these dreams about Mom… almost every night. I haven't thought this much about her in years. You know, it's like…"

Images flooded Henry's mind as Sarah's voice fell away into the distance. Henry and Lydia riding together in their little powder blue Honda Civic—the California freeway stretched out in front of them—a large green sign in the distance: *San Diego—17 miles*. He realized this was exactly what he had been dreaming minutes ago when the phone rang with Sarah on the other end.

"What are you up to this weekend, honey?" Henry interrupted, "Should be great weather for a drive, and I'd love to see your new place. How'd you like a visitor?"

1 From the text, we can infer that Henry's wife Lydia _____ .

   a is a photographer

   b recently moved away

   c died several years ago

   d is divorced from Henry

2 From the text, we can infer that Sarah _____ .

   a is a recent college graduate

   b has started her own company

   c feels angry towards her mother

   d still lives at home with Henry

3 From the text, we can infer that _____ .

   a Sarah will move back home soon

   b Henry and Sarah will see each other soon

   c Henry has lived in San Diego

   d Henry and Sarah do not get along

Part 6   Combined Skills

Read the text. Then circle the letter of the best way to complete each sentence.

Opening a bank account in the US

US banks offer services to international students. However, choosing the right bank and the right type of account can be confusing. Some banks have branches and ATMs on campus for added convenience. Whichever bank you choose, you will need to present certain documents and information in order to meet government financial rules. Contact the bank to find out which documents you need in order to open an account, and be sure to allow some time to complete the process.

What type of account should I open?

Banks generally offer clients a choice of opening a checking account or savings account. The primary purpose of a checking account is for everyday money transactions such as paying bills and making purchases; you can pay bills and make frequent deposits and withdrawals without a lot of additional fees. You will receive a set of checks as well as a debit card, which you can use to make purchases online or in stores, as well as to withdraw cash from ATMs. These accounts tend to be more flexible and offer greater convenience for students. Some banks charge a monthly maintenance fee. Many offer no fee accounts for students. Check with your financial institution to learn if you can qualify for a "no fee" checking account.

The primary purpose of a savings account is to save money (for emergency use, for future purchases, or to invest). Therefore, savings accounts are mainly for deposits, which will earn interest. Interest rates and fees differ from bank to bank; however, a savings account typically pays a higher interest rate than an interest-bearing checking account. Many banks limit the number of withdrawals per month and charge additional fees for frequent withdrawals. For this reason, a checking account may be best; however, if you have a large sum of money, you may also need a saving account.

1 The text is from _____ .
   a a bank employee manual
   b a university economics textbook
   c a handbook for university students
   d a finance magazine

2 The main purpose of the passage is to _____ .
   a introduce a problem and suggest a solution
   b compare two or more things
   c give instructions for how to do something
   d describe a cause and its effect

3 From the text we can infer that most international students

_____ .
   a keep their money in their home countries
   b choose to open a checking account
   c do not have enough money to open bank accounts
   d prefer the convenience of savings accounts

Part 7   Combined Skills

Read the text. Then circle the letter of the best answer.

Can nuclear power be safer?

One of the dangers of nuclear power is the use of radioactive materials like uranium and plutonium. These materials aren't burned completely during the energy-production process, and the leftover material can't be recycled or reused, so they have to be stored underground. If underground pipes and waste pools aren't maintained, those nasty toxins can escape and seep into the ground, affecting our water supply and putting all of us at risk.

Nuclear reactors use cold water to cool down the fuel in order to prevent the core from melting down and avoid an explosion. This is why nuclear plants are generally built near the coast or by rivers. During fission, the process used to create nuclear electric power, it's neutrons that fly around and split the atoms. The use of water as a cooling agent slows down the neutrons, which results in less uranium and plutonium being used. Consequently, a shocking 95% of uranium and other radioactive elements end up as waste in this process.

However, what most people don't know is that water-cooling isn't the safest or most efficient option available. There's actually a more environmentally safe way to produce nuclear energy. It's called an "integral fast reactor." Instead of the traditional water-cooling method, in integral fast reactors, the fuel rods are cooled in a liquid sodium or lead bath. These substances allow neutrons to pass faster and more freely, resulting in a better, more complete burning of uranium and all the other disgusting, unhealthy elements. Consequently, with an integral fast reactor, the process uses up about 80% of the nuclear material, as opposed to 5% with traditional reactors.

When I first heard about it, I thought it was a joke. It sounded like some kind of miracle cure you read about on the Internet. It seems too good to be true, but after looking into it further and doing lots of homework on the subject, I've come to the conclusion that it's real, and I believe it's possible to have safe nuclear power in our lifetime. Nuclear scientists have been working on this technology for over a decade, and many experts are convinced that integral fast reactors are the way of the future. Even more than some other alternative energy sources, such as solar and wind power, safe production of nuclear energy through integral fast reactors will provide an efficient, cost-effective option in times to come.

1 The tone of the passage is _____ .

   a academic

   b humorous

   c casual

   d professional

2 The author's intends to _____ .

   a persuade people to take action

   b express an opinion

   c announce an event

   d advertise a product

3 The overall pattern of the whole passage _____ .

   a explains a cause and its effects

   b describes a problem and a solution

   c compares two or more objects

   d gives instructions for how to do something

4 Paragraph 3 primarily _____ .

   a explains causes and effects

   b describes problems and solutions

   c compares two or more objects

   d gives instructions for how to do something

5 Which statement best describes the author's opinion?

   a Nuclear power is unsafe and should be replaced with wind or solar power.

   b Most people are unaware of the true dangers of nuclear power.

   c Methods of nuclear power can be altered to be more efficient and safer.

   d Nuclear scientists have not put enough effort into finding alternative energy sources.

Part 8 Understanding Paragraphs

Circle the letter of the best supporting information to complete each paragraph.

1 New research has shed light on the purpose of sleep and its power to clear the mind. A recent study conducted at the University of Rochester has shown that the brain uses the time we are asleep to flush toxic material out of its cells. _____ The study suggests a biological purpose for sleep, showing that it results in waste disposal in the brain, thus restoring healthy brain function on a daily basis. This information could have far-reaching implications for the treatment of brain degenerative diseases such as Alzheimer's.

   a Every animal species, from the largest whale to the tiniest insect, needs some amount of sleep regularly.

   b These findings show that the brain's unique method of self-cleaning—called the glymphatic system—becomes highly active during sleep.

   c In other parts of the body, it is the lymphatic system that gets rid of waste build up in the cells.

2 The purpose of sleep has perplexed scientists and scholars since ancient times. Every animal species, from the largest whale to the tiniest insect, needs some amount of sleep regularly. However, being asleep can present significant disadvantages to a species, such as leaving animals vulnerable to attacks by predators, and limiting time spent hunting or mating. Previous research proved that sleep helps the brain store memories and consolidate information, but most experts agree that these benefits still do not outweigh the disadvantages of spending numerous hours asleep every day. _____

   a Researchers also found that during sleep the brain's cells become smaller, allowing waste to be removed more effectively.

b As we sleep, our brain goes to work clearing away toxic substances that can build up in the brain and cause trigger neurological disorders, such as Alzheimer's disease.

c This led scientists to conclude that sleep must have a more fundamental and necessary biological function.

3 Unique to the brain, the glymphatic waste disposal system works by pumping spinal fluid through brain tissue, flushing toxins out of the brain and into the blood and liver. A series of studies on laboratory mice revealed that this process, while functional when the mice were awake, was more active while they slept. _____ Scientists concluded that, while awake, the brain may simply be too busy processing information to perform the necessary clean-up tasks. Therefore, it takes care of the "housework" while we are asleep.

a Certain hormones, such as the so-called "stress-hormone" noradrenaline was also found to be less active during sleep.

b In fact, the glymphatic system turned out to be almost 10 times more active during sleep.

c When we are awake, the brain's cells are larger and closer together, resulting in restricted flow of spinal fluid.

Part 9 Understanding Paragraphs

Read the text. Then circle the letter of the best answer on p. 87.

New research has shed light on the purpose of sleep and its power to clear the mind. A recent study conducted at the University of Rochester has shown that the brain uses the time we are asleep to flush toxic material out of its cells. These findings show that the brain's unique method of self-cleaning—called the glymphatic system—becomes highly active during sleep. The study suggests a biological purpose for sleep, showing that it results in waste disposal in the brain, thus restoring healthy brain function on a daily basis. This information could have far-reaching implications for the treatment of degenerative brain diseases such as Alzheimer's. The purpose of sleep has perplexed scientists and scholars since ancient times. Every animal species, from the largest whale to the tiniest insect, needs some amount of sleep regularly. However, being asleep can present significant disadvantages to a species, such as leaving animals vulnerable to attacks by predators, and limiting time spent hunting or mating. Previous research proved that sleep helps the brain store memories and consolidate information, but most experts agree that these benefits still do not offset the disadvantages of spending numerous hours asleep every day. This led scientists to conclude that sleep must have a more fundamental and necessary biological function. Unique to the brain, the glymphatic waste disposal system works by pumping spinal fluid through brain tissue, flushing toxins out of the brain and into the blood and liver. A series of studies on laboratory mice revealed that this process, while functional when the mice were awake, was more active while they slept. In fact, the glymphatic system turned out to be almost 10 times more active during sleep. Scientists concluded that, while awake, the brain may simply be too busy processing information to perform the necessary clean-up tasks. Therefore, it takes care of the "housework" while we are asleep.

1 Choose the best topic for the passage.
   a neuroscience and human health
   b new research on sleep and the brain
   c how the glymphatic system works

2 Which statement best describes the main idea?
   a Research shows that mice have brain function similar to that of humans.
   b New scientific evidence proves that sleep serves an important biological function.
   c Scientists have learned that sleep is even more complex than previously thought.

3 According to the article, the purpose of sleep is to _____ .
   a encourage animal species to hunt and mate
   b remove harmful substances from the brain
   c increase the size of brain cells

4 According to the article, which of the following is true?
   a Previous research showed that sleep had no effect on the brain.
   b The glymphatic system only works when we are asleep.
   c Besides the brain, the glymphatic system does not operate in other areas of the body.

5 Which of the following is NOT mentioned in the article?
   a how the human glymphatic system removes waste from cells
   b the number of hours of sleep different animal species need each night
   c possible future indications for the new research findings

VOCABULARY BUILDING

Word Parts

ROOTS

Presentation

Latin Roots

Many words in English come from other languages, especially Latin and Greek.

Studying the meanings of Latin roots is useful because it will help you guess the meanings of many unfamiliar words in English.

Some Latin roots can stand alone as words, but most need prefixes, which come before the root word, or suffixes, which come after the root word. For example:

Root	Meaning	Prefix		Root		Suffix	
labor	work	col	+	labor	+	ate	= collaborate (work together)
frig	cold	re	+	frig	+	erator	= refrigerator

Practice 1

Study the Latin roots in the chart and circle the letter of the correct vocabulary word to complete the sentence on pp. 89 and 90.

Root	Meaning	Examples
ab-, a-, abs-	away from	abnormal, absent
acu-	sharp or pointed	acupuncture, accurate
ben-	good, well	benefit, benefactor
cap-, -cip-, capt-, -cept-	hold, take	capture, concept, recipient
deb-	owe	debit, debt, debtor
fug-, fugit-	flee	centrifuge, refugee
juven-	young, youth	juvenile, rejuvenate
medi-, -midi-	middle	medieval, medium
nasc-, nat-	born	native, nation
sed-, -sid-, sess-	sit	reside, session
sol-	alone, only	isolated, solo
tard-	slow	retard, tardy
terr-	earth	terrace, terrain
urb-	city	suburbanite, urban
ver-	true	aver, verify

1 When you _____ from something, you stay away from it.

   a abstain

   b reside

   c verify

2 A _____ place is a lonely place without any people.

   a benefit

   b desolate

   c medieval

3 An _____ quality is one which you were born with.

   a accurate

   b innate

   c urban

4 _____ is small stones, sand, or other kinds of particles that sit on the bottom of water.

   a Debt

   b Sediment

   c Terrace

5 _____ hall is a place where young people must go if they have been found guilty of a crime.

   a Accurate

   b Juvenile

   c Refugee

6 A flame-_____ piece of clothing burns slowly if it catches fire.

   a juvenile

   b retardant

   c urban

7 If your apartment is _____, you live under the earth—underground.

   a isolated

   b native

   c subterranean

8 A/An _____ pain is a sharp pain.

   a acute

   b captive

   c isolated

9 When a small town becomes _____, it becomes more like a city.

   a abnormal

   b rejuvenated

   c urbanized

10 When you check the _____ of statement, you check to find out if it is true.

   a debtor

   b terrain

   c verity

11 A _____ from the law is someone who is fleeing the police.

   a concept

   b debtor

   c fugitive

12 When something holds people's attention, you can say they are a/an _____ audience.

   a absent

   b captive

   c urban

13 The _____ number is the one in the middle of a range of numbers.

   a isolated

   b median

   c native

14 A _____ volcano is one that has not been active for a long time, as if it has been sleeping.

   a dormant

   b juvenile

   c native

15 When you are _____ to someone, you owe them a favor in return for something they did for you.

   a captive

   b indebted

   c innate

Presentation

Greek Roots

Many words in English come from other languages, especially Latin and Greek.

Studying the meanings of these roots is useful because it will help you guess the meanings of many unfamiliar words in English.

A few Greek roots can stand alone as words, but most need a prefix, which comes before the root word, and a suffix, which comes after the root word. For example:

Root	Meaning	Prefix		Root		Suffix	
myth	story			myth	+	ical	= mythical (from a story)
path	suffering	em	+	path	+	etic	= empathetic (relate to suffering)

Practice 2

Study the Greek roots in the chart and draw a line to match the two halves of the sentence.

Root	Meaning	Examples
acr-	height, summit, tip	acrobat, acronym
astr-	star, star-shaped	astrology, astronomy
chlor-	green	chlorine, chloride
-cracy, -crat	government, rule, authority	democracy, autocratic
cycl-	circular	bicycle, cyclical
derm-	skin	epidermis, hypodermic
ethn-	people, race, tribe, nation	ethnic, ethnicity
hydr-	water	hydraulic, hydrophobia,
ide-	idea; thought	ideogram, ideology
log-	thought, word, speech	logic, monologue
neur-	nerve	neurology, neurosurgeon
opt-	eye	optic, optical, optician
peri-	around	peripheral, periscope
tele-	far, end	telegram, telephone
zo-	animal, living being	zoo, protozoa

1 Something that is illogical is   the substance that makes plants green.

2 The perimeter is   you have a fear of high places.

3 A student of zoology   nervous about many things.

4 A neurotic person is   to see objects that are far away.

5 A cyclone is   a person who has official authority.

6 An asterisk is   takes care of people's eyes.

7 A telescope allows you   a star-shaped symbol.

8 If you suffer from acrophobia,   different cultures of people.

9 A dermatologist is   the border around a particular area.

10 Chlorophyll is   a doctor who treats skin problems.

11 An ethnographer studies   studies animals.

12 A bureaucrat is   a strong wind which moves in a circular pattern.

13 To hydrate means   to drink water.

14 An optician   done without clear thought.

PREFIXES

Presentation

Prefixes

A *prefix* is a group of letters added to the beginning of a root to make another word. Adding a prefix to a root changes the word's meaning. For example, adding the prefix, *il-* to the root word *legal* creates the word *illegal*. It changes the meaning to "not legal."

English has many different prefixes that mean *not*. These prefixes make the new word the opposite of the root word.

Practice 1

Study the chart. Read each sentence. Add a prefix from the box to the word in parentheses to form a new word that completes each sentence. Write the complete word in the blank.

Negative Prefix	Meaning	Example
a- ab-	not	atypical
dis-	not	disapprove
il-, im-, in-, ir-	not	illegal, impossible, inconceivable, irresponsible
mis-	badly, wrongly	misunderstand
non-	not	nonsense
un-	not	unable

ab-	im-	il-	un-
a-	in-	mis-	
dis-	ir-	non-	

1 The university students were expelled for their _____ (orderly) conduct.

2 Unfortunately, the meeting was quite _____ (productive). We didn't reach an agreement in the end.

3 The _____ (symmetrical) lines and shapes are characteristic of this painter's work.

4 She couldn't help her reaction; it was completely _____ (voluntary).

5 Your question about the professor's age was totally _____ (appropriate).

6 The flood damaged many of the documents, making them _____ (legible).

7 Ivan seems angry with me. I think he may have _____ (interpreted) my comment.

8 The test results showed signs of _____ (normal) heart function.

9 To some people, even a slight _____ (perfection) in their skin causes them embarrassment.

10 Is Gina OK? Her recent behavior seems completely _____ (rational).

Practice 2

Prefix	Meaning	Example
bi-	two	bicycle
cent-	hundred	century
dec-	ten	decade
du-	two	dual
kilo-	thousand	kilogram
mil-	thousand	milligram
mono-	one	monopoly
multi-	many	multi-colored
quad-	four	quadrangle
semi-	part, half	semicircle
tri-	three	triangle
uni-	one	unicycle

Study the chart. Then write a prefix to correctly complete each sentence.

1 The parade is a _____ annual event. It happens every two years.

2 Old photos were _____ chrome. They only use one color.

3 Our school is celebrating its _____ ennial year. It was founded one hundred years ago.

4 There are ten different sports in the Olympic _____ athlon.

5 The business _____ rupled in size. The company expanded its client list from 100 to 400 customers in just 6 months.

6 The university is changing to a _____ mester schedule next year. The year will be divided into three academic periods with breaks in between.

7 Electricity is often measured in _____ watts. That's units of 1000 watts of power.

8 The decision was made _____ laterally. Only one side had the real power.

9 Have you been to the new _____ plex cinema? It has so many theaters!

10 Wayne was only _____ enthusiastic about his family's travel plans. Half of him wanted to just stay home and relax.

Practice 3

Study the chart. Then circle the letter of the correct word to complete each sentence. Use the clue in parentheses to help you.

Prefix	Meaning	Example
anti-	against	antiwar
en –, em-	to make something change in some way	enlarge
extra-	out, outside, beyond	extraordinary
over-	too much	overwork
post-	after	postpone
pre-	before	preview
re-	again	redesign
sub-	under	substitute
super-	above	supervisor
trans-	across	transatlantic

1 His incredible strength _____ him to lift the large stone off the woman's leg. (made him able)

   a embellish

   b enabled

   c submerse

   d extraction

2 A lot of _____ art focuses serves as a type of political commentary. (after the war)

   a transnational

   b prehistoric

   c re-establish

   d postwar

3 Ronaldo collapsed from _____ after planting trees all day in the hot sun. (too much hard work)

   a embellish

   b antihistamine

   c extraction

   d overexertion

4 For those suffering from allergies, a prescription for an _____ can make a major difference. (drug that works against allergies)

   a postwar

   b embellish

   c antihistamine

   d enabled

5 A simple fresh coat of paint can do wonders to _____ even the dreariest of rooms. (make beautiful)

   a extraction

   b embellish

   c prehistoric

   d overexertion

6 We are a _____ company, serving North, Central, and South America. (across many countries)

   a extraction

   b prehistoric

   c transnational

   d reestablish

7 Ancient cave paintings can give fascinating clues to the day to day lives of _____ peoples. (before written history)

   a postwar

   b transnational

   c embellish

   d prehistoric

8 After a serious argument, it can take time to _____ a trusting relationship with the other person. (create again)

   a embellish

   b submerge

   c extraction

   d reestablish

9 The dentist prepared the necessary instruments to perform the tooth _____ . (taking out)

   a transnational

   b enabled

   c extraction

   d reestablish

10 DANGER. Do not _____ this appliance in water. (put under)

   a antihistamine

   b extraction

   c postwar

   d submerge

SUFFIXES

Suffixes

When a *suffix* is added to the end of a root, it can change the word's part of speech or verb tense. This doesn't always change the overall meaning of the word. Usually, it changes how the word is used in a sentence. For example:

Root		Suffix		
kind (adjective)	+	*-ness*	=	kindness (noun)
apprehend (verb)	+	*-sive*	=	apprehensive (adjective)

Some suffixes change the form **and** the meaning of a word. For example:

Root		Suffix		
tall (adjective)	+	*-est*	=	tallest (superlative adjective)

This section focuses on English suffixes that change words to nouns.

Practice 1

Study the chart. Then use a noun form suffix to make a new word that fits in the sentence. Write the new word. Use the word in parentheses to help you.

Suffix	Example
-ance, -ence	confidence, attendance
-ation -sion, -tion	creation, confusion, emotion
-ian, -er, -or	politician, baker, advisor
-ism	racism
-ist	racist
-ity	gravity
-ment	enjoyment
-ness	greatness
-ship	relationship

1 Ivory Coast gained _____ from France in 1960. (independent)

2 Rachel is a _____ . She generally follows what others do. (conform)

3 Pets that experience abuse or _____ may never trust humans again. (abandon)

4 Both of our companies offer different services that complement each other. We should consider a _____. (partner)

5 It's important to give employees _____ that they are doing a good job. (affirm)

6 It takes fresh ideas and a lot of _____ to succeed in business these days. (diligent)

7 Freddie works long hours as a night _____ at Bay Town High School. (custody)

8 These kinds of situations must be handled with _____ to avoid hurting someone's feelings. (sensitive)

9 I apologize for my _____ on the phone yesterday; I was extremely busy. (abrupt)

10 Critics of modern economic policies say we should be moving away from _____ and toward the more conservative policies of the past. (consumer)

Practice 2

Study the chart. Use an adjective form suffix to make a new word that fits in the sentence. Write the new word. Use the word in parentheses to help you.

Suffix	Example
-able, -ible	understandable, incomprehensible
-al	emotional
-ed	talented
-ful	wasteful
-ic	historic
-ious, -ous	gracious, famous
-ing	interesting
-ive	responsive
-less	relentless
-y	tacky

1 Sometimes it's difficult to make a _____ decision. You have to consider all options carefully. (ration)

2 Karen has always been very _____ about food. Even as a small child, she would only eat a few things. (pick)

3 It's a good idea to try new things and stay physically active, _____ of your age. (regard)

4 Our hotel room was quite _____ and had a fantastic view of the Dubai skyline. (space)

5 I couldn't complete the last question on the test; I was too _____ by the noise all the other students were making. (distract)

6 The restaurant's new decor is very _____ . It was designed by a Parisian interior decorating firm. (taste)

7 In a televised speech yesterday, the president vowed to focus on _____ recovery. (economy)

8 Sadly, animal shelters around the country are filled with dogs and cats that have been rescued from their _____ owners. (abuse)

9 Beware when purchasing _____ items, such as signed baseballs, photos, documents, or other so-called "authentic" autographed items online. A large percentage of them are fake. (collect)

10 Whether or not the CEO should be held responsible for the company's failure is _____ . The poor economy may also have been a factor. (debate)

11 The news report revealed several _____ details about the case. (surprise)

12 Karl's grades suffered when he began to attend private school. The academic work was much more _____ than he was used to. (rigor)

Practice 3

Study the chart. Then complete the table by writing the verb form of the word in the left column. Some words have more than one possible form.

Suffix	Example
-ate	agitate
-ify	personify
-ize	rationalize

Root / Other Form	Verb Form	Root / Other Form	Verb Form
refrigerator	_____	priority	_____
person	_____	triangle	_____
class	_____	real	_____
energy	_____	patron	_____
active	_____	ample	_____
sign	_____	initial	_____
minimal	_____	beauty	_____

WORD FORMS AND FAMILIES

Presentation

Word Families

A *word family* is a group of words that are all formed from the same root. Words in the same family usually have similar meanings, but they can be used differently in the sentence. For example:

Noun	Verb	Adjective	Adverb
freedom	free	free	freely

*Note that sometimes a word may have the same form but different parts of speech. As in the example above, *free* is both a verb and an adjective.

There also may be more than one word for the same part of speech. For example, the word *care* has several adjectives, including negative adjective forms:

Noun	Verb	Adjective	Negative Adjective	Adverb
care	care	careful, carefree, caring	careless, uncaring	carefully

Studying the different forms in word families will help to expand your vocabulary and help you improve your reading and listening skills in English.

Practice 1

Complete the chart with the missing forms. Some parts of speech have more than one form. An "X" means a form is rare or does not exist.

Noun	Verb	Adjective	Negative Adjective	Adverb
reason	_____	_____	unreasonable	_____
_____	avoid	avoidable	_____	X
integration	_____	_____	disintegrated	X
_____	doubt	X	X	_____
_____	X	political	_____	politically
treatment	_____	treated	untreated	X
_____	X	courageous	X	_____
response	respond	_____ responsive	irresponsible _____	irresponsibly
placement	_____	placed		X
enthusiasm _____	enthuse	enthusiastic	unenthusiastic	_____
_____	manage	_____	unmanageable	managably
disruption	disrupt	disruptive	X	disruptively
desire	_____	desirable	_____	desirably
_____	rationalize	rational		_____

Practice 2

Circle the letter of the correct form of the word for each sentence.

1 This type of _____ behavior will not be tolerated in class.
  a disruption   **b** disrupt   **c** disruptive

2 Kelly finally decided to leave her job after her workload became _____ .
  a management   **b** unmanageable   **c** manage

3 This TV show is for teenagers. It doesn't have much _____ for older audiences.
  a appealing   **b** appeal   **c** unappealing

4 It will be a while before technology becomes fully _____ in the classroom.
  a integrated   **b** disintegrate   **c** integration

5 As a rule, I try to keep my social networking profiles and comments _____ .
  a politics   **b** apolitical   **c** politically

6 When the test results came back from the lab, the results were _____ .
  a courage   **b** courageously   **c** discouraging

7 John is doing _____ well, considering what he's been through.
  a reason   **b** reasonably   **c** reasoning

8 This product is the only one of its kind. There is nothing _____ on the market.
  a comparable   **b** compare   **c** comparison

9 Tran's Noodle Bowl is _____ the best Vietnamese restaurant in the city.
  a doubt   **b** doubtful   **c** undoubtedly

10 Don't make a quick decision. Let's think about this _____ .
  a irrational   **b** ration   **c** rationally

Inferring Meaning from Context

USING CONTEXT

Presentation

Finding the Right Meaning

Often, a word has more than one definition (meaning) listed in the dictionary. The part of speech for each definition can be the same or different. You can use the words around it (called the *context*) to help you figure out which definition is the correct one.

When a word had more than one definition in the dictionary:

1. Read the sentence where you found the word and determine the word's part of speech.
2. Read all of the dictionary definitions for the word (with the same part of speech).
3. Think about the meaning of the word in the sentence and look for the definition that best matches that meaning. Use the example sentences in the dictionary to help you.

Practice 1

Read the sentence and think about the meaning of the underlined word. Then circle the letter of the correct definition.

1 Coal and natural gas are the two energy sources with the greatest percent share of electricity generation.
  a n. age group
  b n. production
  c n. percentage

2 Coal and natural gas are the two energy sources with the greatest percent share of electricity generation.
  a n. part, portion, piece of something
  b v. to tell something to someone, usually something private
  c v. to divide into portions

3 Greg and Louise just bought a lovely new home in the country. It's in a very private spot on a country road.
  a adj. confidential, remote
  b adj. privileged, restricted
  c n. lowest ranking member of the military

4 In order to succeed in today's world, businesses have to focus on the things that really matter: service, people, and values.
  a n. an issue or situation that you must think about or deal with
  b v. to be important; having a major effect on other things
  c n. a substance; anything in the universe that has mass, including solids, liquids, and gasses

5 A <u>private</u> in the Australian army wears no emblem or symbol on his or her uniform.
   a adj. secret, confidential
   b adj. privileged, restricted
   c n. lowest ranking member of the military

6 When added to the garden, organic <u>matter</u> such as decaying leaves or manure improves the soil structure for growing.
   a n. an issue or situation that you must think about or deal with
   b v. to be important; having a major effect on other things
   c n. a substance; anything in the universe that has mass, including solids, liquids, and gasses

7 The retiring CEO explained that she was not ready to reveal her plans publicly yet. She wanted to <u>share</u> them with those close to her first.
   a n. part, portion, piece of something
   b v. to tell something to someone, usually something private
   c v. to divide into portions

8 Some archeological sites have been built over many times as later <u>generations</u> build on top of the work of their ancestors.
   a n. age groups
   b n. productions
   c n. creations

Practice 2

Read the sentence and think about the meaning of the underlined word. Then circle the letter of the correct definition.

1 Although many in the courtroom believed the suspect's <u>account</u>, several members of the jury felt that it lacked some key details.
   a n. a written or spoken description which gives details of an event; a story
   b n. a written agreement with a bank or other service provider (Internet server, email, etc.)
   c v. (account for) to be the reason why something happens

2 A virus may remain dormant inside its <u>host</u> for a long period, and then become active and cause serious disease or even death.
   a v. to hold a party or other social event for invited guests
   b n. a large number of things
   c n. an animal or plant on or inside which a smaller organism lives

3 Following the application review process, students will be notified of <u>admission</u> by April 30th.
   a n. the cost of entrance to a concert, sports event, etc.
   b n. a statement in which you admit that something is true or that you have done something wrong
   c n. permission given to someone to become a member of an organization, enter a university, etc.

4 The consumption of foods, such as yogurt, which contain the bacteria *lactobacillus casei* helps the digestive system <u>function</u> naturally.

   a v. to work correctly or properly

   b n. a large party or ceremonial event, such as a wedding or a funeral

   c n. a result of something else

5 Climate change has created an entire <u>host</u> of environmental problems, from melting glaciers in the Arctic to an increase in dangerous bacteria and insects around the world.

   a v. to hold a party or other social event for invited guests

   b n. a large number of things

   c n. an animal or plant on or inside which a smaller organism lives

6 According to economics expert James Turk, inflation has a <u>function</u> of diminishing demand for currency as well as increasing supply.

   a v. to work correctly or properly

   b n. a large party or ceremonial event, such as a wedding or a funeral

   c n. a result of something else

7 The young woman's testimony and her eventual <u>admission</u> of guilt shocked the courtroom and the community.

   a n. the cost of entrance to a concert, sports event, etc.

   b n. a statement in which you admit that something is true or that you have done something wrong

   c n. permission given to someone to become a member of an organization, enter a university, etc.

INFERRING THE MEANING OF WORDS

Presentation

Inferring Meaning from the Larger Context

Sometimes it is difficult to infer the meaning of a word simply from the context of one sentence. In these situations, you need to read more of the passage and gather more clues to infer the meaning.

To infer meaning from the larger context:

- Determine the part of speech of the word.
- Think about the meaning of the sentence and the overall topic of the passage.
- Check to see if the word is repeated elsewhere in the passage. If so, read those sentences and check to see if you can infer the meaning from there.
- Infer the general meaning of the word.
- Try reading the sentence with your meaning instead of the word. Ask yourself if it makes sense.

Practice 1

Read the excerpt from *A Secret Garden* by Frances Hodgson Burnett, as well as other excerpts. Circle the letter of the meaning of the underlined word or phrase.

Mary put down her candle on the table near the bed and sat down on the cushioned stool. She did not want to go away at all. She wanted to stay in the mysterious hidden-away room and talk to the mysterious boy.

"What do you want me to tell you?" she said.

He wanted to know how long she had been at Misselthwaite; he wanted to know which corridor her room was on; he wanted to know what she had been doing; if she disliked the moor as he disliked it; where she had lived before she came to Yorkshire. She answered all these questions and many more and he lay back on his pillow and listened. He made her tell him a great deal about India and about her voyage across the ocean.

She found out that because he had been an <u>invalid</u> he had not learned things as other children had. One of his nurses had taught him to read when he was quite little and he was always reading and looking at pictures in splendid books.

Though his father rarely saw him when he was awake, he was given all sorts of wonderful things to amuse himself with. He never seemed to have been amused, however. He could have anything he asked for and was never made to do anything he did not like to do. "Everyone is obliged to do what pleases me," he said indifferently. "It makes me ill to be angry. No one believes I shall live to grow up."

1   **a**   sick person
     b   teacher
     c   world traveler

Over the past couple of decades, the Internet has literally opened up the world, <u>paving the way</u> for citizens of the world to freely express their ideas and opinions and exchange information with others around the globe, but all this virtual freedom hasn't come without a price. Terrorists, cyber-spies, bootleggers, and other cyber-criminals are constantly finding new ways to use information on the web to their advantage, creating a desperate need for heightened Internet security.

2   **a**   making it difficult
     b   creating opportunities
     c   giving a reason

With hundreds of accidents and fatalities every year resulting from the use of cell phones while driving, it's no surprise that nearly all US states now have passed laws restricting cell phone use and texting while operating motor vehicles. However, officials in cities across the country have decided to take an even more <u>drastic</u> step — "distracted walking" laws, which ban people from texting while crossing the street. Yes, that means walking—not driving—across the street.

3   **a**   realistic
     b   unnecessary
     c   extreme

Ecotourism, also known as "ecological" or "green" tourism, has become a popular way to travel in recent years. It is one of the fastest-growing sectors of the tourism industry, growing annually by 10–15% worldwide (Miller, 2007). Ecotourism refers to an eco-conscious travel experience with the aim of learning about and having a positive impact on the local people and environment. Supporters of ecotourism say it's both fun and educational; however, this relatively recent travel trend has not been without its detrimental side effects.

4 a psychological
   b unexpected
   c harmful

There are two primary factors that differentiate asteroids from comets: chemical composition and orbit. Firstly, terms of chemical composition, comets contain a volatile material on the surface. This material produces a temporary atmosphere when the comet passes near the Sun and solar radiation and winds cause the comet's surface to lose some of this compound. In contrast, asteroids do not produce any type of atmosphere at all. With regard to orbit, asteroids have a fairly regular, elliptical orbit path, and therefore they remain within approximately the same distance from the Sun, wherever they are in that path. Comets, on the other hand, have an irregular orbit, so their distance from the Sun tends to vary greatly.

5 a oval-shaped
   b up and down
   c confusing

Discovered and claimed for Spain in 1499, Aruba was acquired by the Dutch in 1636. Aruba seceded from the Netherlands Antilles in 1986 and became a separate, autonomous member of the Kingdom of the Netherlands. Movement toward full independence was halted at Aruba's request in 1990.

The island's economy has been dominated by three main industries. A 19th century gold rush was followed by prosperity brought on by the opening in 1924 of an oil refinery. The last decades of the 20th Century saw a boom in the tourism industry. Tourism and offshore banking are the mainstays of the small open Aruban economy. The rapid growth of the tourism sector over the last decade has resulted in a substantial expansion of other activities. Over 1.5 million tourists per year visit Aruba with 75% of those arriving from the US. Construction continues to boom with hotel capacity five times the 1985 level. Tourist arrivals rebounded strongly following a dip after the September 11, 2001 attacks.

6 a beginning
   b expansion
   c removal

Practice 2

Read the passage and circle the letter of the definition of the vocabulary word.

Stem cells have the remarkable potential to develop into many different cell types in the body during early life. In addition, in many <u>tissues</u>, they serve as a sort of internal repair system, dividing essentially without limit to <u>replenish</u> other cells as long as the person or animal is still alive. When a stem cell divides, each new cell has the potential either to remain a stem cell or become another type of cell with a more specialized function, such as a muscle cell, a red blood cell, or a brain cell. In some organs, such as the <u>gut</u> and bone marrow, stem cells regularly divide to repair and replace worn out or damaged tissues.

Stem cells are capable of dividing and renewing themselves for long periods. Unlike muscle cells, blood cells, or nerve cells—which do not normally replicate themselves—stem cells may <u>proliferate</u>. A starting population of stem cells that proliferates for many months in the laboratory can yield millions of cells.

Given their unique <u>regenerative</u> abilities, stem cells may offer new potential for treating diseases such as diabetes and heart disease. However, much work remains to be done in the laboratory and the clinic to understand how to use these cells for regenerative therapies to treat disease.

1 The word *tissues* means _____ .
  a medical research studies
  b concepts in the human mind
  c cells inside the body

2 The word *replenish* means _____ .
  a repulse
  b replace
  c remember

3 The word *gut* means _____ .
  a important fact
  b scientific expert
  c stomach and intestine

4 The word *proliferate* means _____ .
  a multiply quickly
  b work extremely hard
  c be in favor of

5 The word *regenerative* means able to _____ .
  a be removed
  b change shape
  c grow again

Collocations and Idioms

COMMON COLLOCATIONS AND PHRASAL VERBS

Common Academic Collocations

Collocations are words that are used together frequently so they become a familiar phrase. There are a number of collocations that are commonly used in academic texts. It is helpful to recognize them to help you efficiently process the information in academic articles, reports, textbook passages, etc.

Some common collocations in academic English follow these structures:

Noun + (preposition) + noun:

The period of civil unrest finally resulted in government intervention.

Noun + verb:

Research shows that people are remaining healthier longer in life.

The lab results indicated that the source of the bacteria was a farm in the Midwest.

Verb + noun:

Professor Mayahara received a grant to conduct research at the university. Scientists are just beginning to assess the impact of climate change.

Verb + adverb:

The study showed that laboratory rats behave differently in different environments.

Students must be able to communicate effectively and make their point clear.

Adjective + noun:

The prosecution made a compelling argument; however the suspect was found not guilty.

The patterns in these rock formations are caused by fluctuating temperatures and other environmental factors.

Phrasal verb (verb + preposition):

NATO is an alliance that consists of 28 member countries.

Students must adhere to the policies and procedures in the University's Student Handbook.

Practice 1

Underline the phrases that are collocations.

According to a recent study conducted at Michigan State University, brief interruptions of even a few seconds—such as the time it takes to view a text message on a smartphone—can have a negative effect on our ability to perform tasks with accuracy. According to the study, these interruptions can cause people to make errors in the workplace, sometimes with serious consequences.

These types of interruptions during the workday are extremely common in today's tech-dependent society, between email, text messages, and notifications from social networking sites. However, the resulting errors could be fatal in some work environments, such as air traffic controllers, food inspectors, or emergency medical technicians.

For the study, researchers asked 300 people to perform a series of tasks on the computer while responding to a number of short interruptions of about three seconds each. The study found a dramatic increase in errors during the performance of the participants who were forced to cope with interruptions. In short, the interruptions effectively doubled the rate of errors.

Erik Altmann, lead researcher of the study and associate professor of psychology at MSU, said his team was surprised to find that such short interruptions would have a major effect. "The findings prove that even momentary interruptions can seem jarring when they occur during a process that takes considerable thought," he said.

Altmann's findings indicate that the public's health and safety depends largely on how often the people who are responsible for protecting it get interrupted during their work.

A possible solution for the future would be for workplaces to institute more frequent break times, so that employees are less tempted to multitask while at work.

Practice 2

Write the missing verbs *have*, *raise*, or *pose* to complete the academic collocation.

1 It is still unknown whether genetically modified foods will _____ an impact on human health.

2 During today's discussions with university officials, the students plan to _____ the issue of unfair grading policies.

3 Higher university tuition _____ problems for students from low-income backgrounds.

4 The report will likely _____ expectations that scientists will someday find a cure for cancer.

5 Only the president or the vice president _____ the authority to make that decision.

6 It has been proven that exposure to secondhand smoke does _____ a risk to non-smokers.

7 Expanded international trade routes _____ a challenge for scientists working to stop the spread of invasive species.

8 The senator wishes to _____ a point about coastal erosion on the National Seashore.

9 It has been proven that the use of insecticides containing the chemical DEET _____ an effect on the nervous system.

10 Climate change continues to _____ a threat to wildlife, especially in Arctic areas.

11 Musicians and other celebrities can sometimes _____ a major influence on politics and society.

12 The results of this study may _____ doubts about the origin of this new strain of virus.

Presentation

Phrasal Verbs

Phrasal verbs are very common in English. A phrasal verb consists of a verb + a preposition (also known as a *particle*). It is important to study phrasal verbs because their meanings are often idiomatic; that is, the actual meaning of the verb and preposition combination may be different from the meaning of the verb and preposition separately.

Take these two examples:

- *Please <u>bring up</u> the basket of laundry when it's finished.* The words *bring up* **do not** form a phrasal verb. You can understand the separate meanings of *bring* = to carry and *up* = to a room upstairs in the house.
- *Never <u>bring up</u> the topic of vacation time at a job interview.* Here, the words *bring up* form a phrasal verb. The words *bring* and *up* come together to mean to talk about or to introduce a topic of conversation.

Phrasal verbs may consist of two words:

- My car **broke down** on the way home.
- **Call** me **back** when you get this message.
- After the school fire alarm **went off**, it took a long time for the children to **calm down**.

Or they may have three words:

- Every time I go swimming, I **come down with** a nasty cold.
- It's important to **stand up for** what you believe in.
- The professor wasn't feeling well, so she asked her assistant to **take over for** her.

Practice 3

Read the example sentences and think about the meaning of the phrasal verb. Then draw a line to match the phrasal verb to the definition.

- In his latest article, Howard Gutzman **puts forward** the idea that vaccinations are dangerous.
- After **carrying out** a series of experiments, the research team concluded its work.
- By the year 2030, people aged 65 and older are expected to **make up** the majority of the world's population.
- The primary aim of the document was to **point out** weaknesses in the public education system.
- The author of the article **set out** to prove that the economic problems were caused by irresponsible government spending.
- The professor gave us more time to **work on** our final projects.
- Days after the accident, Karen was still too upset to **go into** all the details of what happened.
- The committee was asked to **lay out** a campus-wide plan for energy conservation.
- It took representatives from both companies several weeks to **work out** an agreement.
- Although many employees disagreed with the manager's decision, no one dared to **go against** her.

1 put forward		do, complete
2 carry out		create and present
3 make up		propose
4 point out		be a part/percentage of
5 set out		continue, make progress
6 work on		discuss and agree on
7 go into		intend
8 lay out		bring attention to
9 work out		explain
10 go against		disagree with

Practice 4

Study the three-word verbs with *get* and their meanings. Then write in the missing particle to complete the verb in the sentence.

Verb	Meaning	Example
get around to	find the time to do something	Maybe this weekend, I'll get around to cleaning the closet.
get away from	leave a something behind, usually a bad situation	Sarah took a vacation alone to get away from the stress of work.
get away with	avoid blame for something you did wrong	Most criminals feel confident that they will get away with their crimes.
get back at	punish someone who has done something bad to you	Jen told her brother she would get back at him for telling her secret.
get by with	be able to deal with the difficulty of not having exactly what you need.	We can get by with our old car for now, but we'll need to buy a new one soon.
get on with	continue with something, make progress	Let's take a short break and then we'll get on with the rest of the presentation.
get out of	not be responsible for something you don't want to do	How did Ken get out of working this weekend?
get (something) over with	finish something quickly, usually something unpleasant	My surgery is scheduled for next week; I just want to get it over with.

1 We don't need any special accommodations tonight. We can get _____ _____ sleeping bags on the floor.

2 Max embarrassed me in front of the whole class. Don't worry; I'll get _____ _____ him somehow.

3 I'm so nervous about my presentation. I just want to get it _____ _____.

4 Now that your back is feeling better, you can't use that as an excuse to get _____ _____ helping me carry the groceries.

5 Many people feel the jury's decision was wrong, and that the suspect got _____ _____ the robbery.

6 Julia should forget about Tom. She really needs to get _____ _____ her life.

7 By the time I got _____ _____ calling Fran back, she had already left her house.

8 Ken wanted to get _____ _____ the corporate lifestyle, so he quit his job and opened his own café.

IDIOMS

Presentation

Idioms

An *idiom* is a type of collocation. It is a group of words (or a phrase) that has a special meaning when used together. You usually cannot tell the meaning of an idiom just by understanding the separate words in the phrase. That is why it is important to make idioms part your vocabulary study. Idioms are not only useful, but they are also fun to learn.

Here are some examples of common idioms in English and their meanings:

- Yolanda said she was **sick and tired** of waiting for Roberto to call. (frustrated and impatient)
- You don't have to make a decision now. Why don't you **sleep on it** and give me your answer tomorrow? (wait until the next day)
- The test was a **piece of cake**. Every student got an 'A'. (very easy)

There are a number of idioms that include parts of the body. The idioms in this exercise use the words *leg*, *arm*, *shoulder*, *eye*, or *hand*.

Practice 1

Read the sentences and circle the letter of the correct part of the body to complete the idiom. Each answer is used twice.

1 The court case was over quickly. The defendant didn't have a(n) _____ to stand on; he was clearly guilty.

   a leg

   b arm

   c eye

   d hand

   e shoulder

2 Please keep a(n) _____ on little Bobby. He often wanders off in a crowd.

    a leg

    b arm

    c eye

    d hand

    e shoulder

3 Professional athletes make money _____ over fist. It hardly seems fair.

    a leg

    b arm

    c eye

    d hand

    e shoulder

4 Seiji will be successful at everything he does. He's got a good head on his _____.

    a legs

    b arms

    c eyes

    d hands

    e shoulders

5 My mother always knew when we were doing something wrong. She has _____ in the back of her head.

    a legs

    b arms

    c eyes

    d hands

    e shoulders

6 She'll have a(n) _____ up on the other job applicants because of her overseas work experience.

    a leg

    b arm

    c eye

    d hand

    e shoulder

7 Thank you for listening to me when I was upset. I just needed a(n) _____ to cry on.

    a leg

    b arm

    c eye

    d hand

    e shoulder

8 Can you give me a(n) _____ with this? It's really heavy.

    a leg

    b arm

    c eye

    d hand

    e shoulder

9 I'm not sure I trust Ann's new boyfriend. I think she should keep him at _____ length.

    a leg's

    b arm's

    c eye's

    d hand's

    e shoulder's

10 My new smartphone cost a(n) _____ and a leg, but it's worth it.

    a leg

    b arm

    c eye

    d hand

    e shoulder

Practice 2

Read the sentences and circle the letter of the best meaning for the idioms about school and studying in bold.

1 Rei is **a brain**. She hardly ever studies, but she still gets excellent grades.

    a very intelligent

    b very busy

    c very hard-working

2 Carla **aced** her math **test**. She only got one problem wrong.

    a got an excellent grade on

    b refused to take

    c did poorly on

3 Elena hasn't come to French class for weeks. She's going **to bomb** tomorrow's **test**.

    a fail

    b forget

    c be late for

4 **Cramming** might help you pass an exam, but you won't really learn the information.

    a studying hard the night before

    b asking many questions

    c leaving studies until later

5 I won't make it home for dinner tonight. I've really got to **hit the books**.

    a buy books

    b study

    c destroy books

6 Jamal is **a quick study**. He often helps the teacher explain things to the rest of the class.

    a someone who doesn't study much

    b someone who studies a lot

    c someone who learns quickly

7 I'm not worried about the presentation. I usually **perform well under pressure**.

    a do well when stressed

    b feel nervous

    c misunderstand things

8 There's no way I'm going to finish all this reading, unless I **pull an all-nighter**.

    a go to sleep now

    b close the book

    c stay up until the next morning

9 As a result of her health problems, Terry decided to **drop out of** school this semester.

    a come back

    b leave

    c try harder at

Practice 3

Read the sentence and figure out the meaning of the underlined idiom about work and business. Write the correct meaning from the box below.

is a strict boss	increase control over	in charge
cause the negotiations to fail	were unable to continue	limit
from person to person	extremely hard	

1 At the end of a long day of meetings, the negotiations hit a wall.

_____

2 John has been working like a dog since he got his promotion.

_____

3 More companies are beginning to put women at the helm.

_____

4 Larry runs a tight ship.

_____

5 A few irresponsible people caused the company to crack down on employees arriving late.

_____

6 Green's attitude at the meeting just may blow the deal.

_____

7 Due to the decrease in budget, the sales department was forced to cut back on international travel.

_____

8 The news that this product is available is likely to travel quickly by <u>word of mouth</u>.

___

COLLOCATIONS AND IDIOMS IN CONTEXT

Presentation

You will encounter collocations and idioms in all types of reading, from fiction, to textbook passages, to company memos. These set phrases are everywhere, which makes them extremely useful and important to learn.

The exercises in this section will help you practice recognizing phrases such as collocations and idioms in a variety of contexts.

Practice 1

Read the company memo and write the missing phrases from the box in the correct places.

put forward	serious consequences	depends largely on
According to	negative effects	cut back on

Company Memo
To: All employees
Date: August 16
Re: Meeting about upcoming policy changes

In an effort to _____ waste and expenditures, the board of directors has _____ a plan to streamline systems and conserve energy and resources. These changes will allow us to operate more efficiently and avoid the _____ of the current economic challenges facing companies like ours. _____ a recent review conducted by an external committee, failure to make these adjustments could result in _____ for the company and all its employees.

There will be a mandatory all-staff meeting to discuss these changes on Friday, August 30th from 10 AM to noon in the west conference room. The future success of our company _____ the cooperation of all employees.

Thank you for your kind attention to this matter.

Senior Management

Practice 2

Read the email and write in the missing words from the box to complete the collocations.

around	tight	pressure
shoulder	arm's	eyes

New Message

To: Sarah Henke

From: Marla Griggs

Subject: New job

Hi Sarah, I'm so sorry it has taken me so long to get _____ to replying to your email. I've been so busy with my new job, I haven't had a moment to relax. This has been a difficult month—moving to a new city, starting a new job—and I guess I've been feeling kind of lonely. Thanks a lot for keeping in touch. I'm lucky to have your _____ to cry on.

My new company is very well organized. My boss, Mr. Neilson, runs a pretty _____ ship. He works very hard and the employees all have a lot of respect for him. In fact, most of us are actually a little afraid of him. He seems to know what everyone is doing at all times. It's almost like he has _____ in the back of his head.

I haven't made any real friends yet. It's a small company, and the other employees are all quite close, so they seem to be keeping me at _____ length.

I have to give a presentation at a staff meeting this Friday, so I'm hoping to impress everyone then. That's only three days away, and I haven't even begun preparing, so I'd better get going. I'm not too worried, though. As you know, I work well under _____ !

Practice 3

Read the article. Write the correct words from the box in the blanks.

recent	have	found	by
impact	out	forward	researcher
risks	leg	dramatic	

According to a _____ study carried out by a group of researchers in Denmark, regular jogging can have an _____ on how long a person lives.

Lead _____, Peter Schnor and his team at Bispebjerg University Hospital in Copenhagen set out to answer the question, Does regular jogging have a significant influence on life expectancy?

The technological revolution of the past several decades has led to a more sedentary lifestyle, with more and more people sitting in front of a computer for extended periods of time and engaging in much less physical activity than our ancestors. These facts of modern life are resulting in higher obesity rates, heart attacks, and a whole host of other problems. In short, this less active lifestyle poses serious _____ to our health and longevity.

The results of Schnor's study were put _____ last spring at a meeting of the European Society of Cardiology. The study _____ that there is a _____ increase in life expectancy among those who jog at a moderate pace several times per week. Men have a slight _____ up on women, with an increase of 6.2 years, compared to women's 5.6 years. The good news is that you can get _____ with a fairly small amount of jogging and it will still _____ a positive effect.

Today's busy, overly scheduled society poses challenges for those wishing to increase their activity levels. However, Schnor's study results point _____ the importance of making time for regular exercise.

Following Ideas in Text

SIGNAL WORDS AND PHRASES

Signal Words and Phrases

Certain words and phrases are used to signal new ideas, examples, and how one idea relates to another in a passage. Studying signal words and phrases can help you understand the flow of ideas better when you are reading. Here are some common signal words and phrases used in English.

Practice 1

Purpose in the Passage	Signal Words and Phrases
Giving an example	*for example, for instance, in particular, to give an example*
To explain causes, and results or effects	*as a result, because of, due to, therefore, so, consequently*
To add a new idea to a series of ideas	*in addition, furthermore, moreover, as well as, another*
To explain steps in a sequence or events in time	*at first, first, then, finally, next (year), In 1945, last (month), recently*
Introducing a contrasting idea	*however, but, although, while*
To give a fact or detail to clarify a point	*in fact, as a matter of fact*

Circle the letter of the correct signal word or phrase to complete each sentence.

1 The company saw a marked downturn in sales this year. _____ , several branch offices will be closing this year.

    a As a result   **b** As well as   **c** At first

2 _____ the building sustained major damage in the earthquake, it will need to be demolished.

    a In addition,   **b** Since   **c** Therefore,

3 Because of the contract negotiations, the workers refused to enter the building. _____ they stated that they would not return to work until the matter was resolved.

   a Although,   **b** Moreover,   **c** So,

4 Today's children spend too much time in front of the computer. _____ , the average teen spends 8 hours in front of a screen.

   a As a matter of fact   **b** Finally   **c** So

5 The trend is for young people to move to urban areas for college and work. _____ , the population in rural areas is rapidly dwindling.

   a Consequently   **b** For instance   **c** However

6 The author has completed several novels, and a collection of original poetry, _____ numerous essays and articles.

   a although   **b** as well as   **c** therefore

Practice 2

Read the passage and underline the signal words and phrases.

The use of electronic devices as a source of entertainment has increased drastically in recent years, especially among children 12 and under. In fact, recent research has shown that most children between the ages of 8 and 12 spend three to five hours per day watching videos or playing games online, even on days when they attend school. Moreover, some children spend an hour or more texting their friends during the afternoon and evening hours. In the past, children used to spend much more time outdoors, engaging in spontaneous play with other children. For instance, it was common for children from the same neighborhood to gather in the street after school to play kickball or street hockey until their parents called them in to dinner. However, today those same neighborhood streets remain quiet and empty, as children stay inside in front of a screen of some type.

While some blame this trend on the technology, saying that video games are just more interesting to kids than real life, most child psychologists disagree. After all, it's parents who are allowing their children to stay indoors instead of saying, "Go outside and play," the parents' mantra of the past. News stories about various dangers to children have become more common these days. From speeding traffic, to bullying peers, to creepy strangers, the news is constantly fueling parents' worst fears. Consequently, say experts, parents are keeping their kids inside in an effort to protect them.

But are children really safer staying indoors? Not really. Research has shown that while the nature of the possible dangers to children may have changed since the past, today's children aren't really at any more risk than their peers 50 years ago. Actually, the negative health effects of a lack of exercise and outdoor play may be far more dangerous. In addition, there are other potential dangers online, for instance, cyberbullying and Internet predators, to name just a couple.

Practice 3

Write the signal words and phrases in the correct box.

For example	Therefore	After all
Due to	Finally	Consequently
So	In fact	Moreover
As a result	However	another
In particular	Although	Furthermore
As a matter of fact	Actually	In 1945
In addition	At first / First	Next
For instance	Conversely	To illustrate
In recent months	Since	In contrast
While	as well as	But

Signals for Giving an Example	Signals for Explaining Causes and Results or Effects	Signals for Adding a New Idea to a Series of Ideas

Signals for Explaining Steps in a Sequence or Events in Time	Signals for Introducing a Contrasting Idea	Signals for Giving a Fact or Detail to Clarify a Point

PRONOUNS AND REFERENTS

Presentation

Pronouns

In order to be a fluent reader, it is not enough to just understand the words. You also need to understand the way writers connect ideas. You also need follow the flow of ideas and meaning through the text. One way writers connect ideas and avoid repetition is by using various types of pronouns and pronoun-like words, such as possessive adjectives or demonstrative adjectives. (See chart below.)

Pronouns and pronoun-like words (like possessive adjectives and demonstrative adjectives) can take the place of words, phrases, or whole ideas in the text. This word, phrase, or idea is called the referent – the idea the pronoun refers back to. For example, in these sentences the pronouns (or pronoun-like words) are in bold; the referents are underlined:

In the past, children from the same neighborhood gathered in the streets after school to play kickball or street hockey until **their** parents called **them** in to dinner. Today, **those same streets** remain quiet and empty, as children stay inside in front of a screen. While some blame this on the technology, most child psychologists disagree.

- Both the possessive adjective *their* and the object pronoun *them* refer back to the referent *children* from the same *neighborhood*.
- Those same streets refers back to the referent *streets* (*where the children gathered after school*).
- The demonstrative pronoun *This* refers to the trend of *empty streets and children staying inside in front of a screen.*

Practice 1

First, read the passage. Then follow the instructions on p. 123 and write the answers.

Marina Abramović

(1) Art can achieve many things. On one hand, it can help the viewer
(2) understand the artist's feelings or view of the world; on the other,
(3) some art forms seem as though they were specifically designed to
(4) change the viewer's perspective and make him or her see the world
(5) in new ways. In order to accomplish this, some artists take their work
(6) to extreme levels, even using their art to shock or scare viewers. This
(7) seems particularly true in performance art, which typically features
(8) some type of performance or show starring the artist him or herself. It
(9) may be viewed live or via video.
(10) Marina Abramović is known as the "grandmother of performance
(11) art." This nickname is well-deserved, as she has performed
(12) thousands of shows around the world over the past four decades.
(13) Originally from Serbia, she now lives and works in New York City.
(14) Abramović's career began in Europe in the 1970s, when she was in
(15) her early 20s. At that time, performance art was gaining popularity
(16) internationally. Over the years, her performances have ranged from
(17) simply strange to completely shocking. They are designed to test
(18) viewers' limits and encourage them to step outside their own "comfort zones."

1 A subject pronoun in line 1: _____

2 A subject pronoun in line 3: _____

3 Two object pronouns in line 4: _____ , _____

4 A demonstrative pronoun in line 5: _____

5 A possessive adjective in line 5: _____

6 A relative pronoun in line 7: _____

7 A demonstrative adjective in line 11: _____

8 A possessive adjective in line 15: _____

9 A subject pronoun in line 11: _____

10 A demonstrative adjective in line 15: _____

11 An object pronoun in line 18: _____

Practice 2

Read the passage. Then circle the letter of the correct referent for each numbered pronoun.

Art can achieve many things. On one hand, (1) **it** can help the viewer understand the artist's feelings or view of the world; on the other, some art forms seem as though (2) **they** were specifically designed to change the viewer's perspective and make (3) **him or her** see the world in new ways. In order to accomplish (4) **this**, some artists take their work to extreme levels, even using their art to shock or scare viewers. (5) **This** seems particularly true in performance art, (6) **which** typically features some type of performance or show starring the artist him or herself. (7) **It** may be viewed live or via video.

1 The referent for **it** is _____ .

  a art

  b hand

  c many things

2 The referent for **they** is _____ .

  a feelings

  b art forms

  c viewers

3 The referent for **him or her** is _____ .

  a viewer

  b perspective

  c artist

4 The referent for **this** is _____ .

  a understanding the artist's feelings

  b changing the viewer's perspective

  c taking work to extreme levels

5 The referent for **This** is _____ .

   a performance art

   b using art to shock or scare viewers

   c seeing the world in new ways

6 The referent for **which** is _____ .

   a extreme levels

   b shocking or scary art

   c performance art

7 The referent for **it** is _____ .

   a performance or show

   b artist him or herself

   c video

Presentation

Relative Pronouns

A relative pronoun introduces a relative clause, which is a dependent clause that modifies a word, phrase, or idea in the main clause of the sentence. For example, the relative pronouns are: *that, who, whom, whose, which, where, when,* and *why.*

Who, whom, and *that* can refer to people:

- Pierre de Coubertin was the French educator and historian <u>who</u> started the modern-day Olympics.

The referent for *who* = Pierre de Coubertin

- She was the same customer service representative <u>that</u> I had spoken to the day before.

The referent for *that* = the same customer service representative

Which and *that* can refer to objects:

- We're planning to stay at the hotel <u>that</u> we stayed at last year.

The referent for *that* = the hotel

- There are many books now <u>which</u> are available for free online.

The referent for *which* = many books

Which can also refer to ideas:

- Howard has decided to start saving money, <u>which</u> is an entirely new concept for him.

The referent for *which* = saving money

Whose indicates possession:

- Mrs. Hobbs, <u>whose</u> son, Mike, is the class president, has offered to host the graduation party this year.

The referent for *whose* = Mrs. Hobbs (shows possession of "son, Mike,")

Practice 3

Read each paragraph of the book review and write the relative pronoun from the box in the correct place.

that	which	who

1 *The Art of Hearing Heartbeats* is a beautiful story of true love, heartbreak, and a young woman's quest to find out what happened to her father, a respected New York attorney, _____ disappeared when she was 10 years old. The book, _____ was translated to English from German, has been on the best-seller lists in a number of European and Asian countries for several years. With his poignant, poetic writing style, German author Jan-Philipp Sendker has succeeded in writing a story _____ is touching, suspenseful, and thought-provoking.

who	whose	that

2 The narrator of the story 20s Julia, _____ father was born and raised in Burma, is a woman in her early 20s. Ten years earlier, Julia's father, Tin Win, went missing without any explanation to his family. His whereabouts remained a mystery until Julia finds a love letter _____ her father had written to a woman named "Mi Mi" in Burma. The letter prompts Julia to travel to her father's small hometown in Burma to find out what happened to him. There she meets U Ba, an elderly man _____ tells Julia he has been waiting for her. U Ba asks Julia to sit down and then begins to tell her the remarkable story of Tin Win's life.

that	whose	who

3 U Ba's story is about the love story between Tin Win and Mi Mi _____ lasted 50 years, even though they were separated when they were young. As a young boy, Tin Win was abandoned by his mother, _____ was told by an astrologer that her son's birth would bring bad luck. Tin Win is cared for by a kind neighbor as a young boy. Then, at age 10, he becomes ill and loses his eyesight. His caretaker finds him a home at a nearby monastery, where he will be safe and able to study. At the monastery, Tin Win meets Mi Mi, a girl _____ legs are disabled and is unable to walk.

which	who	that

4 Tin Win and Mi Mi, _____ are both disabled, form a strong bond and soon become literally inseparable. Because of the nature of their disabilities, the two complement each other. Mi Mi can see, an ability _____ Tin Win lacks. Tin Win has the ability to walk, _____ is the one thing that Mi Mi cannot do on her own. As though they are one person, Tin Win begins to carry Mi Mi on his back everywhere. In Tin Win's ear, Mi Mi whispers the way forward, telling Tin Win to avoid obstacles in their way and when to walk faster or more slowly, turn left, right, or go straight. Together the two lovers can go anywhere and do anything.

who	which	that

5 The story takes a tragic turn, when Tin Win receives an unexpected telegram. The message, _____ was sent by Tin Win's rich uncle _____ lives in Burma's capital city of Rangoon, tells Tin Win he must prepare to come and live with him in the city. Tin Win must say the one word _____ he never imagined he would say to Mi Mi: "Goodbye."

whose	who	that

6 Listening to U Ba tell Tin Win and Mi Mi's story, Julia begins to recall a different kind of love, one _____ has been buried inside her for years—her own love for her father. Like any child _____ parent abandons them, Julia felt anger and resentment toward her father. But through her journey in his path, she comes to understand the man _____ had always been a mystery to her.

Vocabulary Building Practice Test

Part 1   Inferring Meaning from Context

Circle the letter of the correct word to complete each sentence.

1 So many jobs today involve sitting in front of a computer for hours. This _____ lifestyle is having seriously negative effects on our health.

   a sedentary

   b solo

   c suburban

2 Carlos Sosa is the _____ of the Most Valuable Employee Award.

   a refugee

   b recipient

   c resident

3 Some young children seem to have a/an _____ fear of insects, even if they have never seen bugs before.

   a isolated

   b ideological

   c innate

4 A _____ engineer helps build dams and finds ways to make water flow safely.

   a hypodermic

   b hydraulic

   c hemispheric

5 Our car wouldn't make it up the rough _____ on the mountain, so we had to get out and hike.

   a terrain

   b tardy

   c telepathic

Part 2   Inferring Meaning from Context

Circle the letter of the correct definition for the underlined word.

1 Nuclear power involves the <u>generation</u> of energy using radioactive materials.

   a n. age group

   b n. production

   c n. communication

2 Attendance at a <u>private</u> high school does not automatically guarantee admission to a top tier college.

   a adj. secret, confidential

   b adj. privileged, restricted

   c n. lowest ranking member of the military

3 The rainforest floor consists primarily of decaying plant <u>matter</u>.

    a n. an issue or situation that you must think about or deal with

    b v. to be important; having a major effect on other things

    c n. a substance; anything in the universe that has mass, including solids, liquids, and gasses

4 There is a whole <u>host</u> of reasons why I've decided to quit my current job and return to my hometown.

    a v. to hold a party or other social event for invited guests

    b n. a large number of things

    c n. an animal or plant on or inside which a smaller organism lives

5 The driver's <u>account</u> of the accident varied greatly from that of the witness who called police when it occurred.

    a n. a written or spoken description which gives details of an event; a story

    b n. a written agreement with a bank or other service provider (Internet server, email, etc.)

    c v. (account for) to be the reason why something happens

6 The drama's season ended with the main character's <u>admission</u> that he loved his wife's sister.

    a n. the cost of entrance to a concert, sports event, etc.

    b n. a statement in which you admit that something is true or that you have done something wrong

    c n. permission given to someone to become a member of an organization, enter a university, etc.

Part 3   Word Parts

Circle the letter of the correct prefix to complete the word in parentheses.

1 Email and texting make it easy to _____ (interpret) the meaning of people's messages.

    a dis-

    b mis-

    c de-

2 The judge was cited for having an _____ (appropriate) relationship with one of the jurors.

    a im-

    b in-

    c mis-

3 Valentine's Day is one of the few _____ (religious) holidays celebrated in the US.

    a a-

    b non-

    c un-

4 The furniture store offered us a discount on the sofa because there were some slight _____ (perfections) in the fabric.

    a im-

    b mis-

    c un-

5 Swimming, biking, and running are the typical events in a(n) _____ (athlon).
   a tri-
   b bi-
   c deca-

6 The author claims that the book is _____ (autobiographical). He based it half on his own life, and half on that of a fictional character.
   a cent-
   b semi-
   c multi-

7 _____ (theistic) religions believe in the existence of only one God.
   a Mono-
   b Multi-
   c Semi-

Part 4   Word Parts

Circle the letter of the correct suffix to complete the word in parentheses.

1 Before claiming lost luggage, you must give proof of (owner) _____ .
   a -ness
   b -ity
   c -ship

2 How quickly you are able to build muscle depends on the (intens) _____ of your workouts.
   a -ity
   b -er
   c -ness

3 Sometimes it seems the traditions of old-fashioned (polite) _____ and good manners have been lost over the years.
   a -ity
   b -er
   c -ness

4 Stay away from that cat; he's (feroc) _____ .
   a -ious
   b -ous
   c -al

5 All characters in this program are entirely (fiction) _____ .
   a -ive
   b -ial
   c -al

Part 5   Word Parts

Circle the letter of the correct form of the word to complete the sentence.

1   Terrence needs an interior decorator. The paint colors he has chosen are completely

_____ .

   a   appeal

   b   appealing

   c   unappealing

2   Georgio's Pizzeria is the only place in town to get a _____ priced meal anymore.

   a   reasonable

   b   reasonably

   c   unreasonable

3   We had a fantastic trip to Guam. _____ we'll return there someday.

   a   Doubt

   b   Doubtful

   c   Undoubtedly

Part 6   Inferring Meaning from Context

Circle the letter of the best meaning for the underlined word.

1   Gabon, a beautiful country on the West African coast, is a <u>haven</u> for many different species of plants and wildlife. About three-quarters of Gabon's land is covered by dense rainforest, which is home to gorillas, antelopes, and many tropical birds. In addition, Gabon is home to more than half of Africa's 40,000 forest elephants.

   a   safe place

   b   unknown place

   c   noisy place

2   Unfortunately, the lush, <u>pristine</u> environment that makes Gabon an ideal home for animals also attracts some very unwanted guests: poachers. A growing demand for ivory products, particularly in Asia, has fueled a rapid rise in poaching in recent years, leading to the illegal killing of many animals in Gabon's national parks.

   a   urban

   b   clean; perfect

   c   strange-looking

3   The study suggests a biological purpose for sleep, showing that it results in waste disposal in the brain, thus restoring healthy brain function on a daily basis. This information could have far-reaching implications for the treatment of <u>degenerative</u> brain diseases such as Alzheimer's.

   a   worsening

   b   rare

   c   modern

4   The purpose of sleep has <u>perplexed</u> scientists and scholars since ancient times. Every animal species, from the largest whale to the tiniest insect, needs some amount of sleep regularly. However, being asleep can present significant disadvantages to a species, such as leaving animals vulnerable to attacks by predators, and limiting time spent hunting or mating. Previous research proved that sleep helps the brain store memories and consolidate information, but most experts agree that these benefits still do not outweigh the disadvantages of spending numerous hours asleep every day.

a considered

b confused

c entertained

5 The purpose of sleep has perplexed scientists and scholars since ancient times. Every animal species, from the largest whale to the tiniest insect, needs some amount of sleep regularly. However, being asleep can present significant disadvantages to a species, such as leaving animals <u>vulnerable to</u> attacks by predators, and limiting time spent hunting or mating. Previous research proved that sleep helps the brain store memories and consolidate information, but most experts agree that these benefits still do not outweigh the disadvantages of spending numerous hours asleep every day.

a aware of

b in danger of

c unfamiliar with

Part 7   Collocations and Idioms

Circle the letter of the correct word or phrase to complete each sentence.

1 After last year's budget disaster, the town's treasurer put _____ a new plan to keep the fiscal situation on track.

a in

b over

c on

d forward

2 As I have pointed _____ in class many times, participation is 40% of your final grade.

a out

b over

c on

d at

3 I don't have a good suit to wear to the wedding this weekend. Do you think I could get by _____ some nice pants and a sweater?

a for

b with

c at

d under

4 Raoul wasn't able to keep his 2.5 grade point average. _____, the coach cut him from the soccer team.

a As a result

b As well as

c In addition to

d As a matter of fact

5 The acceleration performance of this car is excellent; _____ , its fuel consumption is relatively low.

    a moreover

    b as a result

    c whatever

    d forever

6 I always carry a first aid kit with me in case there's an accident. _____ , my son fell off his bike yesterday, and I had everything he needed right in my purse.

    a As a result

    b As well as

    c In addition to

    d As a matter of fact

7 The museum houses several of Van Gogh's landscapes, and a collection of his portraits, _____ numerous smaller paintings and sketches.

    a as a result

    b as well as

    c instead of

    d as a matter of fact

Part 8   Following Ideas in Text

Circle the letter of the correct word or words to which the underlined word or phrase refers.

1 Banks generally offer clients a choice of opening a checking account or savings account. The primary purpose of a checking account is for everyday money transactions such as paying bills and making purchases; you can pay bills and make frequent deposits and withdrawals without a lot of additional fees. You will receive a set of checks as well as a debit card, which you can use to make purchases online or in stores, as well as to withdraw cash from ATMs. <u>These accounts</u> tend to be more flexible and offer greater convenience for students. Some banks charge a monthly maintenance fee. Many offer no fee accounts for students. Check with your financial institution to learn if you can qualify for a "no fee" checking account.

    a some banks

    b deposits and withdrawals

    c additional fees

    d checking accounts

2 Nuclear reactors use cold water to cool down the fuel in order to prevent the core from melting down and avoid an explosion. <u>This</u> is why nuclear plants are generally built near the coast or by rivers. During fission, the process used to create nuclear electric power, it's neutrons that fly around and split the atoms. The use of water as a cooling agent slows down the neutrons, which results in less uranium and plutonium being used. Consequently, a shocking 95% of uranium and other radioactive elements end up as waste in this process. But what most people don't know is that water-cooling isn't the safest or most efficient option available.

    a Nuclear reactors use cold water to cool down the fuel.

    b Nuclear plants are generally built near the coast or by rivers.

    c Neutrons fly around and split the atoms.

    d Water slows down the neutrons.

3 New research has shed new light on the purpose of sleep and its power to clear the mind. A new study conducted at the University of Rochester has shown that the brain uses the time we are asleep to flush toxic material out of its cells. These findings show that the brain's unique method of self-cleaning—called the glymphatic system—becomes highly active during sleep. The study suggests a biological purpose for sleep, showing that it results in waste disposal in the brain, thus restoring healthy brain function on a daily basis. This information could have far-reaching implications for the treatment of degenerative brain diseases such as Alzheimer's.

   a sleep results in waste disposal in the brain

   b the brain's unique method of self-cleaning called the glymphatic system

   c treatment of degenerative brain diseases such as Alzheimer's

Part 9   Following Ideas in Text

Circle the letter of the correct relative pronoun to complete each sentence.

1 About three-quarters of Gabon's land is covered by dense rainforest, _____ is home to gorillas, antelopes, and many tropical birds. In addition, Gabon is home to more than half of Africa's 40,000 forest elephants.

   a who

   b which

   c that

2 The demand and the market for ivory products will most likely always exist. However, if governments in the countries _____ import ivory take a stand, the future of Central African elephants may stand a chance.

   a that

   b who

   c whose

3 You will receive a set of checks as well as a debit card, _____ you can use to make purchases online or in stores, as well as to withdraw cash from ATMs.

   a who

   b which

   c whose

4 The primary purpose is to save money (for emergency use, for future purchases, or to invest). Therefore, savings accounts are mainly for deposits, _____ will earn interest.

   a which

   b whose

   c who

5 Our extended eight-week international tour is designed for those _____ love the art of great filmmaking and want to explore our wonderful planet.

   a who

   b whose

   c which

READING FASTER

Introduction: Strategies for Reading Faster

Read the instructions. Next, read the text. Then circle the letter of the correct answer. You have 20 minutes.

Instructions for Timed Reading

1 Print a copy of the Reading Rate Table and the Reading Rate Log from the Appendix.

2 Write your exact start time (minutes and seconds) on the Reading Rate Log.

3 Start the timer.

4 Preview the passage by skimming it quickly.

5 Read the passage, skipping over unknown words or guessing their meaning.

6 Stop the timer and write your exact Finish time on the Reading Rate Log.

7 Answer the comprehension questions—**Do not** look back at the passage—and write the number of correct answers on the Reading Rate Log.

8 Calculate your reading time (your Finish Time minus your Start Time) and check your reading rate on the Reading Rate Table.

9 Mark a check next to your reading rate on the Reading Rate Log.

10 Check your reading rate progress after a few passages. The number should get higher. If not, challenge yourself to read faster.

America's Fast-Food Fixation

Americans have never been unhealthier, according to some recent statistics. Every year, more people in the U.S., including children, are diagnosed with diet-related disorders, ranging from obesity, to heart disease, to diabetes. These figures have resulted in some health advocacy groups, as well as members of the general public, calling for more government regulations, especially of one of America's most profitable industries—fast-food. The U.S. government has already imposed new rules and restrictions, such as requiring fast-food restaurants to display the number of calories and grams of fat for each menu item, and eliminating "super-size" options. Fast-food giants like McDonald's and Burger King have been quick to respond, advertising the use of "no-trans-fat" oils for their frying and adding low-calorie alternatives on their menus in an effort to appeal to more health-conscious Americans. Some areas of the country seem more prone to diet-related health issues, in particular across the southern portions of the U.S., most likely as a result of socioeconomic factors. Researchers have noted that in areas with low average household incomes, there are higher incidences of obesity and other diet-related health problems. This is because fast food tends to be a low cost meal option, which makes it a popular choice for many low income families.

In recent years, a section of Los Angeles has received a lot of negative attention. For the past five years, a 32-square mile area of South L.A. has been the subject of a heated debate among health activists, politicians, and fast-food executives. With its lack of grocery stores offering healthy food options and high concentration of fast-food restaurants, South L.A. has gained a reputation as a "food desert" – an area with almost no nutritional value, leaving residents with little choice but to eat fast food three meals a day.

In 2008, the L.A.-based health advocacy group, Community Health Councils, released statistics that showed shocking rates of diet-related health issues among residents of South L.A. The report stated that over 30% of the residents of South L.A. were obese and 11.7% had diabetes, rates far above those in the rest of the city.

While some accused Community Health Councils of creating unnecessary panic, some residents themselves acknowledged that with so many nearby fast-food restaurants to choose from, it was a challenge to keep from eating unhealthy, high-fat meal options. "To be honest, it's all we eat," local man, Rey Merlan, said during his lunch hour at a Kentucky Fried Chicken. "Everywhere, it's fast food everywhere."

L.A.'s City Council took the report seriously and immediately took action, passing a ban on the opening of any new fast-food restaurants within the South L.A. area. The rationale behind the ban, explained councilmember, Jan Perry, was to allow space for grocery stores and other types of restaurants—those serving healthier options—to be established in the area. "These restrictions are a fair, common-sense way of providing South L.A. residents additional food choices that exist in other parts of the city," Perry said when the regulations were passed.

Fast-food executives were angered by the ban and called the restrictions unfair and unnecessary. They cited their commitment to offering healthier items on fast-food menus, such as Asian chicken salads and yogurt granola parfaits. Many local and national business leaders said the ban overstepped the government's power. In a free-market society, they said, businesses should be able to open where it is profitable for them to operate. While councilmembers recognized these arguments, officials responded that they felt the local government should be responsible for promoting health and ensuring that all areas of Los Angeles offered ample healthy alternatives as well as fast food options. Banning additional fast-food establishments for a period of time and making room for healthier places would be effective in addressing South L.A.'s diet-related health issues, they said.

But several years later, most health advocates, including those from Community Health Councils, now say the ban has had little impact on health in the South L.A. community. Yang Lu, a research professor at the University of Southern California explains that having more healthy options doesn't necessarily mean people will choose to eat them–especially when dietary habits and family food budgets are already in place. "Even when people know what's good for them, sometimes fast-food is so addictive," Lu said. According to Lu, decreasing the number of fast-food restaurants is a good start toward decreasing obesity and other health problems, but she and other experts have recommended that the L.A. city council design programs to educate the public about the dangers of eating fast food frequently, along with a reminder of the old proverb, "You are what you eat."

1 What caused people to call for more government regulation of fast food?

   a a decrease in children being born in the U.S.

   b an increase in diet-related health problems

   c an increase in profits in the fast food industry

2 How have fast-food chains responded to existing government regulations?

   a They have fought them.

   b They have followed them.

   c They have ignored them.

3 Which of the following is NOT mentioned as a current regulation?

   a displaying calorie counts on menus

   b decreasing the number of desserts

   c eliminating "super size" options

4 According to the article, the southern U.S. has higher obesity rates because there are more _____ .

   a fast food restaurants

   b low-income families

   c expensive meal options

5 South L.A. has been called a "food desert" because there are _____.
 a more restaurants than people
 b hardly any restaurants there at all
 c so few places to get healthy food

6 L.A.'s city government reacted to the Community Health Council's report by

_____.

 a passing a ban on new fast-food restaurants
 b calling a meeting with fast-food executives
 c warning residents of the dangers of fast food

7 Professor Yang Lu concludes that _____.
 a most people prefer healthy food to fast food
 b some people are unable to stop eating fast food
 c fast food is not a significant cause of obesity

8 Which of the following can be inferred from the article?
 a The issue in South L.A. will soon be resolved.
 b L.A.'s City Council will try other methods.
 c The fast-food industry will decline in the U.S.

Timed Reading Practice

PRACTICE 1: CRIME-SOLVING TECHNIQUES THROUGHOUT HISTORY

Timed Reading 1

Read the text. You have 20 minutes.

A Brief History of Forensics

From Arthur Conan Doyle's *Sherlock Holmes* to modern popular TV shows like *CSI*, people have always had a fascination with criminal investigation and crime-solving techniques. Modern methods have become increasingly high-tech as investigators are now able to apply elements of medical science and computer technology to analyze evidence and compare large amounts of complex data. This is the world of forensic science, but it wasn't always so sophisticated.

The field of forensics uses a wide variety of technological tools and scientific approaches in order to investigate crimes after they have occurred. Investigators collect and analyze pieces of evidence—from objects, to fingerprints, to tiny fabric fibers, to single strands of hair or skin cells, and try to piece together a picture of what happened during the crime. The word *forensic* is Latin in origin, meaning "in front of the forum." In Ancient Rome, when a crime was committed, the accuser and the accused were required to appear in the public square called the "forum." Both individuals would tell their side of the story before a group of public citizens, who would then decide the accused's punishment—one of the earliest examples of a trial jury. This method, of course, was unreliable and often resulted in punishing the wrong person or setting the criminal free. Today, however, much more definitive evidence and proof is required for a jury to decide a criminal case.

Through the centuries, scientific-minded individuals have used a variety of creative methods to try to prove a person's guilt or innocence. In the Second Century BCE, the Greek physicist Archimedes helped to catch a thief who had tried to cheat the King. The story goes that King Hiero II had commissioned a goldsmith to make him a crown. The King himself supplied the craftsman with enough pure, solid gold to complete the work. When the crown was delivered, the King asked Archimedes to check the crown's purity and make sure the goldsmith had not substituted the gold with silver or some other metal, in order to keep some of the valuable gold for himself. He could not melt the crown to determine its metal content; he had to find a way to fulfill the king's request without destroying the crown. By submerging the crown in water and calculating its volume, mass, and density, Archimedes was successful in proving that the dishonest goldsmith had, indeed, used some silver in the crown.

Records from ancient China show that inspection of the mouth and tongue and the measurement of saliva levels were used to determine guilt or innocence. A person accused of a crime was asked to fill his or her mouth with dry rice and then spit it back out. If a large amount of rice remained in the person's mouth, it was determined that he or she could be guilty. While this test sounds unscientific, there is some logic behind it: a guilty person would be likely to be stressed or nervous during the investigation and therefore, likely to produce less saliva, causing the interior of the mouth to be dry, causing more rice to stick in the mouth. Middle Eastern investigators applied this same principle by requiring suspects to place their tongues briefly on a hot metal rod. A more serious burn indicated a dry mouth, and therefore, probably guilt.

In 250 BCE, the Greek anatomist Erasistratis was the first to use a person's heart rate to detect guilt. Erasistratis, an expert on the heart, knew that a person's pulse grew faster when he or she was lying. Erasistratis used this method when asked by the Greek emperor Nicator to determine whether or not his son was in love with the emperor's new wife. On being interviewed, the son's heart beat rapidly when asked about his feelings for his father's second wife, thereby proving his love for her.

In cases of murder, modern forensics often relies on the study of blood. The first written account of this method came from China in 1248. A person was killed by the use of a sickle (a sharp object with a long handle, used for cutting crops). The medical expert, Sung Tzu, asked the villagers to bring their sickles and lay them out in one location. Eventually, flies, attracted by the smell of fresh blood, gathered on one sickle. Consequently, the owner of the sickle confessed to the murder.

Forensics experts continue to conduct research and pioneer new methods in order to decrease the margins of doubt and ensure that justice prevails. If any of the founding fathers of forensics mentioned above were alive today, one wonders how they would react to our modern crime-solving techniques. No doubt they would be as fascinated as we are.

Reading 1   Comprehension Questions

Circle the letter of the correct answer.

1 Based on what you read, crime investigation techniques have

_____.

    a become more complex over time

    b not changed much in recent years

    c haven't always been a popular subject of study

2 In Ancient Rome, accused criminals had to

_____.

    a confess their crimes or go to jail

    b defend themselves to a public audience

    c decide their own form of punishment

3 Which of the following is NOT stated in the passage?

    a Innocent people are sometimes punished for crimes.

    b The majority of accused criminals are found guilty.

    c Forensic science is likely to change in the future.

4 Which principles of science did Archimedes use in the case described in the passage?

    a energy and motion

    b volume and density

    c gravity and force

5 Which most likely happened to the accused in Archimedes case?

    a He was given a place to live in the King's palace.

    b He was ordered to be killed by the king.

    c He was asked to make a new crown for the King.

6 From the passage, it can be inferred that

_____.

    a some ancient forensic methods were somewhat effective

    b many ancient crime-solving techniques are still used today

    c the Chinese were the first to use modern forensics

7 Erasistatis was the founding father of

_____.

    a heart disease medication

    b the lie detector test

    c a singles dating agency

8 The story of Sung Tzu

_____.

    a is the first written record of insects being used in forensics

    b was written before the sickle was invented

    c shows that blood is a reliable form of evidence in a murder investigation

Timed Reading 2

Read the text. You have 20 minutes.

Animals in Crime Investigation

From large dogs to tiny insects, humans have long looked to the animal world for assistance with their crime-solving endeavors. Throughout history, many crimes would neither have been discovered nor solved without the use of some animal-related evidence or data.

"K-9" Units

Archaeology has shown that dogs were first domesticated tens of thousands of years ago, in the early days of humankind, around 30,000 BCE. Over the course of human history, we have employed dogs for protection and aggression in wars and conflicts, and as an aid for intimidating and controlling enemies. During the Seminole Indian War of 1835-1842, the US Army organized one of the first official military canine (often abbreviated to "K-9") units. It was the Europeans who first began training dogs to do police work. In the late 1800s, in London, officers of Scotland Yard employed bloodhounds in their efforts to find criminals at large. Several decades later, law enforcement officials in Ghent, Belgium organized the first official training program for police dogs to assist officers with security while they were on duty. Soon, other countries across Western Europe were following the Belgians' lead, with Germany eventually becoming the leader in canine-assisted law enforcement. In his book, "The Police Dog: A Study of the German Shepherd Dog," David Brockwell writes, "In Germany as early as 1911 there were between four and five hundred police stations provided with these specially trained dogs." Today the German shepherd and the Belgian malinois are still the most commonly used breeds in the field of police work around the world.

K-9 units may be deployed for a wide variety of duties, such as locating suspected criminals or missing persons; searching for missing articles such as weapons; detecting drugs, explosives, illegal chemicals, or other dangerous substances; and protecting officers. In addition, officers often bring the dogs to community events and schools for demonstrations aimed at educating the public about police work.

Forensic Entomology

Forensic entomology refers the science of using of insects to investigate details of certain types of crimes, for example to determine the cause and time of a person's death, and other important details from crime scenes. As such, insects have proven to be especially helpful in providing important leads in murder cases. The most common types of bugs used in crime-solving are flies and their larvae, known as "maggots." A species of fly called the blow fly can detect a dead body from several kilometers away, and is attracted to dead flesh within 10 minutes, before it has even begun to deteriorate very much. The flies colonize, lay their eggs, and within a matter of hours, the larvae are born. Maggots feed on decaying matter and therefore are responsible for most of a corpse's decomposition. They live on the corpse until they reach adulthood. It is this life cycle and the knowledge of how long each stage takes that allow forensic entomologists to determine a person's precise time of death within minutes. In some cases, insects may also assist investigators in determining the cause of death, for example, when the cause is a toxic substance in the body such as drugs or poison. Traces of these substances may only remain in the body for a short period of time. However, they may still remain in the digestive systems of the insects, allowing investigators more time to piece together what may have happened.

Pet DNA Databases

After a series of recent crimes were solved by analyzing DNA from strands of cat hair taken as evidence from crime scenes, an international team of forensics experts established an official cat DNA database, in hopes that it will help solve additional crimes in the future. The natural oils in cats' skin combined with static electricity mean that anyone who enters a home where a cat lives is bound to attract cat fur. In fact, it would be nearly impossible to leave the home without carrying out numerous cat hairs on one's shoes, clothing, skin, etc. In addition, if the perpetrator of the crime is a pet owner, he or she is likely to leave strands of his or her own cat's fur at the scene of the crime. If the DNA from these hairs can be analyzed, located in the database, and matched to the correct owner, this information could help investigators get to the bottom of many cases. According to researcher Robert Grahn, "The increasing popularity of the domestic cat as a household pet has unknowingly fostered the distribution of potential crime scene evidence across millions of households. Cat fur obtained from a crime scene has the potential to link perpetrators, accomplices, witnesses, and victims."

Reading 2   Comprehension Questions

Circle the letter of the correct answer based on what you read.

1 Humans have had dogs as pets _____ .
 a for many centuries
 b since the 1800s
 c since the early days of the military

2 The first people to use dogs for police work were _____ .
 a soldiers in the US army
 b detectives in England
 c law enforcement officials in Germany

3 Which of the following is NOT mentioned in the passage?
  a Police dogs are often mistreated by their trainers.
  b Blow flies have a remarkable sense of smell.
  c Cat DNA has already been used to solve criminal cases.

4 "Maggots" are the _____ of the blow fly.
  a eggs
  b young
  c adult form

5 From the passage, it can be inferred that

_____.

  a investigators only use forensic entomology in murder cases
  b blow flies and their larvae often eat poison and other toxins
  c forensic entomology can determine the place of death

6 Why is cat DNA especially useful to investigators?
  a Millions of criminals have cats as pets.
  b Cats often travel between different households.
  c Cat fur sticks easily to shoes, clothing, skin, etc.

7 Which of the following is NOT discussed in the passage?
  a what police dogs are usually used for
  b how investigators determine time of death
  c whether investigators use dog fur to solve crimes

8 It can be inferred from the passage that

_____.

  a police will continue to expand the cat DNA database
  b the use of pet DNA to solve crimes is only temporary
  c many police departments do not believe in the use of cat DNA

Timed Reading 3

Read the text. You have 20 minutes.

How DNA Evidence Works

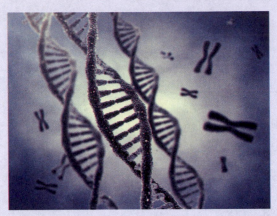

Without a doubt, the most riveting discovery to influence criminal investigation in the past century has been the development of techniques for analyzing DNA evidence. Human DNA has now been used in numerous cases around the world to identify suspects and to exonerate those who have been wrongly accused of crimes.

On the morning of September 10, 1984, British geneticist Professor Sir Alec Jeffreys of the University of Leicester was in his lab. Jeffreys was viewing an X-ray of a DNA experiment that compared differences and similarities in the DNA of different members of his colleague's family. Realizing that each image was unique, like the individual's fingerprint, Jeffreys understood the possibilities that this technique, now known as genetic fingerprinting, had for medical and forensic science. Over the next few years, Jeffreys and his team refined their research, gradually finding ways to isolate tiny variables in individuals' DNA. This new method, called genetic profiling, was more sensitive, more accurate, and allowed the lab to create a more detailed database. It is now the standard method of forensic DNA analysis for detective work. Jeffreys's systems are also instrumental in paternity testing, identifying who is the father of a particular child or individual.

For most of the modern history of forensics, fingerprinting was the most definitive and precise way of linking a suspect to a crime scene. Nowadays, DNA has become the most desirable form of evidence. A sample of DNA extracted from a single hair or a tiny droplet of saliva, when matched to a suspect, can be enough to prove guilt or innocence. With DNA, the evidence is also easier to collect because it can be found anywhere. Even if a criminal takes precautions such as wearing gloves, DNA samples may still be extracted from any miniscule bit of tissue or cells left at the crime scene.

Crime scene investigators must be specially trained and follow strict procedures to avoid contaminating possible DNA evidence. They must wear gloves and use disposable tools for evidence collection, and must avoid touching areas where DNA-containing evidence may be found. In addition, they avoid talking, sneezing, or coughing, as their own DNA may contaminate the evidence. When they find a piece of evidence, it must be placed in an envelope or paper bag, not in a plastic bag. This is because plastic bags retain moisture, which can destroy the sample. They label each sample carefully, including the exact location where it was found and where it should go for laboratory processing. The validity of the entire court case and whether the DNA evidence is admissible in court depends on these systems being strictly followed.

Once the evidence arrives at the forensic laboratory, technicians process each piece carefully to extract the DNA. Scientists use a process known as polymerase chain reaction, or PCR, to make copies of the DNA, so they can observe and compare them. In order to identify the owner of a DNA sample, scientists must match the DNA "fingerprint" to DNA from a suspect, or to another DNA profile from a database. In cases where one or more suspects have been identified, there are three types of scenarios possible following DNA analysis:

1) DNA from the crime scene matches the suspect's DNA. This is known as "inclusion," meaning that the suspect must be included in the continuing investigation.

2) DNA from the crime scene does not match the suspect's DNA. This results in "exclusion," indicating that the suspect can be eliminated from the investigation.

3) If the DNA has been contaminated or does not give a full profile for some other reason, the results are called "inconclusive" and the evidence cannot be used in the investigation. When there is no suspect, DNA samples may be processed by computer in order to find a match in the database system. This quick, efficient system is capable of comparing millions of DNA profiles until it locates matching information.

Thanks to DNA analysis techniques, today's law enforcement officials can move ahead with increased confidence in their investigations. Fewer mistakes are made with regard to false accusations and incorrect convictions. In many instances, people who have been sent to prison for crimes they did not commit have been set free as a result of DNA profiling.

Reading 3   Comprehension Questions

Circle the letter of the correct answer.

1 Sir Alec Jeffreys discovered genetic fingerprinting while
_____ .

    a he was a student at the University of Leicester
    b conducting research on a co-worker's DNA
    c trying to find out the identity of his own father

2 The process known as genetic fingerprinting
_____ .

    a preceded the development of genetic profiling
    b is more sensitive and accurate than genetic profiling
    c is less well-known than genetic profiling

3 DNA is a desirable form of evidence because
_____ .

    a it can be collected without the use of gloves
    b criminals do not take precautions to avoid it
    c only a small amount of it is necessary

4 Which of the following is NOT discussed in the passage?
    a training procedures for crime scene investigators
    b required methods of DNA evidence collection
    c typical results of DNA lab analysis

5 PCR refers to _____ .
    a the computer software used to create a DNA database
    b the way in which DNA evidence is collected
    c the method scientists use to analyze DNA evidence

6 When no suspect has been identified,
_____ .

    a DNA evidence is no longer useful
    b a computer database is used to compare DNA
    c investigations are usually unsuccessful

7 It can be inferred from the passage that
_____ .

    a DNA evidence is still not allowed in murder cases
    b fingerprints are still an important form of evidence
    c investigators are frustrated by strict procedures

8 Which of the following is NOT discussed in the passage?
    a DNA evidence has changed the field of criminal investigation.
    b DNA evidence may be used after a suspect has been sent to prison.
    c DNA evidence processing procedures are likely to become stricter.

PRACTICE 2: ROCK LEGENDS: PEOPLE WHO MADE A DIFFERENCE IN MUSIC

Timed Reading 1

Read the text. You have 20 minutes.

The Roots of the Beatles

It's an indisputable fact that the Beatles have had an immense impact on both music and popular culture that still continues today. While John, Paul, George, and Ringo certainly deserve due credit for their talents, it's important to note that these musical innovators were influenced by others who came before them. Without that spark of inspiration to ignite their passion for music, the history of rock may have taken a different course.

Throughout the band's career, the Beatles also incorporated styles from other artists, which enriched and diversified their own sound. Growing up in Liverpool, a bustling port city on England's west coast, the budding musicians had access to some goods still unavailable in other parts of post-war England. Sailors on ships coming in and out of the city on a daily basis brought with them goods from their home countries. Among those were recordings of American blues, jazz, and rock and roll music. Eventually, these songs made their way to the ears of the young Beatles and fueled their desires to become rock musicians themselves. Here are just a few of the artists who influenced the Beatles and helped carve the path of music history:

Elvis Presley- On the night of May 11, 1956, 15-year-old John Lennon was at home listening to the radio. The DJ played a song called "Heartbreak Hotel," by 21-year-old Elvis Presley. When John heard the rough sound of Elvis's guitar, his low, sultry voice, and the lonely lyrics about the breakup of a relationship, he knew this was something different. In the weeks to come, John sought out pop music magazines and kept his ear on the radio, hoping to learn and hear more about Presley. He transformed his own appearance, mimicking Elvis's hairstyle, sideburns, and tight jeans. John's Aunt Mimi, with whom he lived, recounts this period when it seemed Elvis was all John cared about. "He became a mess almost overnight, and all because of Elvis Presley, I say. He had a poster of him in his bedroom. There was a pajama top in the bathroom, the trousers in the bedroom, socks somewhere else, shirts flung on the floor. Oh, John was a problem in those years!" Later, John himself acknowledged the spell that he was under, stating, "Nothing really affected me until Elvis. Rock and roll was real, everything else was unreal."

James Jamerson- Paul McCartney, the Beatles' bass player is famous for his inventive fingering style on the bass. However, as with all art forms, the inspiration for this originality also had some outside sources. Growing up, Paul was especially fond of the style of music that became known as "Motown," named after the record label by the same name. Motown Records featured mainly African-American artists like Smokey Robinson, the Four Tops, and the Temptations. It was while listening to those artists that Paul first heard bass player James Jamerson. Jamerson did not have a band of his own, nor a solo career. He played in Motown Records' "house band," meaning he was called in as needed to play during other artists' recording sessions. Jamerson died at the age of 47, having received almost no public credit during his lifetime. It wasn't until well after his death that his influence on the Beatles became known when a question came from a curious fan on Paul McCartney's website. "Who was the biggest influence upon your bass playing?" Paul answered, "James Jamerson."

Ravi Shankar- Later in the Beatles' career, the band's style began to reflect more of the individual interests of the four members. The first-time guitarist George Harrison heard a recording of Indian musician, Ravi Shankar, he had a feeling the two would meet someday. Shankar, the father of jazz singer Norah Jones, played the sitar, a traditional Indian instrument that is played while the musician is seated on the floor. After meeting Shankar in Los Angeles in 1967, George asked if he could travel to India to study sitar with him. At first, Shankar was hesitant. "It is strange to see pop musicians with sitars. I was confused at first," he said. "But I was charmed by George's sincerity. I found he really wanted to learn." George's sitar playing is featured on several of the Beatles' songs, including "Norwegian Wood," "Tomorrow Never Knows," and "Within You, Without You." George expressed his respect for Shankar, saying, "He was the first person who ever impressed me in my life."

Reading 1   Comprehension Questions

Circle the letter of the correct answer.

1 The main topic of the passage is _____ .
   a how the Beatles' music changed during their career
   b how the Beatles achieved international stardom
   c how the Beatles were inspired by other artists

2 It can be inferred from the passage that the author _____ .
   a dislikes the music on the Beatles' later albums
   b agrees that the Beatles were highly influential
   c thinks that the Beatles were not original enough

3 The members of the Beatles were aided by _____ .
   a access to a variety of music at an early age
   b being able to travel to foreign countries on ships
   c sailors from America who came to hear them play

4 Which of the following is NOT mentioned in the passage?

   a John Lennon was a teenager when he heard Elvis Presley.

   b Not all of Presley's influence on John Lennon was positive.

   c Lennon met Elvis Presley at a party at Presley's house.

5 James Jamerson performed _____ .

   a live concerts with several prominent Motown bands

   b a variety of instruments on different Beatles albums

   c with different bands in the Motown Records studios

6 From the passage, it can be inferred that

_____ .

   a The Motown Records label never featured any white musicians

   b James Jamerson probably never met Paul McCartney in person

   c Paul McCartney's website offers downloads of Jamerson's songs

7 It can be inferred from the passage that Ravi Shankar

_____ .

   a approached George Harrison and offered to teach him

   b had never heard pop music before the Beatles

   c felt it was important to respect traditional music

8 The passage states that later in the Beatles' career _____ .

   a the members often argued about style

   b their music became more diverse

   c some songs were written by other artists

Timed Reading 2

Read the text. You have 20 minutes.

Bob Marley: The Father of Reggae

A mere mention of the word "Jamaica," the name of the fifth largest island-country in the Caribbean, and you can almost begin to hear the soothing, infectious beat of the musical genre that was made famous there: reggae. And for most people, Bob Marley, with his trademark long dreadlock hairstyle and distinctive, powerful voice, will forever be the reigning king of reggae music.

Nesta Robert Marley was born on February 6, 1945 on his grandmother's farm in Saint Ann's Parish, Jamaica. His father was a white Jamaican of British descent, and his mother was Afro-Jamaican. Although Marley embraced his mixed ethnicity, he identified most strongly with his black African roots. Marley was passionate about music from an early age. When he befriended Neville Livingston at school, the two boys began playing music and writing songs together and collaborating with other musicians who shared their dreams of someday being recording artists. In 1963, Marley, Livingston, and four other musician friends formed the reggae band the Wailers. The Wailers and other Jamaican groups at the time were experimenting with a fresh style of beat that combined American rhythm-and-blues and traditional African drum rhythms; the beat that became known as reggae.

In his book, *The History of Popular Music*, author Piero Scaruffi describes what set reggae apart from other popular genres. "The reggae beat mimics the heartbeat," Scaruffi writes. "Compared with rock, reggae basically inverted the role of bass and guitar. The paradox of reggae, of course, is that this music 'unique to Jamaica' is actually not originally Jamaican at all, having its foundations in the USA and Africa." The term reggae is thought to have originated with the Jamaican expression rege-rege, meaning rough and ragged.

By the late '60s, reggae was an international phenomenon, and The Wailers were competing with bands like Toots and the Maytals and Jimmy Cliff for recognition from radio stations and record companies. Finally, The Wailers were signed by Island Records and released their first major label album, *Catch a Fire*, in April 1973. It wasn't until their second album, titled *Burnin'*, which included the now classic hits "Get Up Stand Up" and "I Shot the Sheriff," that Marley gained true celebrity status. Marley's lyrics, which often featured calls for peace and political and social change, were perfectly timed for the "hippie" era of the late '60s and early '70s. Young people, poor people, and others on the fringes of society felt that Marley shared their views and gave them a voice. In an article in *Rolling Stone Magazine*, Mikal Gilmore said, "Marley wasn't singing about how peace could come easily to the world, but rather how hell on Earth comes too easily to too many. His songs were his memories; he had lived with the wretched, he had seen the downpressors and those whom they pressed down."

In 1976, a series of events in Jamaica contributed even further to Bob Marley's icon status. On December 5, Bob Marley and the Wailers were scheduled to play at a free concert organized by Jamaican Prime Minister Michael Manley. Two days before the concert, masked gunmen broke into Marley's home, seriously injuring Marley's wife, Rita, and wounding Marley in the chest and arm. The attempt on Marley's life was said to be carried out by political rivals of the prime minister. As planned, on the 5th of December, despite having no back-up band (the Wailers had all gone into hiding after hearing of the attack on Marley), Bob Marley appeared on stage before a crowd of over 80,000 fans, announcing, "The people who are trying to make this world worse aren't taking a day off. How can I?"

In July 1977, Bob Marley was diagnosed with a malignant form of cancer. Citing religious reasons, Marley declined surgery, opting instead for a controversial treatment that primarily involved avoiding certain foods and drinks. Despite his continued illness, Bob Marley and the Wailers embarked on another world tour in 1980. During the tour, Marley's health continued to deteriorate, eventually causing the end of the tour. On September 23rd of that year, Marley played his last concert in Pittsburgh, Pennsylvania. He passed away at the age of 36 on May 11, 1981, receiving a state funeral in Jamaica. In a speech in honor of Marley, Jamaican Prime Minister Edward Seaga described the artist in these words: "His voice was an omnipresent cry. . . . His sharp features, majestic looks, and prancing style a vivid etching on the landscape of our minds . . . Such a man cannot be erased from the mind. He is part of the collective consciousness of the nation."

Reading 2   Comprehension Questions

Circle the letter of the correct answer.

1 The passage states that Bob Marley _____ .
   a is primarily of African descent
   b has a mixed ethnic background
   c was raised by his white grandmother

2 Marley's musical interests intensified when he _____ .
   a became a solo artist
   b started playing music with friends
   c first heard reggae music

3 According to Piero Scaruffi, the reggae beat is similar to _____ .
   a the sound of the human heart
   b that of other popular genres
   c a piece of old torn clothing

4 The Wailers became famous _____ .
   a in the US before they were known in Jamaica
   b when one of the members shot a police officer
   c after the release of their second album

5 Marley's music was inspiring to those who _____ .
   a were worried or troubled
   b had difficulty understanding lyrics
   c felt music should not be political

6 Following an incident involving an attempt on Marley's life, _____ .
   a he retreated from public life
   b his level of fame increased
   c the Wailers performed in his honor

7 Despite his illness, toward the end of Marley's life, _____ .
   a he continued to travel and play live concerts
   b he started an organization to help cancer victims
   c he began a career in politics

8 As a result of Marley's death, _____ .
   a cancer treatment began to improve
   b people listened to reggae much less
   c the Jamaican government honored him

Oum Kalthoum: The Lady of Egypt

Nearly four decades after her death, Oum Kalthoum is still widely recognized as the greatest female Arabic singer of all time. She was a young girl from a poor peasant family, but her voice carried her to unsurpassed levels of stardom and gave her eternal status as the national voice of Egypt. Even today, Kalthoum's music is played everywhere in Egypt, from cafes, to elevators, to taxi cab radios, and many of her recordings still outsell those of popular contemporary artists from the Middle East.

Born in a small town in the Nile delta, she was the daughter of a village religious cleric. With her father, she learned to recite verses from the *Koran*, and succeeded in memorizing the entire book by the age of 12. Noticing his daughter's immense talent for memorization and her strong voice, Kalthoum's father began taking her on trips with her older brother, during which they would chant the *Koran* to help the family earn money. Kalthoum had to dress in boy's clothing, as it was not customary for girls to sing in front of strangers in the conservative rural Egyptian tradition. During her teen years, Kalthoum had the opportunity to meet famous composer Zakariyya Ahmad, who recognized her great potential and invited her to come to Cairo to study and perform. Ahmad introduced her to some of the musical elite in the capital city, and it quickly became clear that if she wanted to pursue a singing career, she would need to come to Cairo.

Kalthoum's entire family moved to Cairo in 1923 in order to support her training and help launch her career. At first, Cairo was a cold place. While Kalthoum's powerful voice received positive reviews, the snobbish city arts crowd laughed at her simple cotton dresses and country ways. Driven and determined to earn their respect, Kalthoum began to cultivate her inner star. She studied classical French literature, Egyptian music and poetry, and she mimicked the style of the wealthy Cairo socialites who came to her performances. Over time, she succeeded in crafting her image as a sophisticated artist with traditional roots that stemmed deep in the heart of Egypt. Kalthoum's nickname *Al-Sitt* means *The Lady*, and conveys the public's reverence for her.

Though Kalthoum's musical origins came from reciting verses from the *Koran*, the songs that made her famous were not religious in nature. Instead, they are like epic romantic poems about love, loneliness, desire, and loss. A single song may last several hours. During the height of her career, between the 1930s to the early 1970s, Kalthoum sang concerts live on Egyptian national radio on the first Thursday of every month. All around the Arab world, there was a hush. Stores closed. Families gathered around the radio in their homes while the voice of The Lady filled their hearts and minds for several hours. Many who were fortunate enough to see Kalthoum perform live say the experience was nothing short of life-changing.

Kalthoum's stage presence, the power of her voice, and the passion with which she told stories with her songs, cast a spell over the audience. Kalthoum's English biographer, Virginia Daniels, explains the Arab word *tarab*. "*Tarab* is a concept of enchantment," Danielson says. "It's usually associated with vocal music, although instrumental music can produce the same effect, in which the listener is completely enveloped in the sound and the meaning in a broad, experiential sense, and is just completely carried away by the performance."

Kalthoum's career spanned four decades, during which she cast her spell over kings, queens, and world leaders from all corners of the globe, as well as millions of adoring fans across the Arab world. She was, and still remains, a national treasure of Egypt. She is the only entertainer ever to receive Egypt's highest level honor by King Farouk I of Egypt, a decoration that is given only to politicians and members of the royal family. When Oum Kalthoum died in 1975, at age 76, her funeral was a national event, attended by four million Egyptians who lined the streets of Cairo to pay their respects. Today, Kalthoum fans can visit the museum in her honor, located on Roda Island, near the country villa where she lived. The displays capture Kalthoum's glamour and allure, with her diamond-studded sunglasses, stylish dresses, and scarves. Museum manager Dr. Walid Shosha says it's an honor to help others learn about the fascinating Kalthoum. "Visitors spend hours," he says, "listening to Oum Kalthoum, getting to know her, reading intimate articles about her life and the way she lived."

Reading 3   Comprehension Questions

Circle the letter of the correct answer.

1 Oum Kalthoum can best be described as _____ .
   a a rising star in Arabic music
   b a classical Egyptian vocalist
   c a popular religious musician

2 In Kalthoum's first public appearances, she _____ .
   a was not well-received
   b sang religious verses
   c charged a lot of money

3 Which of the following is NOT mentioned in the passage?
   a where Kalthoum studied music
   b when Kalthoum died
   c whom Kathoum married

4 When she first arrived in Cairo, Kalthoum _____ .
   a was treated like an outsider
   b felt like she was not talented
   c wanted to return to the countryside

5 From the passage, it can be inferred that _____ .

   a Kalthoum's fame is beginning to fade

   b Kalthoum's music will always be well-known

   c Kalthoum's family did not support her career

6 The height of Kalthoum's career _____ .

   a spanned four decades

   b came after she left Cairo

   c has not yet been reached

7 Which of the following is NOT mentioned in the passage?

   a the meaning of Kalthoum's songs

   b the length of Kalthoum's songs

   c the titles of Kalthoum's songs

8 The Arabic word *tarab* refers to _____ .

   a a pleasant feeling

   b a surprising sound

   c a sense of confusion

PRACTICE 3: UNEXPLAINED PHENOMENA

Timed Reading 1

Read the text. You have 20 minutes.

The Voynich Manuscript

The Voynich manuscript is one of the most fascinating and mysterious pieces of ancient literature ever to exist. Named after the Polish rare book dealer, Wilfrid Voynich, who purchased it in 1912, the manuscript is about 240 pages long. The text is written on *vellum*, a type of paper made from cow hide that was commonly used for book-making in medieval times. Recent carbon-dating tests on the book have placed its origins in Europe in the early 15th century, somewhere between 1404 and 1438. Beyond that, after 600 years of research conducted by various experts around the world, not much else about the book has been proven to be certain. Although there have been many theories, no one knows for sure who wrote the Voynich manuscript or why it was written.

On the surface, it looks like some kind of medical encyclopedia or guide to the natural world. The pages contain hundreds of detailed diagrams and whimsical drawings of plants, creatures, and various complex geographic patterns. Strangely, none of the illustrations or diagrams seems to represent real items actually found in nature. In contrast, they seem to be drawn purely from the artist's imagination. The plants cannot be identified or matched to existing species with any certainty, and many illustrations combine elements of several different species. For example, the roots of one plant, combined with the leaves of another, and the flower of a completely different species appear on one plant. In one drawing, instead of flowers, a plant blooms with two human heads, with faces looking shocked and terrified. In other scenes in the Biology section, tiny human figures wearing only crowns slide down giant tubes and climb over amorphous blobs that vaguely resemble humans' internal organs. If this sounds strange, just wait. The mystery gets even more intriguing when you consider the fact that no one in history has ever be able to read the Voynich manuscript. The text is written in an unknown script and a language unlike any seen before. No one, not even the most experienced code-breakers from World War I and World War II, has successfully deciphered its meaning.

The manuscript was donated to the Rare Book Library at Yale University in 1969 by well-known rare book dealer Hans P. Kraus. The first known owner of the Voynich Manuscript was 16th century Roman Emperor Rudolf II, who reportedly purchased the book from its previous owner for a fee of 600 ducats—about ninety thousand dollars in today's money. (At the time of the emperor's purchase, the book was already well over a century old.) From there, over the course of several more centuries, it changed hands numerous times, each new owner hoping to be the one to finally crack the code. Analysts have determined that the text was written from left to right and consists of about 20–30 simple symbols, which are repeated in different patterns to form what appear to be words. Longer sections of text are divided into paragraphs; however, there is no sign of punctuation. Some researchers have identified "spelling" patterns in the symbols. For example, they found that certain symbols are only found at the beginning or end of a word, and that some symbols may be doubled, while others may not. Despite centuries of research, no links have been found between the manuscript and any existing languages. Some speculate that the Voynich text is made-up nonsense. After all, how could hundreds of attempts by numerous experts over hundreds of years turn up absolutely nothing?

The most recent study conducted in 2013 by Marcelo Montemurro of the University of Manchester and Damian Zanette of the Bariloche Atomic Centre identified a clear semantic pattern in the text. Their paper, published in the journal *New Scientist*, suggests that the Voynich manuscript contains a coded message within the text. Whether there is, in fact, a message, what that message may be, and for whom it was intended, still remains a mystery. Various blogs and websites have been devoted to the topic, and messages from contributors, both amateur and professional, pour in daily from around the globe. Perhaps one day, one of them will have the key to understanding the mystery of this ancient, one-of-a-kind book. But, perhaps some things are better left unknown. *New York Times* writer Reed Johnson writes, "As much as each of us strives to be the one to crack the code, I think few of us would truly like to see it solved. The book's resistance to being read is what sets it apart. And no matter how thrilling such a text might be, it will remain a disappointment for being closed off, completed—for being, in the end, no longer a mystery."

Reading 1 Comprehension Questions

Circle the letter of the correct answer.

1 When was the Voynich manuscript created?
- **a** between 240 and 600 BCE
- **b** in the early 1400s
- **c** in the 20th century

2 The drawings in the Voynich manuscript _____ .
- **a** are not based on objects found in reality
- **b** represent many ancient plants and creatures
- **c** appear to have been drawn by small children

3 It can be inferred from the passage that _____ .
- **a** the author did not want the public to read the book
- **b** the book was written by Wilfrid Voynich
- **c** a living person knows the purpose of the book

4 Which of the following is NOT mentioned in the passage?
- **a** Both experts and non-experts have attempted to understand the book.
- **b** Yale University wants to pay someone to crack the book's code.
- **c** Research on the book has been done relatively recently.

5 The Voynich manuscript contains _____ .
- **a** a key that explains its symbols
- **b** a style of text that has never been seen before
- **c** a message within the drawings

6 It can be inferred from the text that Emperor Rudolf II
_____ .
- **a** purchased the book from Hans P. Kraus
- **b** believed that the book was very valuable
- **c** requested that the book be donated to Yale

7 The research of Montemurro and Zanette points to the notion that
_____ .
- **a** the book was used to create atomic energy
- **b** the text has some meaning and purpose
- **c** the text should not be removed from the library

8 Reed Johnson's statement at the end of the passage means that
_____ .
- **a** people are too easily frustrated
- **b** most people prefer not knowing
- **c** the answers will soon be found

Timed Reading 2

Read the text. You have 20 minutes.

The Placebo Effect

The placebo effect is one of the most baffling and least-understood phenomena in the field of human psychology and physiology. *Placebos*, from the Latin for *I shall please*, were used by doctors in the early days of modern medicine to try to satisfy patients who demanded medication when there was no effective treatment available for their illnesses. In those days, the doctor would prescribe a pill that was made mainly of salt or sugar and water, knowing that it would not cure the patient's illness, but aiming instead to help relieve stress and anxiety. In some extreme cases of placebo medicine, doctors even performed "sham surgery," basically cutting the patient open and sewing him or her back up without performing actual surgery on any organs. Interestingly, over time, doctors noticed that there was often a significant improvement in patients immediately after receiving a placebo. The phenomenon, known as the placebo effect, began to be studied by psychologists and physicians, and research found conclusive evidence that humans can, in fact, cure ourselves of an illness simply because we believe we are being treated for it. Our brains can actually be tricked into believing we are getting healthy, which in turn can affect our body chemistry and actually cause us to heal. Placebos have been proven effective in about 30 percent of patients.

Some experts believe that the placebo effect is purely psychological—that the act of taking medicine simply makes one feel better, but does not actually have significant power to improve physical health. Throughout history, however, there have been numerous incredible examples of placebos' effect on physical well-being. One famous story, presented in a 1957 report by psychologist Bruno Klopfer of the University of California, Los Angeles, tells the story of a cancer patient named Mr. Wright. Wright was in the terminal stages of lymphoma, a cancer affecting the lymph glands. Large tumors had been found throughout Wright's body, and doctors had tried every available treatment. Independently, Mr. Wright had researched a new cancer drug called Krebiozen and believed it would work for him. He requested that the doctors give him the new drug. The hospital agreed to try Krebiozen on Mr. Wright and its other terminal cancer patients. What happened next defied logic. Within two days of beginning his treatment, Mr. Wright, who had been confined to a bed and barely able to breathe, began to improve, was sitting up and joking with doctors and nurses. After another few days, he got out of bed and was walking around the cancer ward. After 10 days, tests revealed that he his tumors had shrunk by 50%, at which point he was sent home to continue his recovery. Oddly, no other patient in the hospital made any improvements whatsoever while on Krebiozen.

Researchers explain that the placebo effect has to go with the brain's expectation of what happens when we take medicine. In short, we expect relief when we take a pill, so before we even put the pill in our mouth—placebo or not—the brain is already preparing us to feel better, and we do begin to feel better—immediately. The brain-conditioning theory is strengthened further by the fact that the outer appearance of the placebo affects its effectiveness. For instance, certain color placebos are more effective than others for treating certain illnesses. Green pills relieve anxiety, while white pills help calm digestive issues. Bright yellow placebos work best for treating depression, and red pills cause us to be more awake and alert. Pills that have their brand name stamped on them also have a greater effect than pills that have nothing written on them.

In the same way that our expectations can cause our brain and our body to respond positively to a placebo, they can also cause negative side-effects. This opposite of the placebo phenomenon is known as the "nocebo effect." In one study in Italy, people who had a sensitivity to lactose (a type of sugar found in milk) were given lactose-free milk to drink, but were told it was regular milk. Forty-four percent of the participants reported stomach cramps and indigestion. In a clinical study on depression, a patient ingested 26 placebo pills, which he thought were anti-depressants, in an attempt to commit suicide. Although the pills were totally harmless, the patient's blood pressure dropped to a dangerously low level. Whether the effects are positive or negative, it's clear that placebos offer a way to harness the seemingly unlimited power of the human mind to bring about changes to our own health and well-being.

Reading 2 Comprehension Questions

Circle the letter of the correct answer.

1 Placebos have been used _____ .
   a only in a few very recent cases
   b when patients did not want medicine
   c throughout the course of medical history

2 Types of placebos have included _____ .
   a a glass of water containing salt or sugar
   b both medication and surgical procedures
   c drugs that can actually cause illness

3 It can be inferred from the text that _____ .
   a Some patients' lives have been extended by placebos.
   b The effect of placebos is purely psychological.
   c Doctors must notify patients when they prescribe placebos.

4 Research has shown that placebos _____ .
   a work in fewer than half of patients
   b are only effective for certain illnesses
   c can usually be used in place of medication

5 Which of the following is NOT mentioned in the passage?

   a The placebo effect can begin to work very quickly.

   b The drug Krebiozen was ineffective for most patients.

   c The cancer patient named Mr. Wright is still alive.

6 The placebo effect is connected to the brain's _____ .

   a reaction to sugar or salt

   b anticipation of results

   c understanding of the body

7 According to the passage, different colored placebos _____ .

   a are manufactured by different companies

   b can affect our ability to see correctly

   c work best on certain types of illnesses

8 It can be inferred from the passage that placebos _____ .

   a will probably be banned from use

   b can be harmful to our health

   c have become more popular recently

Timed Reading 3

Read the text. You have 20 minutes.

Spontaneous Human Combustion

In 1663, Danish anatomist Thomas Bartholin reported the mysterious case of a Parisian woman who had inexplicably suddenly caught fire in her home and "went up in ashes and smoke." According to Bartholin's account, the woman had been sleeping, and her straw mattress showed no signs of being burned or even slightly charred anywhere. The only explanation, it seemed, Bartholin said, was that the woman herself had been the source of the fire. This was the first reported case of the phenomenon now known as spontaneous human combustion (SHC). Since that time, there have been hundreds of reported cases of spontaneous combustion of men and women around the world.

In 1938, a 22-year-old British woman named Phyllis Newcombe was attending a dance with some friends. At the end of the night, as Newcombe headed down the staircase on her way home, witnesses say her dress suddenly became enveloped in flames. Panicking, Newcombe ran back upstairs to the ballroom and collapsed. Although several witnesses ran to help her, she died in the hospital several days later. No evidence was ever found of any source for the fire. In another case from 1966, an electric company employee in Pennsylvania made a service call to the home of 92-year-old Dr. J. Irving Bentley. When Dr. Bentley did not answer the door, the worker entered the home to check on his welfare. Smelling smoke, he rushed toward the back of the house where he found the remains of Dr. Bentley inside the bathroom of his home. However, the only thing to indicate Dr. Bentley's prior presence was his charred slipper next to a round hole burnt into the floor surrounded by a pile of ashes. Nothing else in the bathroom showed any signs of being burned or coming in contact with the flames. Once again, it seemed the source of the fire was the victim himself.

Most cases of SHC share similar characteristics. The victim is usually found inside his or her own home. The person's body has usually been completely or almost completely consumed by the fire, while the immediate surroundings—furniture, walls, etc.—remain untouched. Sometimes, even the clothing worn by the victim is surprisingly intact. In addition, in some cases, police, firefighters, and others responding to the scene have reported a strange, unexplained sweet smell in the air along with the smell of smoke. Not all victims of SHC have died. Those that have survived have experienced a less extreme case of the phenomenon. Rather than bursting into flames, these victims may have had smoke coming from their bodies, with no apparent source. Others have suddenly developed serious burns on their bodies without coming in contact with fire or a heat source.

Is it possible for a human to literally burst into flames or smoke without any outside source of fire? Some scientists say this phenomenon is possible when the chemical conditions inside a person's body are just right. One explanation theorizes that fire can start inside the body when enough of the gas known as methane builds up in the intestines. This flammable gas can then ignite when it comes into contact with certain enzymes in the person's digestive tract. In most instances of SHC, however, the outside of the person's body usually incurs the greatest damage, casting doubt on this hypothesis. Others have presented the theories that a build-up of static electricity or some geomagnetic force may be responsible for starting the fire.

Although there has never been any conclusive evidence to prove or disprove the possibility of spontaneous human combustion, many say that the phenomenon is simply scientifically impossible. Many scientists have offered the "wick effect" as a possible explanation. In cases of SHC, this theory says that when the human body comes into contact with a heat source, such as a lit cigarette, it becomes like an inside-out candle. The person's body fat is like the wax of a candle, the flammable substance, and their hair and clothing acts as the wick—the material that the fire travels along as it burns the flammable fat. This, scientists assert, explains why victims' bodies are burned while their surroundings are largely untouched. The existence or non-existence of true spontaneous human combustion has yet to be proven. Until a definitive explanation can be established, the incredible stories of the unfortunate victims will continue to fuel our curiosity and desire to solve this mysterious phenomenon.

Reading 3 Comprehension Questions

Circle the letter of the correct answer based on what you read.

1 The first case of spontaneous human combustion _____ .
   a was proven to be false
   b involved a European woman
   c was caused by a straw mattress

2 The reported cases of SHC have occurred in _____ .
   a the victims' homes
   b European countries
   c different parts of the world

3 Dr. J. Irving Bentley _____ .
   a has conducted research on SHC
   b is an elderly victim of SHC
   c worked for an electric company

4 Cases of SHC are especially mysterious _____ .
   a when they involve younger victims
   b because the surroundings are not damaged
   c if the source of the fire is identified

5 It can be inferred from the passage that _____ .
   a not everyone believes in SHC
   b certain chemicals in foods can cause SHC
   c there is clear scientific evidence for SHC

6 Which of the following is NOT mentioned in the passage?
   a a variety of possible causes of SHC
   b the number of reported SHC cases
   c a description of a typical SCH case

7 The "wick effect" _____ .
   a suggests that there is wax in the human body
   b compares the victim's body to a candle
   c explains why some SHC victims survive

8 It can be inferred from the passage that the author

_____ .
   a has experienced SHC him or herself
   b believes an explanation will be found
   c is confused by the different theories on SHC

STUDY SKILLS

Storing and Studying New Words

Vocabulary Notebooks

Are you an active vocabulary learner? What do you do when you find a new word or phrase in your reading? Many students use vocabulary notebooks to store and study new words. This is a good way to remember vocabulary and improve your English skills.

There are many ways to organize a vocabulary notebook. You can organize new words by date, by parts of speech, by topic, or alphabetically—like the dictionary. You can write the words in a notebook, on index cards, or in a computer file. The important thing is to choose a way that is convenient and makes it easy for you to find and study new words.

Below is a basic example of a vocabulary notebook entry. Read the instructions and look at the sample.

- Draw a line down the middle of the page.
- Write the new word on the left side of the page.
- Beside the new word, write its part of speech (noun, verb, adjective, adverb).
- Write the definition of the word on the right side of the page.
- Below the word, write the sentence where you found the word. If needed, add another sample sentence from the dictionary.

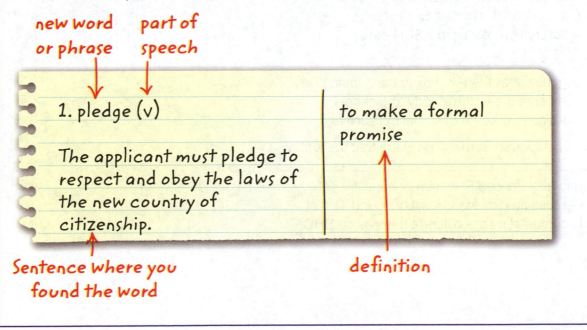

new word or phrase

part of speech

1. pledge (v)

The applicant must pledge to respect and obey the laws of the new country of citizenship.

to make a formal promise

Sentence where you found the word

definition

Practice 1

Read the text below. Choose words that are new to you. Write the following information for each word:

Word

Part of speech

Sample sentence

Definition

There are two primary factors that differentiate asteroids from comets: chemical composition and orbit. Firstly, in terms of chemical composition, comets contain a volatile material on the surface. This material produces a temporary atmosphere when the comet passes near the Sun; solar radiation and winds cause the comet's surface to lose some of this compound. In contrast, asteroids do not produce any type of atmosphere at all. Asteroids have a fairly regular, elliptical-shaped orbit path, and therefore, they remain within approximately the same distance from the Sun, wherever they are in that path. Comets, on the other hand, have an irregular orbit, so their distance from the Sun tends to vary greatly.

There are other secondary ways in which asteroids and comets are different. These have to do with the way the two are named when they are discovered. While asteroids are named by their discoverers, comets are named for their discoverer. For example, the famous comet discovered by English astronomer Edmund Halley, is called Halley's Comet. However, when the first asteroid was discovered by Italian astronomer Giuseppe Piazzi, he named it Ceres.

_____

_____

_____

_____

_____

_____

_____

_____

_____

_____

_____

Practice 2

Read the text below. Choose words that are new to you. Write the following information for each word:

Word

Part of speech

Sample sentence

Definition

It's a fact. The world is getting older. In 2012, 810 million people were ages 60 or over, and by 2050, that number will reach 2 billion. Around the world, advancements in healthcare and medicine are allowing people to stay healthier and live longer than ever before. The fact that these developments have helped to extend our lives may seem like good news, but in the future, the growing elderly population may create serious social and economic challenges around the globe.

The statistics are alarming: Almost 58 million people worldwide will turn 60 this year. By 2050, there will be more old people than children under the age of 15 for the first time in history. The most rapidly growing elderly populations are in developing countries in Africa, Asia, and other regions where resources and access to medical care may already be limited.

The simple truth is this: With so many people living longer, some with disabilities or chronic medical conditions like high blood pressure or diabetes, the caregiving responsibilities of family members will be extended, as will the required medical care costs for each individual. Unless world leaders begin planning how to address the potentially devastating caregiving challenges and financial strain of this demographic shift, there will be grave consequences.

Programs that allow the elderly to continue to be active members of their communities have been shown to keep older members of society healthier and happier for longer. When older people have opportunities to work or volunteer and remain productive in society, they feel valued and respected. Sustained activity and involvement helps them stay physically fit and experience fewer emotional problems such as depression. These programs are also beneficial because they allow others to benefit from their elderly co-workers' wisdom and experience.

Another successful tactic being used in some countries (the Russian Federation, the Slovak Republic, Turkey, the United Kingdom, and Canada) is offering paid allowances for family members who take on caregiving responsibilities for their elderly parents or grandparents. This helps people more easily make the choice to work less at their jobs in order to care for their elderly relatives. As a result, these relatives are able to live independently for longer and fewer elderly end up in government-funded nursing homes.

In an ideal future, we'll be able to have our cake and eat it, too. People will live longer, remain healthy, and be respected members of society in their workplaces, communities, and families well into old age. But whatever the actions, strategic planning must begin now.

_____

_____

_____

_____

_____

_____

_____

_____

_____

_____

_____

_____

_____

_____

_____

_____

_____

Word Maps

Word maps are a good way to collect and store important information about new vocabulary. The more you work with new words and are able to make meaningful connections to them, the faster you will learn and be able to remember them. Creating word maps for new words helps you learn and remember new vocabulary so you can understand and use those words in the future.

Style 1

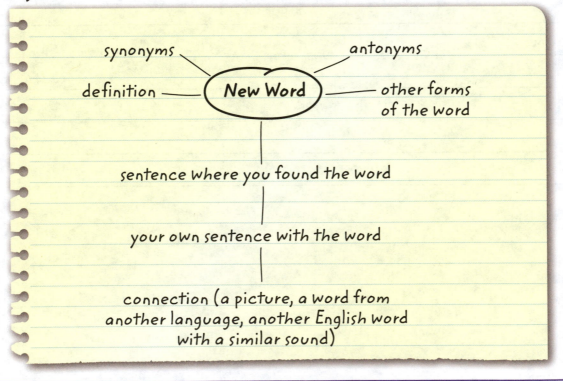

definition in
your own words

synonyms

Vocabulary Word

your own
sentence

connection (a picture,
a word from another
language, another
English word with a
similar sound)

Style 2

synonyms

antonyms

definition —— **New Word** —— other forms
of the word

sentence where you found the word

your own sentence with the word

connection (a picture, a word from
another language, another English word
with a similar sound)

Practice 3

Read the text below. Choose two words that are new to you. Complete the following information about each word. Then use the information to make a word map. Follow Style 1 from the Presentation on p. 166.

New word:

Definition in your own words:

Synonyms.

Your own sentence:

Connection: (another word with a similar sound, another English word)

You're standing on a busy city street corner with a crowd of fellow pedestrians waiting to cross the street. Look around you. Most of the people face straight ahead to the other side of the intersection, watching for the lighted signal to change to "WALK," but invariably these days, you'll also see others with heads bowed downward, each in his or her own little world. They may be smiling or chuckling to themselves as their thumbs move furiously up and down on a smartphone keypad, never looking up, even as the signal changes and the crowd moves forward en masse to cross the street. These citizens are texting while walking, and in the city of Fort Lee, New Jersey, it's breaking the law.

With the jump in traffic accidents and fatalities as a result of cell phone use while driving in recent years, it's not surprising that nearly all 50 US states now have distracted driving laws to restrict cell phone use and texting while operating motor vehicles. But officials in Fort Lee, New Jersey decided to take things a step further. Last spring, the city passed a "distracted walking" law, banning pedestrians from texting while crossing the street. Violators must pay an $85 fine.

_____

_____

_____

_____

_____

_____

_____

_____

_____

_____

_____

Practice 4

Read the text below. Choose two words that are new to you. Complete the following information about each word. Then use the information to make a word map. Follow Style 2 in the Presentation on p. 166.

New word:

Synonyms:

Antonyms:

Definition:

Other forms of the word:

Sentence where you found the word:

Your own sentence:

Connection: (word from your language/word with a similar sound)

A new law in Fort Lee, New Jersey bans pedestrians from texting while crossing the street. The new legislation comes in response to an increase in the numbers of pedestrians being hit by cars while texting and crossing the street. Police Chief Thomas Ripoli explained, "They're not walking in the crosswalks. They're walking against the red light, and they're being struck by vehicles." The city has already had three fatalities this year, and in one three-month period, 23 people were injured, all as a result of being distracted by technology while walking.

While proponents of the law say officials are just doing their job to keep citizens safe, others view it as another example of the government overstepping its boundaries and imposing too many controls on people's behavior. "What's next?" said Fort Lee resident Miyuki Young. "Before you know it, they'll be telling women we can't wear high heels because we might fall down and hurt ourselves. This is getting out of hand."

In fact, Young's prediction may not be too far off. Further south in the seaside town of Wildwood on the famous Jersey Shore, officials have just passed a law banning the wearing of overly saggy pants on its boardwalk. The hip-hop fashion known as "sagging," involves wearing pants very low around the hips, and is a popular style among some of Wildwood's young male residents. The new legislature was prompted by the large number of complaints from visitors, especially families with young children, who said they were offended by the fashion.

Some influential people are encouraging Wildwood "saggers" to fight the system, saying the government doesn't have the right to tell them how to wear their clothes. The hip-hop artist known as "The Game" has offered to personally pay the tickets for the first five violators of the new law, which goes into effect July 2.

Back to Fort Lee resident Miyuki Young's question, "What's next?" Will the rest of the country get in line with New Jersey's policies, or will freedom-loving Americans have their way? We'll just have to wait and see.

_____
_____
_____
_____
_____
_____
_____
_____
_____
_____
_____
_____

Study Cards

Study cards are small cards you can use to study new vocabulary at home, in a café, on the train or bus, or anywhere else.

Use the words in your vocabulary notebook and follow these instructions to make study cards.

- Write the word in big letters in the middle of the card.
- Write the word's part of speech in the top right-hand corner of the card.
- Write a sample sentence below the word.
- Write the definition on the back of the card. Draw a picture that represents the word or make a connection with another word, if possible.

Use your study cards to practice the words. Follow these tips for practicing the words on your own.

- Look at the cards. Say the words aloud and try to remember their meanings. If you don't remember a word, look at the definition on the other side of the card. Put the words you don't know in a separate pile. Review those words again.
- Look at the definition side of each card. Say and spell the words aloud. Put the words you don't know in a separate pile. Review those words again.
- Practice your words with another student. Test each other by saying a word and asking for the definition or by giving a definition and asking for the word.
- Make new cards that have the word on one card and the definition on a different card (single-sided study cards). Play matching games, memory games, or categorizing games with these cards.

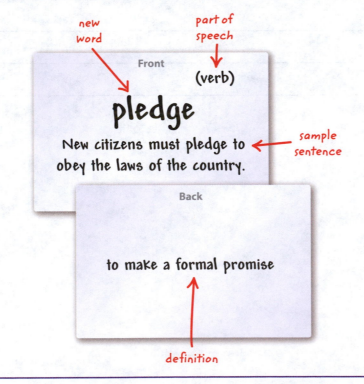

Practice 5

Read the text below and choose five words that are new to you. Write the following information for each word. Then make your own study cards with this information and use them for study and review.

Study Card (front)

Part of speech

Word

Sample sentence

Study Card (back)

Definition

The Black Ships (*kurofune* in Japanese) were the ships that arrived in Japan from the West during the 16th and 19th centuries.

The term "black ships" was first used when Portuguese ships, the first Western vessels which arrived in Japan in 1543, began a trade route between Goa, India and Nagasaki, Japan. These vessels were painted black with tar pitch to enhance waterproofing. This period of peaceful trading with the West lasted approximately a century. Then, in 1639, a rebellion erupted in Japan, which the ruling Tokugawa shogunate blamed on the influence of Christianity. As a result, the shogun closed off trade and contact with Westerners, and enforced a strict isolationist policy, called "Sakoku."

For 200 years, despite the requests of various Western leaders, Japan remained a primarily locked state, and trade with other nations was practically non-existent, aside from China and an allowance of one ship per year from the Dutch East India Company (based in Indonesia).

The End of Self-imposed Isolation

In the present day, the term "Black Ships" refers in particular to the four US Navy warships—*Mississippi, Plymouth, Saratoga,* and *Susquehanna*—commandeered by United States Commodore Matthew Perry, which arrived in the Bay at Edo (present-day Tokyo) in July of 1853. In this case, black refers not only to the color of the sailing vessels, but also to the black smoke from the coal-powered American ships.

Perry's Mission

US president Millard Fillmore sent Commodore Matthew Perry to Japan to try to secure trading rights with Japan for eager American merchants. As well, the American military wanted the Japanese to help shipwrecked sailors who washed up on their shores, who under Japan's isolationist period, had been either killed or left to die. Perry presented the Japanese with a letter from President Fillmore, requesting that Japan open its ports for both diplomatic and commercial purposes.

External Pressure and Internal Revolt

Perry told Japanese leaders he would return the following year, with an even larger fleet, for the shogun's reply. A year later, in July of 1854, Perry arrived with seven ships. This massive display of power, combined with the ships' loud, booming cannons, shocked the shoguns and the Japanese people. After some debate among the shogun's advisors, the Japanese leadership had determined that Japan could not defend itself against the US Navy. The government conceded, marking the end of Japan's two centuries of isolation.

In the Treaty of Kanagawa, the shogun agreed to open two ports to American ships, though at first, not for trade. After a few years, the United States gained trading rights, leading the way for several European nations to do the same. The Japanese people were angered by the terms of the treaties, which they found unequal and humiliating. Many citizens criticized the shogun for not fighting against the aggressive foreign invaders.

_____

_____

_____

_____

_____

_____

_____

_____

_____

_____

Practice 6

Read the text on p. 173. Choose five words that are new to you. Write the following information for each word. Then make your own study cards with this information and use them for study and review.

Study Card (front)

Part of speech

Word

Sample sentence

Study Card (back)

Definition

We take it for granted now, but at the turn of the twentieth century, the use of fingerprints to identify criminals was still in its infancy.

More popular was the Bertillon system, which measured dozens of features of a criminal's face and body and recorded the series of precise numbers on a large card along with a photograph. After all, the thinking went, what were the chances that two different people would look the same and have identical measurements in all the minute particulars logged by the Bertillon method?

Not great, of course. But, inevitably, a case came along to beat the odds.

It happened this way: In 1903, a convicted criminal named Will West was taken to Leavenworth Federal Prison in Kansas. The clerk at the admissions desk, thinking he recognized West, asked if he'd ever been to Leavenworth. The new prisoner denied it. The clerk took his Bertillon measurements and went to the files, only to return with a card for a "William" West. Turns out, Will and William bore an uncanny resemblance (they may have been identical twins). And their Bertillon measurements were a near match.

The clerk asked Will again if he'd ever been to the prison. "Never," he protested. When the clerk flipped the card over, he discovered Will was telling the truth. "William" was already in Leavenworth, serving a life sentence for murder! Soon after, the fingerprints of both men were taken, and they were clearly different.

It was this incident that caused the Bertillon system to fall "flat on its face," as reporter Don Whitehead aptly put it. The next year, Leavenworth abandoned the method and started fingerprinting its inmates. Thus began the first federal fingerprint collection.

In New York, the state prison had begun fingerprinting its inmates as early as 1903. Following the event at Leavenworth, other police and prison officials followed suit. Leavenworth itself eventually began swapping prints with other agencies, and its collection swelled to more than 800,000 individual records.

By 1920, though, the International Association of Chiefs of Police had become concerned about the erratic quality and disorganization of criminal identification records in America. It urged the Department of Justice to merge the country's two major fingerprint collections—the federal one at Leavenworth and its own set of state and local ones held in Chicago.

Four years later, a bill was passed providing the funds and giving the task to the young Bureau of Investigation. On July 1, 1924, J. Edgar Hoover, who had been appointed Acting Director less than two months earlier, quickly formed a Division of Identification. He announced that the Bureau would welcome submissions from other jurisdictions and provide identification services to all law enforcement partners. The FBI has done so ever since.

Study Strategies

Text Marking and Study Outlines

Longer passages, such as research articles or textbook chapters, often include a lot of important information. How do you make sure you understand the key points you need to know for your tests, papers, or other assignments?
Here are some strategies you can use to help you understand and remember information in longer academic passages.

Marking and Underlining

As you read each paragraph, use a pencil or a highlighter to underline or mark the main idea and supporting details. Keep the following in mind when you mark a text:

- Underline only the most important points and ideas. If you underline too much, you will not be able to tell what's important.
- Put a star (*) in the margin next to the sentence that gives the main idea of the paragraph.
- Write comments, questions, or short summaries in the margins.

Look at this example of a student's marked paragraph.

49

The immigration debate

* Immigration has been a <u>major topic of political debate in the last several U.S. presidential elections,</u> fueling the age-old debates about national security, employment, health care, and social security, among others. But another immigration-related <u>question being raised</u> by some is whether the U.S. should create legislature <u>to make both Spanish and English the official languages of the U.S.</u>

Study Outlines

After you read the passage, use the information you underlined to create a brief outline of the main and supporting ideas. This will help you remember the information and use it to write essays or research papers. Look at this sample outline for the passage above:

Paragraph 1
<u>Main idea:</u>
Immigration has long been a subject of political debate in US

<u>Supporting ideas:</u>
Fuels debates about national security, employment, health care, social security
Some feel both Spanish and English should be the official languages of the U.S.

Practice 1

Use the marked information in the following passage to write a study outline for each paragraph. Then submit your work to your teacher. The first paragraph is shown in the Presentation.

What is the official language of the U.S.?

Being the <u>primary language of the U.S. for over 200 years,</u> many might guess that English is the country's official language. However, the truth is that currently <u>the country does not have a</u> <u>legal official language.</u> Though there is no official language, <u>all</u> <u>formal government documents and forms are printed in English as</u> <u>well as Spanish and a variety of other languages</u> common to U.S. citizens.

Foreign Language Viewed as a Threat

Over the years, individuals and groups have proposed the idea of making English the official language, but it has <u>never become</u> official policy. Now <u>some proponents of English as the official</u> <u>language are feeling threatened</u> by the fact that other languages, like Spanish, are becoming <u>prominent in the U.S.</u> They say some formal policy is needed to protect America's English heritage.

Spanish to Overtake English in U.S.

While a large <u>number of proponents</u> would like to make English the one-and-only official language of the United States, there are a growing number of cities and regions around the country—in particular in the <u>Mexican-border states</u>—that are being <u>dominated</u> by <u>Spanish-speakers.</u> Some experts predict that <u>Spanish will</u> <u>overtake English</u> as the most used language in these areas of the country soon. As a result, many <u>jobs require some Spanish-speaking ability,</u> and Spanish is <u>the most commonly studied</u> <u>language among English speakers in the U.S.</u> All of this makes it clear why some groups are suggesting that Spanish should be the official second language of the country.

_____

_____

_____

_____

_____

_____

_____

> ### Presentation
> #### Graphic Organizers and Charts
> Graphic organizers and charts are two ways of representing information visually. You can use these tools to make important information from a reading easier to find and understand.
>
> Charts are especially useful for articles that are organized in a pattern and discuss more than one topic or theme. Charts may have two or more columns, depending on the amount and type of information in the text.

Practice 2

Part A

Read the following article. Then study the sample graphic organizer on p. 177.

Our Aging Planet

It's a fact. The world is getting older. In 2012, 810 million people were age 60 or over, by 2050, that number will reach 2 billion. Around the world, advancements in healthcare and medicine are allowing people to stay healthier and live longer than ever before. The fact that these developments have helped to extend our lives may seem like good news, but in the future, the growing elderly population may create serious social and economic challenges around the globe.

The statistics are alarming: Almost 58 million people worldwide will turn 60 this year. By 2050, there will be more old people than children under the age of 15 for the first time in history. The most rapidly growing elderly populations are in developing countries in Africa, Asia, and other regions where resources and access to medical care may already be limited.

The simple truth is this: With so many people living longer, some with disabilities or chronic medical conditions like high blood pressure or diabetes, the caregiving responsibilities of family members will be extended, as will the required medical care costs for each individual. Unless world leaders begin planning how to address the potentially devastating caregiving challenges and financial strain of this demographic shift, there will be grave consequences.

Programs that allow the elderly to continue to be active members of their communities have been shown to keep older members of society healthier and happier for longer. When older people have opportunities to work or volunteer and remain productive in society, they feel valued and respected. Sustained activity and involvement helps them stay physically fit and experience fewer emotional problems such as depression. These program are also beneficial because they allow others to benefit from their elderly co-workers' wisdom and experience.

Another successful tactic being used in some countries (the Russian Federation, the Slovak Republic, Turkey, the United Kingdom, and Canada) is offering paid allowances for family members who take on caregiving responsibilities for their elderly parents or grandparents. This helps people more easily make the choice to work less at their jobs in order to care for their elderly relatives. As a result, these relatives are able to live independently for longer, and fewer elderly end up in government-funded nursing homes.

In an ideal future, we'll be able to have our cake and eat it, too. People will live longer, remain healthy, and be respected members of society in their workplaces, communities, and families well into old age.

But whatever the actions, strategic planning must begin now.

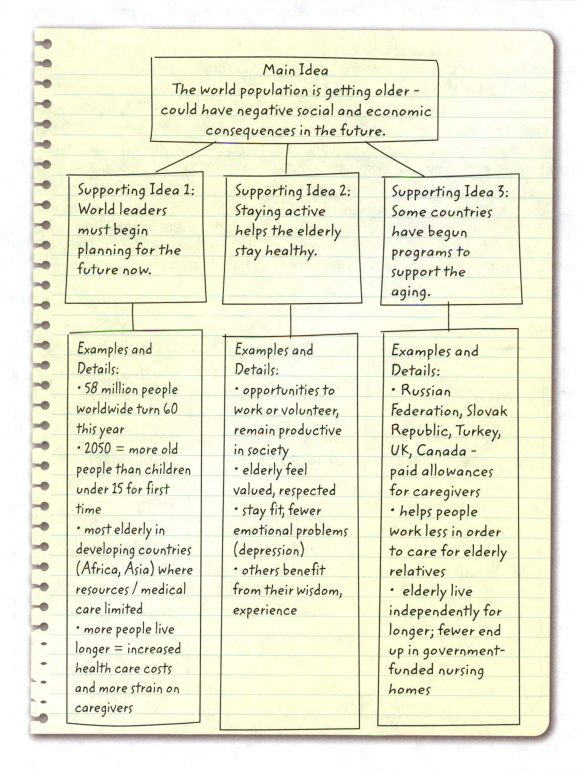

Part B

Read the following article. Then study the sample chart for the article.

Comets and asteroids are two types of celestial bodies found in Earth's solar system. They are, in fact, pieces left over from the time of the solar system's formation.

There are two primary factors that differentiate asteroids from comets: chemical composition and orbit. Firstly, terms of chemical composition, comets contain a volatile material on the surface. This material produces a temporary atmosphere when the comet passes near the Sun and solar radiation and winds cause the comet's surface to lose some of this compound. In contrast, asteroids do not produce any type of atmosphere at all.

With regard to orbit, like the earth, both comets and asteroids travel around the Sun. As a result, there have been instances of both crashing into the earth. Asteroids have a fairly regular, elliptical-shaped orbit path, and therefore they remain within approximately the same distance from the sun, wherever they are in that path. Comets, on the other hand, have an irregular orbit, so their distance from the Sun tends to vary greatly.

There are other secondary ways in which asteroids and comets are different. These have to do with the way the two are named when they are discovered. While asteroids are named by their discoverers, comets are named for their discoverer. For example, the famous comet discovered by English astronomer Edmund Halley, is called Halley's Comet. However, when the first asteroid was discovered by Italian astronomer Giuseppe Piazzi, he named it Ceres.

Asteroids	Comets	Both asteroids and comets
do not produce any atmosphere	contain volatile material on the surface	found in Earth's solar system
regular orbit path; remain same distance from Sun	irregular orbit, distance from Sun varies	left over from solar system's formation
named by their discoverers	named for their discoverer	travel around the Sun
		Have crashed into Earth

Practice 3

Read the text and take notes. Use your notes to create a graphic organizer and a chart.

The placebo effect is one of the most baffling and least-understood phenomena in the field of human psychology and physiology. *Placebos*, from the Latin for *I shall please*, were used by doctors in the early days of modern medicine to try to satisfy patients who demanded medication when there was no effective treatment available for their illnesses. In those days, the doctor would prescribe a pill that was made mainly of salt or sugar and water, knowing that it would not cure the patient's illness, but aiming instead to help relieve stress and anxiety. In some extreme cases of placebo medicine, doctors even performed "sham surgery," basically cutting the patient open and sewing him or her back up without performing actual surgery on any organs. Interestingly, over time, doctors noticed that there was often a significant improvement in patients immediately after receiving a placebo. The phenomenon, known as "the placebo effect," began to be studied by psychologists and physicians, and research found conclusive evidence that humans can, in fact, cure ourselves of an illness simply because we believe we are being treated for it; that is, our brain can be tricked into believing we are getting healthy, which in turn, can affect our body chemistry and actually cause us to heal.

Placebos have been proven effective in about 30 percent of patients. Some experts believe that the placebo effect is purely psychological—that the act of taking medicine simply makes you feel better, but does not actually have significant power to improve physical health. Throughout history, however, there have been numerous incredible examples of placebos' effects on people's physical well-being. One famous story, presented in a 1957 report by psychologist Bruno Klopfer of the University of California, Los Angeles, tells the story of a cancer patient named Mr. Wright. Wright was in the terminal stages of lymphoma, a cancer affecting the lymph glands. Large tumors had been found throughout Wright's body, and doctors had tried every available treatment. Independently, Mr. Wright had researched a new cancer drug called "Krebiozen," and he believed it would work for him. He requested that the doctors give him the new drug. The hospital agreed to try Krebiozen on Mr. Wright and its other terminal cancer patients. What happened next defied logic: within two days of beginning his treatment, Mr. Wright, who had been confined to bed and barely able to breathe, began to improve, was sitting up, and joking with doctors and nurses. After another few days, he got out of bed and was walking around the cancer ward. After 10 days, tests revealed that his tumors had shrunken by 50%, at which point, he was sent home to continue his recovery. Oddly, no other patient in the hospital made any improvement whatsoever on Krebiozen.

Researchers explain that the placebo effect has to do with the brain's expectation of what happens when we take medicine. In short, we expect relief when we take a pill, so before we even put the pill in our mouth—placebo or not—the brain is already preparing us to feel better, and we do begin to feel better—immediately. The brain-conditioning theory is strengthened further by the fact that the outer appearance of the placebo affects its effectiveness. For instance, certain color placebos are more effective than others for treating certain illnesses. Green pills relieve anxiety, while white pills help calm digestive issues. Bright yellow placebos work best for treating depression, and red pills cause us to be more awake and alert. Pills that have their brand name stamped on them also have a greater effect than pills that have nothing written on them.

In the same way that our expectations can cause our brain and our body to respond positively to a placebo, our expectations can also cause negative side effects. This opposite of the placebo phenomenon is known as the "nocebo effect." In one study in Italy, people who had a sensitivity to lactose (a type of sugar found in milk) were given lactose-free milk to drink, but were told it was regular milk. Forty-four percent of the participants reported stomach cramps and indigestion after drinking the milk. In a clinical study for depression, a patient ingested 26 placebo pills that he thought were anti-depressants, in an attempt to commit suicide. Although the pills were totally harmless, the patient's blood pressure dropped to a dangerously low level.

Whether the effects are positive or negative, it's clear that placebos offer a way to harness the seemingly unlimited power of the human mind to bring about improvements to our own health and well-being.

Presentation

Study Summaries

A summary is a shorter version of a passage that includes only the most important facts and ideas.

Writing a study summary helps you check how well you have understood a text and remember the important points. It is also a useful strategy for preparing to write a report or a research paper.

Follow these steps when you write a study summary:

1 Read the text and underline the main ideas and key supporting information. Do not focus on small details.
2 When writing the summary, it's OK to include some key words and phrases from the original, but use your own words as much as possible.
3 Write the ideas in the same order and follow the same pattern of organization as in the original.
4 Don't include any facts, ideas, or opinions that are not in the passage.

Practice 4

Read the passage. Then read the summary below. Notice how the summary follows the guidelines of good summary writing.

In the late 1600s and early 1700s, conflicts arose between the French and the British governments over territory in eastern Canada. Because the land that the French had settled in Canada was a border area between French and British territories, the two powers had started to fight over the right to govern the region known as Acadia. These conflicts resulted in many battles and significant loss of life for British and French forces over a period of about 75 years.

In 1710, the British Navy, led by General Charles Lawrence succeeded in beating the French, leading to a 45-year period of British rule over Acadia. During that time, the French, now known as "Acadians" lived under British rule with few problems. However, everything changed for the Acadians in 1755 at the start of the French and Indian War. Between 1755 and 1763, thousands of Acadians were driven out of Canada by the British. The Acadians' homes and villages were set on fire and burned to the ground, families were separated, with men put on ships and sent away to labor building other new British colonies. Their wives and children were loaded onto other ships and sent back to France or other areas of Europe. Approximately one-third of the Acadians drowned or died from disease during this time.

Many Acadians who survived made their way south to Louisiana, which was still ruled by France at the time. Some made the entire journey on foot, taking many months and relying on kind strangers for food and a bed for the night.

In Louisiana, they were safe. Once again, there was land where they could farm and hunt, and rivers and swamps where they could trap animals and fish. And once again, they made friends and shared the land with the local Native Americans; many from both cultures even married each other. Over time, as the Acadian culture and language blended with the Native American, as well as that of the local Africans who had been brought to Louisiana as slaves, the Louisiana Cajun culture emerged.

Over a 75-year period at the turn of the 17th and 18th centuries, French and British forces were engaged in a fierce conflict over the area of eastern Canada known as Acadia. The British finally won under navy general Charles Lawrence, after which the French Acadians lived relatively peacefully for nearly half a century until the French-Indian War. During this time, the French were forced out of Acadia by the British in a brutal and violent way, which resulted in the deaths of many Acadians. Many of the survivors went to Louisiana, which was still under French rule at the time. There they were able to lead a happy life, farming and fishing. The Acadian French language and culture blended with that of the Native Americans and African slaves, forming the roots of Cajun culture.

Practice 5

Read the article. Take notes on the main ideas and supporting information below. Then write a summary using the guidelines in the Presentation on p. 180.

The use of electronic devices as a source of entertainment has increased drastically in recent years, especially among children 12 and under. In fact, recent research has shown that the average child between the ages of 8 and 12 spends three to five hours per day watching videos or playing games online, even on days when they attend school. Moreover, some children spend an hour or more texting their friends after school. In the past, children spent much more time outdoors, engaging in spontaneous play with other children. For instance, it used to be common for children from the same neighborhood to gather in the street after school to play kickball or street hockey until their parents called them in for dinner. However, today, those same neighborhood streets remain quiet and empty, as children stay inside in front of a screen of some type.

While some blame this trend on the technology, saying that video games are just more interesting to kids than real life, most child psychologists disagree. After all, it's parents who are allowing their children to stay indoors instead of saying, "Go outside and play," the parent's mantra of the past. News stories about various types of dangers to children have become more common these days. From speeding traffic, to bullying peers, to creepy strangers, the news is constantly fueling parents' worst fears. Therefore, say experts, parents are keeping their kids inside to protect them.

But, are children really better off indoors? Not really. Recent research has shown that, while the types of possible dangers to children may have changed since the past, today's children aren't really at any more risk than their peers 50 years ago were.

_____

_____

_____

_____

_____

_____

_____

_____

_____

LANGUAGE IN CONTEXT

Practice 1

Part 1

Look at the words in the box. Which ones do you know? Which ones are new? Read the passage and underline the words from the list in the box. Some words may be in a different form (for example, plural or past tense).

adhere to	constitute	institute	obesity
authority	curb	mandatory	overstep

"Nanny state" is an expression which originated in Britain. The term is used to describe laws and policies that aim to control people's behavior in an effort to protect them from danger. Policies such as mandatory seatbelt laws, motorcycle, and bicycle helmet laws, and high taxes on junk food are examples of the government overstepping its power. According to officials who adhere to these policies, it is the government's duty to protect citizens from their own dangerous behavior. These authorities assume that the government, not the citizens themselves, should be the judge of what constitutes "dangerous behavior." Recent attempts at regulating retail food and beverages are particularly disturbing. Last year, New York City Mayor Michael Bloomberg proposed a ban on selling soft drinks over 16 ounces. Bloomberg defended the ban, saying it would help curb childhood obesity and promote better health in general. Recent research has shown that large sized sweetened drinks are a major contributing factor in childhood obesity. However, a government imposed ban on soda size is likely to be an ineffective response. Instead, the government should institute more programs to educate parents and children about the dangers of junk food and high sugar beverages.

Part 2

Check your comprehension. Read the text. Circle the letter of the correct answer.

1 The term "Nanny State" generally has a negative meaning.
  a True
  b False

2 The passage suggests that government officials do not trust citizens' judgment.
  a True
  b False

3 The author of the passage approves of strict government regulations.
  a True
  b False

4 New York's mayor does not believe the research about childhood obesity.
  a True
  b False

5 The author of the passage feels that banning large soft drinks is not a good solution.
  a True
  b False

Part 3

Read each sentence. Circle the letter of the best meaning for the underlined word.

1 According to officials who <u>adhere to</u> these policies, it is the government's duty to protect citizens from their own dangerous behavior.

    a disagree with

    b follow

    c give up

    d expand on

2 These <u>authorities</u> assume that the government, not the citizens themselves, should be the judge of what constitutes "dangerous behavior."

    a officials

    b students

    c writers

    d strangers

3 These authorities assume that the government, not the citizens themselves, should be the judge of what <u>constitutes</u> "dangerous behavior."

    a confuses

    b represents

    c helps

    d causes

4 Bloomberg defended the ban, saying it would help <u>curb</u> childhood obesity and promote better health in general.

    a follow

    b control

    c create

    d improve

5 Instead, the government should <u>institute</u> more programs to educate parents and children about the dangers of junk food and high sugar beverages.

    a employ

    b study

    c find

    d introduce

6 Policies such as <u>mandatory</u> seatbelt laws, motorcycle and bicycle helmet laws, and high taxes on junk food are examples of the government overstepping its power.

    a required

    b unusual

    c temporary

    d international

7 Recent research has shown that large-sized sweetened drinks are a major contributing factor in childhood <u>obesity</u>.

    a homelessness
    b happiness
    c heaviness
    d health

8 Policies such as mandatory seatbelt laws, motorcycle and bicycle helmet laws, and high taxes on junk food are examples of the government <u>overstepping</u> its power.

    a buying
    b exceeding
    c creating
    d ignoring

Part 4

Write the correct word or phrase from the box to complete each sentence.

obesity	overstepped	institute	curb
authorities	adhere to	constitutes	mandatory

1 If you see a suspicious package, please notify airport _____ immediately.

2 All students must _____ the rules of the dormitory.

3 In an effort to _____ cheating, the school banned all cell phones from the classrooms.

4 Gina felt her boss's comment about her hair _____ the employer-employee relationship.

5 The city plans to _____ a new recycling program.

6 Adult _____ has become a greater problem in our community since five fast-food restaurants opened last year.

7 Could you please explain what _____ a passing grade in this class?

8 Goggles and gloves are _____ in the laboratory.

Practice 2

Part 1

Look at the words in the box. Which ones do you know? Which ones are new? Read the passage and underline the words from the list in the box. Some words may be in a different form (for example, plural or past tense).

concentration	disruptive	function	sustain
diagnosis	extend	hire	tailor

Attention Deficit Disorder (ADD) and Attention Deficit Hyperactivity Disorder (ADHD) are neuro-phychological or behavioral disorders that affect a person's ability to function normally, particularly in situations which require extended periods of sustained concentration. Diagnoses of these disorders are becoming more and more common, affecting up to 16% of school-aged children.

As a result, school officials are looking for ways to better serve the needs of these children. ADD/ADHD and related disorders can create serious challenges for children in traditional school environments. The symptoms may cause an inability to sit or stay at rest, difficulty concentrating for extended time periods, and disruptive behavior. At school, children suffering from ADD may miss important details, have trouble staying organized, daydream, or become easily confused. These issues very often result in serious difficulties in the classroom. Without proper diagnosis and support, they can lead to academic failure. Due to the fact that symptoms and needs vary from individual to individual, many schools have hired additional support staff to work with students with ADD/ADHD. One-on-one support and tailored accommodations can help students stay focused and on task and lead to greater academic success.

Part 2

Check your comprehension. Reread the text. Circle the letter of the correct answer.

1 According to the article, cases of ADD and ADHD are on the rise.
    a True
    b False

2 School officials largely ignore the problem.
    a True
    b False

3 ADD-ADHD is relatively rare in children.
    a True
    b False

4 Students with ADD-ADHD are likely to have trouble on tests.
    a True
    b False

5 Students with ADD-ADHD can succeed in school.
    a True
    b False

Part 3

Read each sentence. Circle the letter of the best meaning for the underlined word.

1 Attention Deficit Disorder (ADD) and Attention Deficit Hyperactivity Disorder (ADHD) are neuro-phychological or behavioral disorders that affect a person's ability to function normally, particularly in situations which require extended periods of sustained <u>concentration</u>.
    a difficulty
    b focus
    c energy
    d enjoyment

2 <u>Diagnoses</u> of these disorders are becoming more and more common, affecting up to 16% of school-aged children.

    a understanding

    b research

    c questioning

    d identification

3 The symptoms may cause an inability to sit or stay at rest, difficulty concentrating for extended time periods, and <u>disruptive</u> behavior.

    a calm

    b unusual

    c confusing

    d distracting

4 Attention Deficit Disorder (ADD) and Attention Deficit Hyperactivity Disorder (ADHD) are neuro-phychological or behavioral disorders that affect a person's ability to function normally, particularly in situations which require <u>extended</u> periods of sustained concentration.

    a far

    b basic

    c long

    d fun

5 Attention Deficit Disorder (ADD) and Attention Deficit Hyperactivity Disorder (ADHD) are neuro-phychological or behavioral disorders that affect a person's ability to <u>function</u> normally, particularly in situations which require extended periods of sustained concentration.

    a perform

    b remember

    c study

    d walk

6 Due to the fact that symptoms and needs vary from individual to individual, many schools have <u>hired</u> additional support staff to work with students with ADD/ADHD.

    a employed

    b entertained

    c enjoyed

    d exercised

7 Attention Deficit Disorder (ADD) and Attention Deficit Hyperactivity Disorder (ADHD) are neuro-phychological or behavioral disorders that affect a person's ability to function normally, particularly in situations which require extended periods of <u>sustained</u> concentration.

    a difficult

    b helpful

    c steady

    d unexpected

8 One-on-one support and <u>tailored</u> accommodations can help students stay focused and on task and lead to greater academic success.

    a personalized

    b finalized

    c realistic

    d misunderstood

Part 4

Complete each sentence with a word from the box.

hire	sustain	extended	concentration
disruptive	tailor	function	diagnosis

1 Please turn off that loud music. It's affecting my _____ .

2 The doctor hesitated slightly before telling the patient his _____ .

3 The class trip was cut short because several students were being too _____ .

4 I sprained my ankle, and the doctor said I shouldn't stand on it for an _____ length of time.

5 My brain does not _____ well if I haven't slept enough.

6 The company plans to _____ 40 more salespeople this year.

7 Justin hasn't had a day off in months. He won't be able to _____ this level of exhaustion for long.

8 A good teacher is able to _____ his or her class to the needs of the students.

Practice 3

Part 1

Look at the words in the box. Which ones do you know? Which ones are new? Read the passage and underline the words from the list in the box. Some words may be in a different form (for example, plural or past tense).

capable	remarkable	replicate	worn out
regenerate	replenish	tissue	yield

Stem cells have the remarkable potential to develop into many different cell types in the body during early life. In addition, in many tissues, they serve as a sort of internal repair system, dividing essentially without limit to replenish other cells as long as the person or animal is still alive. When a stem cell divides, each new cell has the potential either to remain a stem cell or become another type of cell with a more specialized function, such as a muscle cell, a red blood cell, or a brain cell. In some organs, such as the gut and bone marrow, stem cells regularly divide to repair and replace worn out or damaged tissues. Stem cells are capable of dividing and renewing themselves for long periods. Unlike muscle cells, blood cells, or nerve cells—which do not normally replicate themselves—stem cells may proliferate. A starting population of stem cells that proliferates for many months in the laboratory can yield millions of cells. Given their unique regenerative abilities, stem cells may offer new potential for treating diseases such as diabetes and heart disease. However, much work remains to be done in the laboratory and the clinic to understand how to use these cells for regenerative therapies to treat disease.

Part 2

Check your comprehension. Reread the text. Circle the letter of the correct answer.

1 Stem cells are interesting because they never change.

   a True

   b False

2 Stem cells may continue to regenerate after a person or animal has died.

   a True

   b False

3 Stem cells help the body heal itself.

   a True

   b False

4 Other types of cells do not divide as much as stem cells do.

   a True

   b False

5 The research on stem cells is largely complete.

   a True

   b False

Part 3

Read each sentence. Circle the letter of the best meaning for the underlined word or phrase.

1 A starting population of stem cells that proliferates for many months in the laboratory can <u>yield</u> millions of cells.

   a locate

   b select

   c produce

   d damage

2 In addition, in many <u>tissues</u>, they serve as a sort of internal repair system, dividing essentially without limit to replenish other cells as long as the person or animal is still alive.

   a instances

   b organs

   c cases

   d injuries

3 Given their unique <u>regenerative</u> abilities, stem cells may offer new potential for treating diseases such as diabetes and heart disease.

   a experienced

   b peaceful

   c unsurprising

   d renewing

4 Stem cells have the <u>remarkable</u> potential to develop into many different cell types in the body during early life.

  a secret

  b indescribable

  c amazing

  d helpful

5 Stem cells are <u>capable of</u> dividing and renewing themselves for long periods.

  a connected to

  b aware of

  c fond of

  d able to

6 In addition, in many tissues, they serve as a sort of internal repair system, dividing essentially without limit to <u>replenish</u> other cells as long as the person or animal is still alive.

  a replace

  b reduce

  c regret

  d record

7 Unlike muscle cells, blood cells, or nerve cells—which do not normally <u>replicate</u> themselves—stem cells may proliferate.

  a introduce

  b embarrass

  c reproduce

  d remove

8 In some organs, such as the gut and bone marrow, stem cells regularly divide to repair and replace <u>worn out</u> or damaged tissues.

  a closed up

  b used up

  c shut up

  d brought up

Part 4

Complete each sentence with a word from the box.

tissue	capable of	yield	replenish
replicated	remarkable	worn out	regenerate

1 I can't believe Jack is the new CEO. There is no way that he is _____ leading the company.

2 Some animal species, such as sea stars, are actually able to _____ their legs if they are cut off or damaged.

3 Greg is truly a _____ person. He's good at everything he does.

4 Excuse me. Could you please _____ the lettuce on the salad bar?

5 I saw a horrifying science fiction movie last night. This terrifying alien _____ itself hundreds of times in just a few seconds.

6 The surgeon carefully removed the damaged _____ in the patient's heart.

7 You should change your pants before we go out. The knees are all _____ in those ones.

8 Because of this year's rain and cold, the garden did not _____ as many strawberries as usual.

Practice 4

Part 1

Look at the words in the box. Which ones do you know? Which ones are new? Read the passage and underline the words from the list in the box. Some words may be in a different form (for example, plural or past tense).

creepy	engaging in	peers	spontaneous
drastically	fueling	predators	trend

The use of electronic devices as a source of entertainment has increased drastically in recent years, especially among children 12 and under. In fact, recent research has shown that most children between the ages of 8 and 12 spend three to five hours per day watching videos or playing games online, even on days when they attend school. Moreover, some children spend an hour or more texting their friends during the afternoon and evening hours. In the past, children used to spend much more time outdoors, engaging in spontaneous play with other children. For instance, it was common for children from the same neighborhood to gather in the street after school to play kickball or street hockey until their parents called them in to dinner. However, today those same neighborhood streets remain quiet and empty, as children stay inside in front of a screen of some type. While some blame this trend on the technology, saying that video games are just more interesting to kids than real life, most child psychologists disagree. After all, it's parents who are allowing their children to stay indoors instead of saying, "Go outside and play," the parents' mantra of the past. News stories about various dangers to children have become more common these days. From speeding traffic, to bullying peers, to creepy strangers, the news is constantly fueling parents' worst fears. Consequently, say experts, parents are keeping their kids inside in an effort to protect them. But are children really safer staying indoors? Not really. Research has shown that while the nature of the possible dangers to children may have changed since the past, today's children aren't really at any more risk than their peers 50 years ago. As a matter of fact, the negative health effects of a lack of exercise and outdoor play may be far more dangerous. In addition, there are other potential dangers online, for instance, cyberbullying and Internet predators to name just a couple.

Part 2

Check your comprehension. Read the text on page 191. Circle the letter of the correct answer.

1 Children under 12 are using more electronic devices than in the past.

   a True

   b False

2 Children still spend about as much time outdoors as they used to.

   a True

   b False

3 Child psychologists believe that real life is as interesting to children as video games.

   a True

   b False

4 The passage states that some parents are overly concerned about their children's safety.

   a True

   b False

5 It is generally safer to allow kids to play online than go outdoors.

   a True

   b False

Part 3

Read each sentence. Circle the letter of the best meaning for the underlined word.

1 Use of electronic devices as a source of entertainment has increased <u>drastically</u> in recent years, especially among children 12 and under.

   a only a small amount

   b significantly

   c to a small degree

   d unexpectedly

2 News stories about various dangers to children have become more common these days. From speeding traffic, to bullying peers, to creepy strangers, the news is constantly <u>fueling</u> parents' worst fears.

   a forgetting

   b calming

   c increasing

   d finding

3 In the past, children used to spend much more time outdoors, engaging in <u>spontaneous</u> play with other children.

   a prearranged

   b dangerous

   c unplanned

   d unfriendly

4 In addition, there are other potential dangers online, for instance, cyberbullying and Internet <u>predators</u> to name just a couple.

  a tutors
  b stalkers
  c gamers
  d cheaters

5 News stories about various dangers to children have become more common these days. From speeding traffic, to bullying <u>peers</u>, to creepy strangers, the news is constantly fueling parents' worst fears.

  a strangers
  b teachers
  c classmates
  d relatives

6 While some blame this <u>trend</u> on the technology, saying that video games are just more interesting to kids than real life, most child psychologists disagree.

  a tendency
  b tenderness
  c tentativeness
  d temptation

7 In the past, children used to spend much more time outdoors, <u>engaging in</u> spontaneous play with other children.

  a participating in
  b dreaming of
  c complaining about
  d competing in

8 News stories about various dangers to children have become more common these days. From speeding traffic, to bullying peers, to <u>creepy</u> strangers, the news is constantly fueling parents' worst fears.

  a friendly
  b familiar
  c frightening
  d foolish

Part 4

Complete each sentence with a word from the box.

engaging in	creepy	predators	spontaneous
trend	fuel	peers	drastically

1 I've always hated visiting my aunt's house. It's a _____ old place.

2 Of all my college friends, I think Amber has changed the most _____ .

3 Environmentalists are hoping that heightened public awareness will reverse the _____ of global warming.

4 This show is interesting. It's about how the cops catch _____ online.

5 The students were kicked out of the dorms for _____ illegal activities.

6 Our life has become so routine. We never do anything _____ anymore.

7 The president's speech only served to _____ people's anger about the economic crisis.

8 Helen doesn't have the confidence to be different from her _____ . She just follows everything they do.

Practice 5

Part 1

Look at the words in the box. Which ones do you know? Which ones are new? Read the passage and underline the words from the list in the box. Some words may be in a different form (for example, plural or past tense).

aggressive	glare	offensive	random
extreme	intense	prescription	timid

Marina Abramović is known as the "grandmother of performance art." This nickname is well-deserved, as she has performed thousands of shows around the world over the past four decades. Originally from Serbia, she now lives and works in New York City. Abramović's career began in Europe in the 1970s, when she was in her early 20s. At that time, performance art was gaining popularity internationally. Over the years, her performances have ranged from simply strange to completely shocking. They are designed to test viewers' limits and encourage them to step outside of their own "comfort zones." Abramović's early works were some of her most extreme. During these performances, she cut herself with knives, played with fire, and took prescription drugs in front of live audiences. Some called them brilliant works of art; others said they were offensive. During one piece, Abramović stood still and silent in a gallery for six hours. On a table in front of her, she placed 73 random objects. These included pens, a rose, a pair of scissors, a gun, and a single bullet. A sign on the table explained that visitors could approach her and do anything they wanted. They were not required to use the objects, but were allowed to if they wished. In the beginning, audience members seemed timid, not wanting to come near. However, as time went on, some of them began to act aggressively. One man held the gun to her neck. Tears filled Abramović's eyes, but she did not move. Abramović later described the experience, "What I learned was that if you leave it up to the audience, they can kill you." After exactly six hours, I stood up and started walking toward the audience. Everyone ran away." Abramović's more recent performances have been less shocking; nevertheless, they attract thousands of curious viewers. In 2010, New York's Museum of Modern Art (MOMA) presented her exhibition entitled "The Artist is Present." As part of the show, Abramović appeared seated silently at a plain square table, which was placed in the center of a large gallery. Across the table was an empty chair where visitors could sit across from her and stare into her intense eyes for a few silent minutes. People waited in line for hours to sit across from Abramović. Their reactions varied. Some stared at her with no expression. Others suddenly broke down in tears. Still others looked as though they were ready to laugh at any moment. Over the course of the three-month exhibit, Abramović sat in the chair for a total of over 700 hours and glared into over 1,400 pairs of visitors' eyes. Many have questioned whether Abramović's performances can really be considered works of art. As one art critic wrote of the MOMA exhibition, "Whether it's a work of art or not is up to the viewer, but one thing is certain: It is work."

Part 2

Check your comprehension. Read the text on page 194. Circle the letter of the correct answer.

1 Abramović began performing in the US, then moved to Europe.
  a True
  b False

2 People's opinions are divided about Abramović's work.
  a True
  b False

3 Her MOMA exhibition generated emotional reactions from visitors.
  a True
  b False

4 Abramović has never worried for her own safety during a performance.
  a True
  b False

Part 3

Read each sentence. Circle the letter of the best meaning for the underlined word.

1 However, as time went on, some of them began to act <u>aggressively</u>.
  a unwillingly
  b gracefully
  c violently
  d jokingly

2 During these performances, she cut herself with knives, played with fire, and took <u>prescription</u> drugs in front of live audiences.
  a medicinal
  b traditional
  c rare
  d imaginary

3 On a table in front of her, she placed 73 <u>random</u> objects.
  a large
  b stolen
  c dangerous
  d unrelated

4 Some called them brilliant works of art; others said they were <u>offensive</u>.
  a unpleasant
  b fast-paced
  c predictable
  d boring

5 Over the course of the three-month exhibit, Abramović sat in the chair for a total of over 700 hours and <u>glared</u> into over 1400 pairs of visitors' eyes.

   a cried

   b closed

   c stared

   d crossed

6 Across the table was an empty chair where visitors could sit across from her and stare into her <u>intense</u> eyes for a few silent minutes.

   a painful

   b gentle

   c tired

   d powerful

7 Abramović's early works were some of her most <u>extreme</u>.

   a tame

   b unpopular

   c outrageous

   d misunderstood

Part 4

Complete each sentence with a word from the box.

timid	aggressive	intense	glared
offensive	extreme	prescription	random

1 Dogs often become _____ when they are mistreated.

2 I don't think Kelly deserved to be fired for being late. That seems a little _____ .

3 I wanted to get Mack Jackson's autograph after the game, but I was too _____ .

4 The teacher _____ at the class as she announced that someone had been caught cheating.

5 After my surgery, the doctor gave me a _____ painkiller.

6 The woman's voice was _____ and passionate as she spoke about her experiences during the war.

7 You owe me an apology. That comment was terribly _____ .

8 None of the evidence made any sense. Each separate clue seemed completely _____ .

Practice 6

Part 1

Look at the words in the box. Which ones do you know? Which ones are new? Read the passage and underline the words from the list in the box. Some words may be in a different form (for example, plural or past tense).

cultivate	immense	reverence
customary	peasant	unsurpassed
eternal	recite	launch

Nearly four decades after her death, Oum Kalthoum is still widely recognized as the greatest female Arabic singer of all time. She was a young girl from a poor peasant family, but her voice carried her to unsurpassed levels of stardom and gave her eternal status as the national voice of Egypt. Still today, Kalthoum's music is played everywhere in Egypt, from cafés, to elevators, to taxi cab radios, and many of her recordings still outsell those of popular contemporary artists from the Middle East. Born in a small town in the Nile Delta, she was the daughter of a village religious cleric. With her father, she learned to recite verses from the *Koran*, and succeeded in memorizing the entire book at the age of 12. Noticing his daughter's immense talent for memorization and her strong voice, Kalthoum's father began taking her on trips with her older brother, during which they would chant the *Koran* in order to help the family earn money. Kalthoum had to dress in boy's clothing, as it was not customary for girls to sing in front of strangers in the conservative rural Egyptian tradition. During her teen years, Kalthoum had the opportunity to meet the famous composer Zakariyya Ahmad, who recognized her great potential and invited her to come to Cairo to study and perform. Ahmad introduced her some of the musical elite in the capital city, and it quickly became clear that if she wanted to pursue a singing career, she would need to come to Cairo. Kalthoum's entire family moved to Cairo in 1923 in order to support her training and help launch her career. At first, Cairo was a cold place. While Kalthoum's powerful voice received positive reviews, the snobbish city arts crowd laughed at her simple cotton dresses and country ways. Driven and determined to earn their respect, Kalthoum began to cultivate her inner star. She studied classical French literature, Egyptian music and poetry, and she mimicked the style of the wealthy Cairo socialites who came to her performances. Over time, she succeeded in crafting her image as a sophisticated artist with traditional roots that stemmed deep from the heart of Egypt. Kalthoum's nickname, *Al-Sitt* meaning *The Lady* conveys the public's reverence for her.

Part 2

Check your comprehension. Read the text. Circle the letter of the correct answer.

1 Oum Kalthoum's recordings are difficult to find today.

   a True

   b False

2 Her brother first noticed her singing talent.

   a True

   b False

3 Her family encouraged her to pursue a singing career.

  a True

  b False

4 She enjoyed her early experiences in Cairo.

  a True

  b False

5 Following criticism, she withdrew from public life.

  a True

  b False

Part 3

Read each sentence. Circle the letter of the best meaning for the underlined word.

1 Driven and determined to earn their respect, Kalthoum began to <u>cultivate</u> her inner star.

  a develop

  b fight

  c feel

  d remove

2 Kalthoum had to dress in boy's clothing, as it was not <u>customary</u> for girls to sing in front of strangers in the conservative rural Egyptian tradition.

  a expensive

  b promised

  c political

  d traditional

3 She was a young girl from a poor peasant family, but her voice carried her to unsurpassed levels of stardom and gave her <u>eternal</u> status as the national voice of Egypt.

  a near

  b troubled

  c little

  d endless

4 Noticing his daughter's <u>immense</u> talent for memorization and her strong voice, Kalthoum's father began taking her on trips with her older brother, during which they would chant the *Koran* in order to help the family earn money.

  a impossible

  b slight

  c great

  d frequent

5 She was a young girl from a poor <u>peasant</u> family, but her voice carried her to unsurpassed levels of stardom and gave her eternal status as the national voice of Egypt.

  a lawyer

  b farmer

  c faraway

  d large

6 With her father, she learned to <u>recite</u> verses from the *Koran*, and succeeded in memorizing the entire book at the age of 12.

   a narrate

   b listen

   c write

   d copy

7 She was a young girl from a poor peasant family, but her voice carried her to <u>unsurpassed</u> levels of stardom and gave her eternal status as the national voice of Egypt.

   a unmatched

   b inhuman

   c usual

   d unsurprising

8 Kalthoum's nickname, *Al-Sitt* meaning *The Lady* conveys the public's <u>reverence</u> for her.

   a unfamiliarity

   b respect

   c hatred

   d fear

Part 4

Complete each sentence with a word from the box. Write the correct word into the sentence.

eternal	peasant	cultivate	customary
immense	reverence	unsurpassed	recite

1 Your work is _____ . You deserve a raise.

2 It is important for parents to _____ good manners in their children.

3 This decision will have an _____ effect on the community.

4 It is _____ to remove one's shoes when entering a home in Japan.

5 *Fiddler on the Roof* is a musical about a poor Jewish _____ .

6 Frank's bowling championship trophy was an _____ source of pride for him.

7 The students had great _____ for their teacher.

8 For our final project, we had to _____ a poem in French.

APPENDICES

Appendix 1

Tips for Reading Tests

All of the reading practice activities in My English Lab will help you improve your reading skills and lead to greater success on reading tests. Reading regularly in English, especially textbooks and academic texts, will help you build a strong vocabulary and increase your rate of comprehension.

Here are some additional useful tips and suggestions to help you succeed on reading comprehension tests:

General Suggestion

In most testing situations, your time will be limited. This can make you feel nervous and create pressure, making it hard to focus on what you are reading.

- Relax. Take a few deep breaths and clear your mind before you begin.
- Preview the entire test to see how many sections and points there are. Quickly calculate how much time you have to spend on each section.

Previewing Questions

- Read the test questions first. When you know what information you need, you can use time-saving strategies such as skimming and scanning to find it.
- Preview the title and the first and last few lines of each text. Then ask yourself questions about the details of the text. You can use the "five *W*s and an *H*" question words (*Who, What, Where, When, Why, How*) to guide your questions. For example, *Who are the people involved? What happened? What is the main point/author's purpose/author's opinion? Where did the events take place?*

Reading Strategies

- Always skim the whole passage quickly before you read carefully.
- Look for a pattern (sequence, comparison/contrast, cause and effect).
- Scan for transition words to help you.
- After skimming, read the passage carefully and highlight or mark the main idea and important supporting facts and ideas.
- Skip over words and phrases you don't understand, or use the context of the sentence or passage to guess their meanings.
- Make inferences and conclusions using your background knowledge about the topic.
- If there is time, use a chart or graphic organizer to write down the main points from the passage.

Appendix 2

Transition Words and Phrases

Transitions for the Comparison/Contrast Pattern

To show similarities: *similar to, similarly, like, alike, both, also, too, the same, in common, as well as*

To show differences: *different from, unlike, however, while, although, on the other hand, instead, rather than, but, however, instead, in contrast, yet, though*

Transitions for the Cause and Effect Pattern

Causes: *so, cause, help, start, create, produce, affect, make, lead to, result in, responsible for, since, because, as*

Effects: *because of, resulting from, a result of, caused by, due to, as a consequence of, consequently, therefore, thus*

Transitions for the Problem-Solution Pattern

Words that indicate a problem: *problem, situation, trouble, crisis, issue, question, dilemma, debate, deliberate, challenge*

Words that indicate a solution: *solution, solve, resolution, resolve, decide, figure out, work out, determine*

Appendix 3

Reading Rate Table

All of the passages are about 750 words long. To find your reading rate, find the reading time that is closest to yours. Then look across at the reading rate column.

Reading time (minutes)	Reading rate (words per minute)
1:00	750
1:15	600
1:30	500
1:45	429
2:00	375
2:15	333
2:30	300
2:45	272
3:00	250
3:15	230
3:30	214
3:45	200
4:00	188
4:15	176
4:30	167
4:45	157
5:00	150
5:15	142
5:30	136
5:45	130
6:00	125
6:15	120
6:30	115
6:45	111
7:00	107

Appendix 4

Reading Rate Log

Under the Practice Activity number, write your comprehension score (number of correct answers). Then check (√) your reading rate. Write the date at the bottom of the chart.

Exercise	Intro	P1-R1	P1-R2	P1-R3	P2-R1	P2-R2	P2-R3	P3-R1	P3-R2	P3-R3
Comprehension Score										
Reading rate										
750										
600										
500										
429										
375										
333										
300										
272										
250										
230										
214										
200										
188										
176										
167										
157										
150										
142										
136										
130										
125										
120										
115										
111										
107										
Date										

POST-TEST

Part 1 Comprehension Skills

Read the scanning questions. Then scan the text to find the answers. Circle the letter of the correct answer to each question on pp. 205 and 206.

Scanning Questions

1 Where can you buy books at discount prices?
2 What type of event concludes the festival on Friday?
3 Which time slot has the most events?
4 At which event can you check your email?

Festival Schedule: Friday, September 27

10 AM

Feedback from the Experts – City Lights Stage

Hey, amateur writers and poets! Here's your chance for free advice and constructive commentary from two experienced leaders of the city's literary scene. Bring up to four pages of double-spaced prose or poetry for some on-the-spot feedback and suggestions from the experts.

Romance Authors Meet and Greet – Bayside Bookstore

Members of the Romance Writers' Guild will be on hand for a casual meet-and-greet with readers. Come talk about books, receive promotional materials, and browse the bookstore!

Jane Austen Fiction – City Library

This panel will celebrate the 200th anniversary of *Pride and Prejudice* with a discussion and readings of Jane Austen-inspired fiction.

12 PM

Kayenne Jones Concert – Music Stage

Kayenne Jones warms up the Music Stage with her acoustic sounds.

Cooking Demonstrations – Food for Thought Tent

Join Northside Café Chef Kevin Brown as he whips up delicious recipes before your very eyes!

Farmer's Market Food Court – Kendrick Park

Open daily from 10–2, the Farmer's Market Food Court offers a variety of farm-fresh food options for your dining pleasure. Bring your laptop and enjoy free wireless Internet in the dining area, provided by Finelines Computers.

1 PM

Panel Discussion: From Zeus to Zombies – City Lights Stage

Fantasy fiction often draws upon the stories of ancient civilizations around the world. Join our panelists in a discussion of cultural myths and legends that form the rich backdrop for our literature of the fantastic.

Book Sale – City Library

Browse dozens of titles published by Huntington Press. Take advantage of special festival discounts, and meet some of the acclaimed authors from around the region.

Authors' Marketplace – Writer's Tent

The Writer's Tent features local and regional, commercially-published and self-published authors signing and selling their books.

3 PM

The Art of Coffee – Food for Thought Tent

Join Linda Fabian, owner of Linda's Latte Lair, as she talks coffee and the relationship between our favorite hot beverage and books.

Publisher's Forum – City Lights Stage

Learn about the publishing industry from an insider's perspective. The publishing industry has changed dramatically in recent years, with new technology and multi-media projects. What are editors and publishers looking for these days? Find out what's new and what's tried and true.

Writing Historical Fiction – City Library

Authors will talk about the challenges of writing historical fiction, including researching, issues of accuracy, and more.

Paranormal Fiction – Wendell's Bookshop

Authors will talk about why they choose to write paranormal fiction, how to develop concepts for paranormal creatures, and why paranormal romance and characters are popular.

Graphic Novels – Bayside Bookstore

Juan Mendoza and Pierre Parker, creators of the graphic novel series *Wandering Wolf* talk about their experiences with writing a graphic novel.

Putting the Suspense in Horror – Writer's Tent

Various authors will talk about incorporating suspense and mystery into romantic fiction.

4 PM

Reggae Concert by One World Union – Kendrick Park

Live reggae music performed by the city's most popular reggae band!

1 Where can you buy books at discount prices?
   a City Lights Tent
   b Writer's Tent
   c City Library
   d Wendell's Bookshop

2 What type of event concludes the festival on Friday?
   a a live concert
   b a cooking demonstration
   c an author book signing
   d a panel discussion

3 Which time slot has the most events?

   a 10 AM

   b 1 PM

   c 3 PM

   d 4 PM

4 At which event can you check your email?

   a Cooking Demonstrations

   b Farmer's Market Food Court

   c The Art of Coffee

   d Kayenne Jones Concert

Part 2 Comprehension Skills

Skim the text and circle the letter of the best way to complete each sentence.

Recent research suggests that certain animals have much greater intellectual capacity than was previously thought. Scientists define intelligence, as it pertains to animals, as the capacity to learn a new communication system, such as human language, the ability to adapt behavior for enhanced results (for example, the use of tools), and the ability to learn from previous mistakes. Instinctive behavior, i.e., behavior that is automatically programmed into an animal's brain as a result of genetics, is not considered an indicator of intelligence. Some species of animals, such as chimpanzees and dolphins, have long been known to possess above average intelligence. However, there are others whose smarts have gone largely unnoticed until fairly recently. The sea invertebrates known as *cephalopods* (octopi and squid) are one example. These animals' brains share many features with the human brain, such as folded lobes and separate regions for processing tactile and visual information. In addition, they use tools, show high levels of curiosity, and have a general distaste for boredom. Pigs may be one of the most misunderstood animals. According to some experts, they are one of the cleanest animals on Earth, but because pigs don't have sweat glands to keep cool, they roll around in the mud. A series of experiments conducted on several animal species in the 1990s tested the animals' ability to move a cursor on a video screen in order to identify a symbol they had been shown. Using their snouts to perform the task, the pigs learned as quickly as chimpanzees.

1 The passage is about _____ .

   a similarities between humans and animals

   b methods of training animals

   c examples of intelligent animals

   d intelligence levels of different animals

2 The author of the passage intends to _____ .

   a inform people about the topic

   b give an opinion about the topic

   c teach people how to do something

   d persuade people to take some action

Part 3 Comprehension Skills

Read the passage and circle the letter of the answer.

Patents, trademarks, and copyrights are ways to protect the rights of individuals when they create an original product or piece of work. Some people confuse patents, copyrights, and trademarks. Although there may be some similarities among these kinds of intellectual property protection, they are different and serve different purposes.

A patent for an invention is the grant of a property right to the inventor. Generally, the term of a new patent is 20 years from the date on which the application for the patent was filed or, in special cases, from the date an earlier related application was filed, subject to the payment of maintenance fees. Under certain circumstances, patent term extensions or adjustments may be available.

A patent grants the right to exclude others from making, using, offering for sale, or selling the invention. It does not grant the right to make, use, offer for sale, sell or import, but the right to exclude others from making, using, offering for sale, selling or importing the invention. Once a patent is issued, the patent holder is responsible for enforcing the patent.

There are three types of patents: 1) Utility patents may be granted to anyone who invents or discovers any new and useful process, machine, article of manufacture, or composition of matter, or any new and useful improvement thereof; 2) Design patents may be granted to anyone who invents a new, original, and ornamental design for an article of manufacture; and 3) Plant patents may be granted to anyone who invents or discovers and reproduces any distinct and new variety of plant.

A trademark is a word, name, symbol, or device that is used in trade with goods to indicate the source of the goods and to distinguish them from the goods of others. Trademark rights may be used to prevent others from using a confusingly similar mark, but not to prevent others from making the same goods or from selling the same goods or services under a clearly different mark. Trademarks which are used in interstate or foreign commerce may be registered.

Copyright is a form of protection provided to the authors of "original works of authorship," including literary, dramatic, musical, artistic, and certain other intellectual works, both published and unpublished. The law generally gives the owner of copyright the exclusive right to reproduce the copyrighted work, to prepare derivative works, to distribute copies, and to perform or display the copyrighted work publicly. The copyright protects the form of expression rather than the subject matter of the writing. For example, a description of a machine could be copyrighted, but this would only prevent others from copying the description; it would not prevent others from writing a description of their own or from making and using the machine.

1 What is the topic of the article?

  a ways to apply for a patent, trademark, or copyright
  b ways patents, trademarks, and copyrights differ
  c ways people use patents, trademarks, and copyrights

2 Which statement best describes the main idea of the passage?

   a Patents, trademarks, and copyrights are needed to protect original works.

   b Patents, trademarks, and copyrights all serve different purposes.

   c Patents, trademarks, and copyrights are getting more difficult to obtain.

3 Which type of patent is granted for inventors of a new and useful process?

   a utility patent

   b design patent

   c plant patent

4 A trademark can be registered for use in international trade.

   a True

   b False

5 A copyright prevents others from _____ .

   a reproducing works in print

   b using others' ideas

   c making their own machines

Part 4   Comprehension Skills

Read the passage and circle the letter of the answer.

[1] Students in our town's elementary schools are being deprived of the opportunity to think for themselves, and denied the chance to analyze, explore, and be creative. [2] Since 2002, all public schools receiving federal funding have been required by law to administer standardized tests to all students. [3] While testing and assessment is an important part of education, too much emphasis on "teaching to the test" can have dangerous negative consequences for both teaching and learning.

[4] In efforts to standardize the elementary curriculum and ensure that students perform well on these tests, many school districts around the country, including ours, are purchasing "boxed" programs for core subjects, such as reading, math, and science. [5] These programs not only dictate what is taught, but also how it is taught, essentially taking away the individual teacher's choice, creativity, and teaching style, leaving both teachers and students feeling bored and unmotivated.

[6] As concerned parents, teachers, and community members, we need to come together to find a way to take back our children's education from the administrators and politicians who seem determined to take the joy out of the classroom. [7] The next school board meeting will be held Wednesday, October 28th at 6 PM at Green Street School. Please consider attending the meeting or writing a letter to your local school board representative. Our voices must be heard.

1 What is the main purpose of the passage?

   a to explain a new school policy

   b to announce a change in procedures

   c to inform people about an event

   d to persuade people to take action

2 From the passage, we can infer that the writer is _____ .

   a a politician

   b an administrator

   c a parent

   d a school board representative

3 The overall tone of the article is _____ .

   a formal

   b professional

   c opinionated

   d friendly

4 In the first paragraph, which sentence expresses a fact?

   a 1

   b 2

   c 3

5 In the second paragraph, which sentence expresses an opinion?

   a 4

   b 5

Part 5   Comprehension Skills

Read the beginning of a student's research paper. Then circle the letter of the answer.

Research Paper

Todd Coopee

English 101

Professor Timmons

Not Safe Anywhere: How Online Monitoring in the Workplace Is Threatening Employees' Privacy

Since the dawn of the Internet, companies have been rapidly revising and adding new policies to employee manuals in an effort to control workers' use of the Web during working hours. Rules and policies regarding online activity range from blocking employees' access to certain websites to granting the company full access to workers' computers in order to check their Web history, including email messages. Most of these provisions allow the company to conduct regular online monitoring secretly at any time and of any employee. A survey conducted by the ePolicy Institute in 2005 found that 76% of companies engaged in online monitoring and the number of companies that blocked employees' access to certain websites increased 30% since 2001.

1 Choose the best thesis statement for the essay.

   a John Chi, a former top-level manager for Nol-Corp Computers admits that it was common practice at the company to review employees' email accounts to check on their correspondences with important clients and ensure that workers weren't using the accounts for personal purposes.

b Although most employees admit to surfing the Web for personal reasons while at work, the vast majority say that they do so only during their official break times or during their lunch hour, so it does not adversely affect their ability to concentrate or complete their work.

c While Internet usage in the workplace has been shown to decrease worker productivity and can result in security problems for the company, the practice of online monitoring violates employees' rights to privacy and should be reserved only for law enforcement officials when criminal activity is suspected.

d In his book, Open Source, John Coster lists a number of ways companies have violated employees' privacy throughout history, including office video surveillance, mandatory drug testing, lie detector tests, and psychological profiling.

2 From the passage, we can infer that the writer _____ .

    a works for a company that monitors employees online

    b wants companies to stop regular online monitoring

    c feels that online monitoring is necessary in the digital age

    d lost his job as a result of online monitoring

Part 6   Comprehension Skills

Read the passage and circle the letter of the answer to the question.

[1] Last week, National Oil Company announced the creation of the new position of Senior Vice President. [2] The company has appointed Andrea Adams, former CEO of PetrolCorp, to fill the post, and to become a member of the executive team. [3] Adams will be based at National Oil's main headquarters in Morristown and will report to current CEO Phillip Cranston. [4] Cranston, who has led the company for the past 19 years, recently took a 3-month leave of absence for health reasons. [5] The timing of Adams' appointment indicates that she may be the one to take over should Cranston need to step down. [6] Adams will join National Oil in the spring and will oversee the strategic direction, expansion and operation of two new manufacturing facilities scheduled to open in the summer of 2015.

Which sentence expresses an inference (not a fact)?

a 1	**c** 3	**e** 5
b 2	**d** 4	**f** 6

Part 7   Comprehension Skills

Read the passage and circle the letter of the best way to complete the sentence on p. 211.

Although modern appliances and electronics offer many features that are touted as being more convenient for the user, such as "touch" operation as opposed to buttons and knobs, or being manufactured from lighter weight materials, these new products on the market are far inferior in quality and craftsmanship to those that were made years ago. It used to be that even a mid-priced brand refrigerator, blender, or washing machine would last for 20 years or more. Today's consumers are fortunate to get ten years out of a machine before needing to replace it, and even those ten years involve frequent calls for service and repair. Appliances made fifty years ago or more were built with top quality materials and parts, often solid iron and steel, resulting in strong and sturdy construction, whereas today's products are made primarily from plastics and man-made composite materials, which have a much shorter life span. In contrast to modern products, appliances in the past were assembled mainly by people rather than by machines. Nowadays, however, the emphasis is on speed and profit as opposed to maintaining a company's reputation for quality craftsmanship. Products are manufactured from prefabricated materials by machines in record time.

This passage primarily describes _____ .

a a comparison between two things

b a causes and its effects

c a problem and a solution

Part 8 Comprehension Skills

Read the passage and circle the letter of the best way to complete the sentence.

Hydraulic fracturing, also known as "fracking," is the process of drilling and injecting fluid into the ground at a high pressure in order to fracture shale rocks to release natural gas inside. This practice has become increasingly frequent in recent years, offering greater supplies of natural gas and lowering fuel costs for consumers. These few positive side-effects, however, are vastly outweighed by the possible health risks to humans caused by the hydraulic fracturing and gas extraction processes. These dangers include the potential contamination of drinking water supplies as a result of surface spills or underground leaks, air toxicity from improperly sealed vents, as well as noise pollution from truck traffic and constant underground vibration. The fracking process also involves the use of chemicals such as benzene, methanol, and formaldehyde that are known toxins to humans and animals. When inhaled, ingested, or contacted by the skin, these substances disrupt the body's normal function and can cause serious diseases. They have been linked to cancer, Attention Deficit Disorder, autism, infertility, and diabetes. In addition to the toxic chemicals used in fracking, the wastewater that is a byproduct of the drilling process contains dangerous compounds such as radioactive material, barium, magnesium, and other substances which have been proven to cause cancer. Over time, exposure to these carcinogenic toxins can lead to death. Illnesses associated with gas drilling may take months, years, or decades to develop. As such, residents living near fracking sites now may not become aware of the dangers to their own health for years to come, which is too late.

This passage primarily describes _____ .

a a comparison between two things

b a cause and its effects

c a problem and a solution

Part 9   Comprehension Skills

Read the memo and circle the letter of the best way to complete the sentence.

Jackson Street School District
Memo for Parents and Guardians
April 5, 2015
Re: School Violence and Bullying

Recent incidents of bullying and violence on school grounds have prompted school-wide discussions about the best way to prevent these types of incidents from happening in the future. After a series of meetings between school officials, teachers, parents, and student representatives, a Bullying Prevention Committee has been selected to create policies and procedures for bullying and related behavior. The committee has prepared the following statement for parents and guardians:

It is the responsibility of the adults at Jackson Street School to take the issue of bullying seriously and to intervene. If we do not emphasize the gravity of bullying, create rules against it, and follow up incidents with serious consequences, it will continue to escalate and may have devastating effects on individual students and our entire school community. It is not adequate to teach individual victims strategies to better handle bullying situations; in order to truly be effective, a school-wide program needs to be implemented to make clear to students that bullying is not acceptable at school.

The following outline details the committee's initial plan of action and suggested first steps:

1. Determine the role and involvement of adults: Policies around when students should notify adults if they see, hear, or experience bullying should be established and presented to the school at an assembly. Parents should also be made aware of the policies.

2. Increase supervision during recess, lunch time, and other break times: Most victims of bullying report that incidents occur during these unsupervised break periods. Additional adult supervision should be arranged during those periods, and adults should remind students about policies regarding notification of adults if bullying occurs.

3. Create class rules against bullying and hold regular class meetings: Students should be taught what bullying is, what is unacceptable behavior, and the consequences of that behavior. Follow-up discussions should be held in class. Classes should meet weekly to discuss students' experiences and how they feel about the new policies.

4. Meet with victims, bullies and their parents: When bullying occurs, the school should facilitate talks between victims, bullies, and their parents. Agreements about cooperation between school and home can be reached.

Thank you for your cooperation.
The Jackson Street School Bullying Prevention Committee

This passage primarily describes _____ .

a   a comparison between two things

b   a cause and many effects

c   a problem and a solution

Part 10   Vocabulary Building

Circle the letter of the best form of the word to complete the sentence.

1 It's difficult to describe this artist's style. She seems to _____ the styles of several other artists.

   a integrate

   b disintegrate

   c integration

   d integral

2 During the debate, the mayor accused his opponent of making _____ decisions that endangered the general public.

   a rationalize

   b irrational

   c rationally

   d irrationally

3 Although John claims to be an avid rock-climbing _____ , he admits that deep down, he is terrified of heights.

   a unenthusiastic

   b enthusiast

   c enthusiastic

   d enthusiastically

Part 11   Vocabulary Building

Circle the letter of the correct meaning for the underlined word.

1 Pigs may be one of the most misunderstood animals. According to some experts, they are one of the cleanest animals on Earth, but because pigs don't have sweat glands to keep cool, they roll around in the mud. A series of experiments conducted on several animal species in the 1990s tested the animals' ability to move a cursor on a video screen in order to identify a symbol they had been shown. Using their <u>snouts</u> to perform the task, the pigs learned as quickly as chimpanzees.

   a sweat glands

   b monkeys

   c noses

   d animal species

2 Copyright is a form of protection provided to the authors of "original works of authorship" including literary, dramatic, musical, artistic, and certain other intellectual works, both published and unpublished. The law generally gives the owner of copyright the exclusive right to reproduce the original copyrighted work, to prepare <u>derivative</u> works, to distribute copies, to perform or display the copyrighted work publicly.

   a similar

   b original

   c musical

   d unpublished

3 Since the dawn of the Internet, companies have been rapidly revising and adding new policies to employee manuals in an effort to control workers' use of the Web during working hours. Rules and policies regarding online activity range from blocking employees' access to certain websites, to granting the company full access to workers' computers in order to check their browser history, including email messages. Most of these <u>provisions</u> allow the company to conduct online monitoring secretly, at any time and of any employee. A survey conducted by the ePolicy Institute in 2005 found that 76% of companies engaged in online monitoring, and that the number of companies that blocked employees' access to certain websites increased 30% since 2001.

    a websites

    b rules

    c activities

    d companies

4 In addition to the toxic chemicals used in fracking, the wastewater that is a byproduct of the drilling process contains dangerous compounds such as radioactive material, barium, magnesium, and other substances which have been proven to cause cancer. Over time, exposure to these <u>carcinogenic</u> toxins can lead to death.

    a health-conscious

    b unimportant

    c cancer-causing

    d misunderstood

Part 12 Vocabulary Building

Circle the letter of the correct word to complete the paragraph.

1 In _____ to modern products, appliances in the past were assembled mainly by people rather than by machines. Nowadays, however, the emphasis is on speed and profit as opposed to maintaining the company's reputation for quality craftsmanship.

    a conclusion

    b addition

    c opposed

    d contrast

2 The sea invertebrates known as *cephalopods* (octopi and squid) are one example. These animals' brains share many features of the human brain such as folded lobes and separate regions for processing tactile and visual information. In _____ , they use tools, show high levels of curiosity, and have a general distaste for boredom.

    a addition

    b example

    c relation

    d comparison

3 Recent research _____ that certain animals have much greater intellectual capacity than was previously thought. Scientists define intelligence, as it pertains to animals, as the capacity to learn a new communication system, such as human language, the ability to adapt behavior for enhanced results (for example, the use of tools), and the ability to learn from previous mistakes.

   a says

   b knows

   c suggests

   d reminds

Part 13   Vocabulary Building

For each group of sentences, circle the letter of the correct word or words that the underlined word or phrase refers to.

1 The copyright protects the form of expression rather than the subject matter of the writing. For example, a description of a machine could be copyrighted, but <u>this</u> would only prevent others from copying the description; it would not prevent others from writing a description of their own or from making and using the machine.

   a getting a copyright

   b copying the description

   c making and using the machine

2 Hydraulic fracturing, also known as "fracking," is the process of drilling and injecting fluid into the ground at a high pressure in order to fracture shale rocks to release natural gas inside. This <u>practice</u> has become increasingly frequent in recent years, offering greater supplies of natural gas and lowering fuel costs for consumers.

   a hydraulic fracturing

   b offering greater supplies

   c lowering fuel costs

3 Since the dawn of the Internet, companies have been rapidly revising and adding new policies to employee manuals in an effort to control workers' use of the Web during working hours. Rules and policies regarding online activity range from blocking employees' access to certain websites, to granting the company full access to workers' computers in order to check their web history, including email messages. Most of <u>these provisions</u> allow the company to conduct online monitoring secretly at any time and of any employee.

   a employee manuals

   b rules and policies

   c working hours

ANSWER KEY

PRE-TEST

Part 1 p. 1
1. c, 2. c, 3. a, 4. b

Part 2 pp. 2–3
1. b, 2. b, 3. c, 4. b

Part 3 pp. 3–4
1. d, 2. a, 3. b, 4. c

Part 4 p. 4
Sentence 4

Part 5 p. 5
1. c, 2. a, 3. d, 4. b

Part 6 p. 6
1. b, 2. c, 3. b

Part 7 pp. 7–8
1. c, 2. a

Part 8 pp. 8–9
b

Part 9 pp. 9–10
c

Part 10 p. 10
1. b, 2. a

Part 11 p. 10
1. d, 2. b, 3. c, 4. b, 5. b

Part 12 p. 11
1. c, 2. b

Part 13 p. 11
1. b, 2. b

5. Fall break
6. Prof. Jackie Barstow / Jackie Barstow / Prof. Barstow / Professor Jackie Barstow / Professor Barstow
7. 20% / twenty percent / 20 percent
8. Room 321 / 321 / Rm 321 / Rm. 321

Practice 2 pp. 20–21
1. Toronto, Canada / Canada / Toronto
2. June 7, 2014 / June 7
3. Two / 2
4. Fashion buyer
5. Five to seven years / 5–7 years / 5 to 7 years / Five–seven years
6. Four-year college degree / Four year degree / Four year college degree / 4 year college degree / 4-year college degree / 4-year degree / 4 year degree / a four-year college degree / a four year degree / a four year college degree / a 4 year college degree / a 4-year degree / a 4 year degree

COMPREHENSION SKILLS

Previewing, Scanning, and Skimming

PREVIEWING

Practice 1 pp. 12–13
1. b, 2. a, 3. b, 4. a, 5. a

Practice 2 pp. 14–18
1. c, 2. a, 3. c, 4. c, 5. b

SCANNING

Practice 1 pp. 18–19
1. Mondays and Wednesdays / Mondays, Wednesdays / Monday and Wednesday / Monday, Wednesday / Monday Wednesday / Mondays Wednesdays
2. three / 3
3. two / 2
4. Week 14 / fourteen / Week Fourteen / 14

Practice 3 pp. 21–22

1	legal		citizen
	nationality		country
	citizenship		country
	country		nationality
	citizenship		nationality
	country		countries
	citizen		citizens
	countries		citizenships
	legal		citizenships
	country		citizenship
	country	3	citizenship
	citizenship		country
2	Nationality		countries
	citizenship		country
	country		country
	citizenship		

SKIMMING

Practice 1 p. 23

1. b, 2. c, 3. b

Practice 2

Part 1 pp. 24–25

1. a, 2. c, 3. b

Part 2 pp. 25–26

1. c, 2. a, 3. b

Part 3 pp. 26–27

1. a, 2. b, 3. a

Practice 3 pp. 28–29

1. b, 2. c, 3. b

Practice 4 pp. 30–31

1. b, 2. b, 3. a

COMBINED SKILLS: PREVIEWING, SCANNING, AND SKIMMING

Practice 1 pp. 32–33

1. b, 2. c, 3. a, 4. c, 5. a, 6. b, 7. b

Practice 2 pp. 34–35

1. b, 2. b, 3. c, 4. a, 5. b, 6. a

Understanding Paragraphs

IDENTIFYING THE TOPIC OF A PARAGRAPH

Practice 1 p. 36

1. a, 2. a

Practice 2 pp. 37–38

1. b, 2. a, 3. a, 4. c

IDENTIFYING THE MAIN IDEA

Practice 1 pp. 38–39

1. 1   2. 5   3. 2   4. 2   5. 7

Practice 2 pp. 40–41

1. 2   2. 3   3. 1   4. 4

Practice 3 pp. 41–42

1, 2, 5

IDENTIFYING KEY DETAILS

Practice 1 pp. 43–44

1. a, 2. c, 3. b, 4. a, 5. c

Practice 2

Part 1 pp. 44–45

1. b, 2. b

Part 2 p. 45

1. b, 2. c

Practice 3 pp. 45–46

Tom Fredrickson: 1, 3, 4, 9

Carol Newman: 2, 5, 7, 8

Both: 6

Making Inferences

FACTS VS. INFERENCES

Practice 1 pp. 47–48

1. F, 2. F, 3. I, 4. F, 5. I

Practice 2 p. 48

1. F, 2. F, 3. I, 4. F, 5. I

MAKING INFERENCES FROM FICTION

Practice 1 pp. 49–50

1. b, 2. b, 3. a, 4. b, 5. a

Practice 2

Excerpt 1 pp. 50–51

1. b, 2. c, 3. b

Excerpt 2 pp. 51–52

1. a, 2. b, 3. c

Excerpt 3 p. 52

1. a, 2. b

FACTS AND OPINIONS

Practice 1 pp. 53–54

Facts: 1, 5, 6

Opinions: 2, 3, 4, 7, 8

Practice 2 pp. 54–55

Facts: 1, 4, 6

Opinions: 2, 3, 5

TONE AND POINT OF VIEW

Practice 1 pp. 56–57

1. Tom Fredrickson
2. environmental issues
3. against
4. Tom Fredrickson

Practice 2 p. 57

1. b, 2. a, 3. b

Practice 3 p. 58

but all this virtual freedom hasn't been without its price.

desperate need for heightened Internet security.

and with good reason.

governments need to respond quickly to

Patterns of Organization

TEXT ORGANIZATION: THESIS STATEMENTS, MAIN POINTS, AND SUPPORTING DETAILS

Practice 1 p. 59

1. 1	2. 4	3. 4

Practice 2 p. 60

1. 4	3. 1	5. 6
2. 5	4. 3	6. 2

COMPARISON AND CONTRAST PATTERN

Practice 1 p. 61

Asteroids: 2, 3, 5, 8
Comets: 1, 4, 6, 7

Practice 2 p. 62

differences
different
while
as well as
both
On the other hand
larger
In addition

although
similar
In contrast

CAUSE AND EFFECT PATTERN

Practice 1 pp. 62–63

1. b, 2. c, 3. b, 4. a, 5. a

Practice 2 p. 64

results in
reduce
creates
improves
affects
require
As a consequence
helps
leads to
serves to

PROBLEM AND SOLUTION PATTERN

Practice 1 pp. 65–66

1. P, 2. S, 3. P, 4. S, 5. S, 6. P

Practice 2 pp. 66–67

1. b, 2. b, 3. a, 4. c

IDENTIFYING PATTERNS

Practice 1 pp. 67–71

1. a, 2. c, 3. c, 4. b, 5. b, 6. c, 7. a, 8. a, 9. b

SUMMARIZING

Practice 1 pp. 72–74

1, 2, 5

Practice 2 pp. 74–75

a, b, d, e, f, h, i, j

Comprehension Skills Practice Test

Part 1 pp. 76–77

1. c, 2. b, 3. a

Part 2 pp. 77–78

1. d, 2. a, 3. a, 4. c

Part 3 pp. 79–80

1. b, 2. c, 3. b, 4. b, 5. a

Part 4 pp. 80–81

1. b, 2. c, 3. b, 4. a, 5. b

Part 5 pp. 81–82

1. c, 2. a, 3. b

Part 6 p. 83

1. c, 2. b, 3. b

Part 7 pp. 84–85

1. a, 2. b, 3. b, 4. a, 5. c

Part 8 pp. 85–86

1. b, 2. c, 3. b

Part 9 pp. 86–87

1. b, 2. b, 3. b, 4. c, 5. b

VOCABULARY BUILDING
Word Parts
ROOTS

Practice 1 pp. 88–90

1. a, 2. b, 3. b, 4. b, 5. b, 6. b, 7. c, 8. a, 9. c, 10. c, 11. c, 12. b, 13. b, 14. a, 15. b

Practice 2 p. 91

1. done without clear thought.
2. the border around a particular area.
3. studies animals.
4. nervous about many things.
5. a strong wind which moves in a circular pattern.
6. a star-shaped symbol.
7. to see objects that are far away.
8. you have a fear of high places.
9. a doctor who treats skin problems.
10. the substance that makes plants green.
11. different cultures of people.
12. a person who has official authority.

13. to drink water.
14. takes care of people's eyes.

PREFIXES

Practice 1 p. 92

1. disorderly	6. illegible
2. unproductive	7. misinterproted
3. asymmetrical	8. abnormal
4. involuntary	9. imperfection
5. inappropriate	10. irrational

Practice 2 p. 93

1. bi	6. tri
2. mono	7. kilo
3. cent	8. uni
4. dec	9. multi
5. quad	10. semi

Practice 3 pp. 94–95

1. b, 2. d, 3. d, 4. c, 5. b, 6. c, 7. d, 8. d, 9. c, 10. d

SUFFIXES

Practice 1 pp. 96–97

1. independence	6. diligence
2. conformist	7. custodian
3. abandonment	8. sensitivity
4. partnership	9. abruptness
5. affirmation	10. consumerism

Practice 2 pp. 97–98

1. rational	7. economic
2. picky	8. abusive
3. regardless	9. collectible
4. spacious	10. debatable
5. distracted	11. surprising
6. tasteful	12. rigorous

Practice 3 p. 98

Row 1: refrigerate, prioritize

Row 2: personify, impersonate; triangulate

Row 3: classify, realize

Row 4: energize, patronize

Row 5: activate, amplify

Row 6: signify; initialize, initiate

Row 7: minimize, beautify

WORD FORMS AND FAMILIES

Practice 1 p. 99

Row 1: reason, reasonable, reasonably

Row 2: avoidance, unavoidable

Row 3: integrate, integrated

Row 4: doubt; undoubtedly, doubtfully

Row 5: politics, apolitical

Row 6: treat, mistreated

Row 7: courage, courageously

Row 8: responsible, unresponsive

Row 9: place, misplaced

Row 10: enthusiast, enthusiastically

Row 11: management, manageable

Row 12:

Row 13: desire, undesirable

Row 14: rationale, irrational, rationally

Practice 2 p. 100

1. c, 2. b, 3. b, 4. a, 5. b, 6. c, 7. b, 8. a, 9. c, 10. c

Inferring Meaning from Context

USING CONTEXT

Practice 1 pp. 101–102

1. b, 2. a, 3. a, 4. b, 5. c, 6. c, 7. b, 8. a

Practice 2 pp. 102–103

1. a, 2. c, 3. c, 4. a, 5. b, 6. c, 7. b

INFERRING THE MEANING OF WORDS

Practice 1 pp. 104–105

1. a, 2. b, 3. c, 4. c, 5. a, 6. b

Practice 2 p. 106

1. c, 2. b, 3. c, 4. a, 5. c

Collocations and Idioms

COMMON COLLOCATIONS AND PHRASAL VERBS

Practice 1 pp. 107–108

Paragraph 1: According to, recent study, negative effect, serious consequences

Paragraph 2: extremely common, work environments

Paragraph 3: study found, dramatic increase, In short

Paragraph 4: lead researcher, associate professor, major effect, findings prove

Paragraph 5: findings indicate, depends largely on

Paragraph 6: possible solution

Practice 2 p. 108

1. have	7. pose
2. raise	8. raise
3. poses	9. have
4. raise	10. pose
5. has	11. have
6. pose	12. raise

Practice 3 p. 110

1. propose
2. do, complete
3. be a part/percentage of
4. bring attention to
5. intend
6. continue, make progress
7. explain
8. create and present
9. discuss and agree on
10. disagree with

Practice 4 p. 112

1. by with	5. away with
2. back at	6. on with
3. over with	7. around to
4. out of	8. away from

IDIOMS

Practice 1   pp. 112–114

1. a, 2. c, 3. d, 4. e, 5. c, 6. a, 7. e, 8. d, 9. b, 10. b

Practice 2   pp. 114–115

1. a, 2. a, 3. a, 4. a, 5. b, 6. c, 7. a, 8. c, 9. b

Practice 3   pp. 115–116

1. were unable to continue
2. extremely hard
3. in charge
4. is a strict boss
5. increase control over
6. cause the negotiations to fail
7. limit
8. from person to person

COLLOCATIONS AND IDIOMS IN CONTEXT

Practice 1   p. 116

1. cut back on
2. put forward
3. negative effects
4. According to
5. serious consequences
6. depends largely on

Practice 2   p. 117

1. around
2. shoulder
3. tight
4. eyes
5. arm's
6. pressure

Practice 3   pp. 117–118

1. recent
2. impact
3. researcher
4. risks
5. forward
6. found
7. dramatic
8. leg
9. by
10. have
11. out

Following Ideas in Text

SIGNAL WORDS AND PHRASES

Practice 1 pp. 119–120

1. a, 2. b, 3. b, 4. a, 5. a, 6. b

Practice 2 p. 120

Paragraph 1: In fact, Moreover, In the past, For instance, However

Paragraph 2: While, After all, Consequently

Paragraph 3: But, Actually, In addition, for instance

Practice 3 p. 121

Signals for Giving an Example: After all, In particular, For example, For instance, To illustrate,

Signals for Explaining Causes and Results or Effects: Due to, Therefore, As a result, So, Consequently,

Signals for Adding a New Idea to a Series of Ideas: as well as, Furthermore, In addition, Moreover, another

Signals for Explaining Steps in a Sequence or Events in Time: Finally, In 1945, In recent months, Next, At first, / First,

Signals for Introducing a Contrasting Idea: Conversely, But, Although, In contrast, However, While,

Signals for Giving a Fact or Detail to Clarify a Point: Since, As a matter of fact, Actually, In fact,

PRONOUNS AND REFERENTS

Practice 1 pp. 122–123

1. it
2. they
3. him/her, her/him
4. this
5. their
6. which
7. this
8. her
9. she
10. that
11. them

Practice 2 pp. 123–124

1. a, 2. b, 3. a, 4. b, 5. b, 6. c, 7. a

Practice 3 pp. 125-126

1. who, which, that
2. whose, that, who
3. that, who, whose
4. who, that, which
5. which, who, that
6. that, whose, who

Vocabulary Building Practice Test

Part 1 p. 127

1. a, 2. b, 3. c, 4. b, 5. a

Part 2 pp. 127–128

1. b, 2. b, 3. c, 4. b, 5. a, 6. b

Part 3 pp. 128–129

1. b, 2. b, 3. b, 4. a, 5. a, 6. b, 7. a

Part 4 p. 129

1. c, 2. a, 3. c, 4. a, 5. c

Part 5 p. 130

1. c, 2. b, 3. c

Part 6 pp. 130–131

1. a, 2. b, 3. a, 4. b, 5. b

Part 7 pp. 131–132

1. d, 2. a, 3. b, 4. a, 5. a, 6. d, 7. b

Part 8 pp. 132–133

1. d, 2. a, 3. a

Part 9 p. 133

1. b, 2. a, 3. b, 4. a, 5. a

READING FASTER

INTRODUCTION: STRATEGIES FOR READING FASTER pp. 134–137

1. b, 2. b, 3. b, 4. b, 5. c, 6. a, 7. b, 8. b

Timed Reading Practice

PRACTICE 1: CRIME-SOLVING TECHNIQUES THROUGHOUT HISTORY

Reading 1 p. 140

1. a, 2. b, 3. b, 4. b, 5. b, 6. a, 7. b, 8. c

Reading 2 pp. 142–143

1. a, 2. b, 3. a, 4. b, 5. b, 6. c, 7. c, 8. a

Reading 3 p. 146

1. b, 2. a, 3. c, 4. a, 5. c, 6. b, 7. b, 8. c

PRACTICE 2: ROCK LEGENDS: PEOPLE WHO MADE A DIFFERENCE IN MUSIC

Reading 1 pp. 148–149

1. c, 2. b, 3. a, 4. c, 5. c, 6. b, 7. c, 8. b

Reading 2 p. 151

1. b, 2. b, 3. a, 4. c, 5. a, 6. b, 7. a, 8. c

Reading 3 pp. 153–154

1. b, 2. b, 3. c, 4. a, 5. b, 6. a, 7. c, 8. a

PRACTICE 3: UNEXPLAINED PHENOMENA

Reading 1 p. 156

1. b, 2. a, 3. a, 4. b, 5. b, 6. b, 7. b, 8. b

Reading 2 pp. 158–159

1. c, 2. b, 3. b, 4. a, 5. c, 6. b, 7. c, 8. b

Reading 3 p. 161

1. b, 2. c, 3. b, 4. b, 5. a, 6. b, 7. b, 8. b

STUDY SKILLS

STORING AND STUDYING NEW WORDS pp. 162–173

Answers will vary.

STUDY STRATEGIES pp. 174–182
Answers will vary.

LANGUAGE IN CONTEXT

Practice 1

Part 1 p. 183

mandatory, overstepping, adhere to, authorities, constitutes, curb, obesity, institute

Part 2 p. 183

1. a, 2. a, 3. b, 4. b, 5. a

Part 3 pp. 184–185

1. b, 2. a, 3. b, 4. b, 5. d, 6. a, 7. c, 8. b

Part 4 p. 185

1. authorities
2. adhere to
3. curb
4. overstepped
5. institute
6. obesity
7. constitutes
8. mandatory

Practice 2

Part 1 pp. 185–186

function, sustained, concentration, diagnoses, extended, disruptive, diagnosis, hired, tailored

Part 2 p. 186

1. a, 2. b, 3. b, 4. a, 5. a

Part 3 pp. 186–187

1. b, 2. d, 3. d, 4. c, 5. a, 6. a, 7. c, 8. a

Part 4 p. 188

1. concentration
2. diagnosis
3. disruptive
4. extended
5. function
6. hire
7. sustain
8. tailor

Practice 3

Part 1 p. 188

remarkable, tissues, replenish, worn out, capable, replicate, yield, regenerative

Part 2 p. 189

1. b, 2. b, 3. a, 4. a, 5. b

Part 3 pp. 189–190

1. c, 2. b, 3. d, 4. c, 5. d, 6. a, 7. c, 8. b

Part 4 pp. 190–191

1. capable of
2. regenerate
3. remarkable
4. replenish
5. replicated
6. tissue
7. worn out
8. yield

Practice 4

Part 1 p. 191

drastically, engaging in, spontaneous, trend, peers, creepy, fueling, predators

Part 2 p. 192

1. a, 2. b, 3. a, 4. a, 5. b

Part 3 pp. 192–193

1. b, 2. c, 3. c, 4. b, 5. c, 6. a, 7. a, 8. c

Part 4 pp. 193–194

1. creepy
2. drastically
3. trend
4. predators
5. engaging in
6. spontaneous
7. fuel
8. peers

Practice 5

Part 1 p. 194

extreme, prescription, offensive, random, timid, aggressively, intense, glared

Part 2 p. 195

1. b, 2. a, 3. a, 4. b

Part 3 pp. 195–196

1. c, 2. a, 3. d, 4. a, 5. c, 6. d, 7. c

Part 4 p. 196

1. aggressive

2. extreme

3. timid

4. glared

5. prescription

6. intense

7. offensive

8. random

Practice 6

Part 1 p. 197

peasant, unsurpassed, eternal, recite, immense, customary, launch, cultivate, reverence

Part 2 pp. 197–198

1. b, 2. b, 3. a, 4. b, 5. b

Part 3 pp. 198–199

1. a, 2. d, 3. d, 4. c, 5. b, 6. a, 7. a, 8. b

Part 4 p. 199

1. unsurpassed

2. cultivate

3. immense

4. customary

5. peasant

6. eternal

7. reverence

8. recite

POST-TEST

Part 1 pp. 204–206

1. c, 2. a, 3. c, 4. b

Part 2 p. 206

1. c, 2. a

Part 3 pp. 207–208

1. b, 2. b, 3. a, 4. a, 5. a

Part 4 pp. 208–209

1. d, 2. c, 3. c, 4. b, 5. b

Part 5 pp. 209–210

1. c, 2. b

Part 6 p. 210

e

Part 7 pp. 210–211

a

Part 8 p. 211

b

Part 9 p. 212

c

Part 10 p. 213

1. a, 2. b, 3. b

Part 11 pp. 213–214

1. c, 2. a, 3. b, 4. c

Part 12 pp. 214–215

1. d, 2. a, 3. c

Part 13 p. 215

1. a, 2. a, 3. b